Designing Internet of Things Solutions with Microsoft Azure

A Survey of Secure and Smart Industrial Applications

Nirnay Bansal

APRESS®

Designing Internet of Things Solutions with Microsoft Azure: A Survey of Secure and Smart Industrial Applications

Nirnay Bansal
Bothell, WA, USA

ISBN-13 (pbk): 978-1-4842-6040-1   ISBN-13 (electronic): 978-1-4842-6041-8
https://doi.org/10.1007/978-1-4842-6041-8

Managing Director, Apress Media LLC: Welmoed Spahr
Acquisitions Editor: Smriti Srivastava
Development Editor: Matthew Moodie
Coordinating Editor: Shrikant Vishwakarma

Cover designed by eStudioCalamar

Cover image designed by Freepik (www.freepik.com)

Distributed to the book trade worldwide by Springer Science+Business Media New York, 233 Spring Street, 6th Floor, New York, NY 10013. Phone 1-800-SPRINGER, fax (201) 348-4505, e-mail orders-ny@springer-sbm.com, or visit www.springeronline.com. Apress Media, LLC is a California LLC and the sole member (owner) is Springer Science + Business Media Finance Inc (SSBM Finance Inc). SSBM Finance Inc is a **Delaware** corporation.

For information on translations, please e-mail booktranslations@springernature.com; for reprint, paperback, or audio rights, please e-mail bookpermissions@springernature.com.

Apress titles may be purchased in bulk for academic, corporate, or promotional use. eBook versions and licenses are also available for most titles. For more information, reference our Print and eBook Bulk Sales web page at http://www.apress.com/bulk-sales.

Any source code or other supplementary material referenced by the author in this book is available to readers on GitHub via the book's product page, located at www.apress.com/ 978-1-4842-6040-1. For more detailed information, please visit http://www.apress.com/source-code.

Printed on acid-free paper

I would like to dedicate this book to my mother Mrs. Kusumlata, father Mr. Rajkishore, and in-laws Mr. Pradeep and Mrs. Abha for believing that I could do this and supporting me. My gratitude also goes to Anubhav, Anurag, Harshit, Neha, and Nutan.

Table of Contents

About the Author

Nirnay Bansal is a certified solution architect who has been working at Microsoft Corporation in Redmond, WA, since 2015. He graduated in with an undergraduate degree in computer science from BITS, Pilani and an MBA from Louisiana State University. He has been working for more than 15 years on large and complex IT projects. He is a technical specialist in providing architecture, development, and consultancy, using Microsoft technologies including Microsoft Azure. Among his past clients are Frontier Communications, Fidelity, PricewaterHouseCoopers, and Dell.

He is a well-known expert when it comes to designing cloud-based solutions and data scenarios. Additionally, he participates in public events as a speaker for Code Camps. In addition to holding various Microsoft certifications, he is a Microsoft Certified Trainer (MCT) and a certified Solution Architect from IASA. He is cofounder and chief technology officer of the mobile application development company www.TechValens.com, helping small to mid-sized clients across the globe.

When he is not working, he loves trekking and skating. He spends his spare time and holidays with his wife Dharna, his son Neev, his father Rajkishore, and his mother Kusumlata in India.

You can contact him through his Twitter handle @nirnaybansal, on LinkedIn at www.linkedin.com/in/nirnaybansal, or by sending him an e-mail at nirnaybansal@gmail.com.

About the Technical Reviewer

Devendra G. Asane is currently working as a cloud, big data, and microservices architect with a multinational IT firm in Pune, India. Before this, he worked with Microsoft and was part of GTSC for a long time in Bangalore, India.

Devendra lives with his wife Seema and son Teerthak in Pune, India. You can contact him on LinkedIn at www.linkedin.com/in/devendra007.

Acknowledgments

A special note of thanks goes to my wife Dharna for being supportive while I worked on this book after spending hours at the office each day. My lovely little son Neev, who is my world, actually let me write when it was probably time to play or spend time with him.

I would like to give a big shout out to the publisher, Apress, and their team. Special thanks to Acquisitions Editor Smriti Srivastava for support, Coordinating Editor Shrikant Vishwakarma for being so flexible, and wonderful reviewers Matthew Moodie and Devendra Asane for their thoughtful comments and efforts toward improving the quality of the content.

Without the experience and support of my startup partner and team at Techvalens Software (`www.techvalens.com`), this book would not exist.

Special thanks go to a wonderful author and my mentor, Rami Vemula. I am so lucky to have him by my side.

I want to thank God most of all, because without God I wouldn't be able to do any of this.

Introduction

Thank you for choosing to read my book. This book is a deeper dive into the challenges and opportunities every manager and developer faces, in small to large industries across a broad spectrum of business processes. This book is structured with short but meaningful lab activities that help the reader explore each topic area. These realistic use cases are inspired by individual achievers, winning teams, and organizations, who often dream big, but often start small.

There are hundreds of Internet of Things (IoT) success stories: big retailers using facial recognition systems to improve operations, transit monitoring with IoT powered by artificial intelligence (AI), IoT in remote medical patient monitoring, industrial AI software for better predictive maintenance, and gas companies saving millions of dollars by tapping into the power of IoT and AI. These stories prove that AI with IoT empowers intelligence and connectivity, and embedded devices make this technology useful in a wide variety of applications and environments. The use cases designed in this book will help you lay the foundation for a longer IoT journey for your department and business process.

Being an early tech adopter, you have a competitive advantage; that is, you will experience better business outcomes, including increased revenue growth and market position.

Who This Book Is For

This book is for everyone who would like to have a good understanding of IoT and its industrial applications. The content is aimed at software developers, architects, and solution designers who want to learn about the implementation of IoT with Azure Cloud. It is also designed for IT managers, product managers, and business specialists to learn where they should invest in IoT for an immediate, visible impact on security and productivity, as well as to increase customer satisfaction.

At the time of writing this book, LinkedIn had more than 16,000 job results for "Internet of Things in the United States," with more than 5,000 jobs looking for entry-level experience in this technology. In writing this book, I am not targeting any specifc problem, company, or individual. Instead, I hope to prepare you with enough knowledge and wireframe codes to get a head start on success in your job. For managers, I hope I have succeeded in translating industrial use cases of IoT in your industry that can start you on your own journey.

What You'll Learn

This book is broken up into three parts. Here's a summary of what you'll learn.

Setting the Stage

The first two chapters provide readers with an introduction to Industry 4.0 and IoT, covering the concepts, terms, and architecture of an IoT solution.

Preparing an Azure Account

The third and fourth chapters introduce the Microsoft Azure IoT Platform, guiding you through setting up an account, which is required in later chapters. You will learn how we will bring data to the Microsoft Azure cloud with speed, durability, security, and optimized cost. We will be streaming both structured data being collected in relational and NoSQL databases, and unstructured data such as photos or video footage for decision making in business operations.

Industrial Problem and IoT-Based Solution

Progressively while reading this book, you will learn about various industries and how you can solve known problems quickly using IoT. Although a dedicated lab is provided in each industry-based chapter, actually most of the labs are industry-agnostic. Therefore, you should read all the chapters instead of jumping directly to your industry-specific chapter.

Chapter 5 covers predictive maintenance using Azure Solution Accelerator. Chapter 6 covers working with analog-to-digital thermistor sensors and digital humidity sensors using Raspberry Pi and a Windows IoT Core operating system. Chapter 7 covers an image classification model to detect cracks in structural asset using the ML.NET Image Classification API and TensorFlow model. Chapter 8 covers developing a smart mirror using Raspberry Pi and the Raspbian operating system. Chapter 9 covers physical object tracking using radio-frequency identification (RFID). Chapter 10 covers identifying and marking firearms in a live video feed. An IP camera is required, but you need no knowledge of machine learning or programming. Chapter 11 covers analyzing heart rate data from your Apple Watch using Azure Time Series Insight. Chapter 12 covers visual analytics like facial recognition, brand recognition, and virtual dressing using Cognitive Services. Chapter 13 covers logistics monitoring using the Xamarin mobile application using a smartphone. This chapter also covers using an ultrasonic ranging module with Raspberry Pi to implement smart parking.

Security and Risk

The final chapter is dedicated to security and challenges faced for all IoT projects. You will learn how easy it is to use threat modeling and Azure Sphere to solve most of these challenges.

Prerequisites for the Lab
Hardware

This book focuses on using Raspberry Pi; therefore, a basic Raspberry Pi setup is required. Samples in Chapters 4 to 13 make use of Raspberry Pi 3+, but all samples will work with Raspberry Pi 4, too. When working with sensors, you are required to have additional hardware.

The standard setup will consist of Raspberry Pi (Model B); an SD card installed with Windows Core IoT; an SD card installed with Raspbian; a suitable micro USB power supply; and an HDMI-compatible screen, keyboard, and mouse. You will also be required to download and install various software packages. Raspberry Pi should therefore have a working Internet connection (either Wi-Fi or ethernet).

Tools and Account

You need to work in the Microsoft Visual Studio development environment. You can purchase a license or a get a free Microsoft Visual Studio Community at `https://visualstudio.microsoft.com/vs/community/`.

You will need a valid and active Microsoft Azure account for the Azure labs. If you do not have one, you can sign up for a free trial at `https://azure.microsoft.com/en-us/free/`.

If you are a Visual Studio active subscriber, you are entitled to a $50 to $150 credit per month. Refer to `https://azure.microsoft.com/en-us/pricing/member-offers/msdn-benefits-details/` to find out more, including how to activate and start using your monthly Azure credit.

If you are not a Visual Studio subscriber, you can sign up for the free Visual Studio Dev Essentials program to create a free Azure account (includes one year of free services, $200 for the first month) at `https://visualstudio.microsoft.com/dev-essentials/`.

CHAPTER 1

Industry 4.0 Movement

A revolution is defined as a forcible approach for advancement of existing results or introduction of new results. LINQ, for example, signified a revolution in programming languages. Cloud servers are a revolution when compared with on-premises servers. Smart watches could herald a revolution in health care. A decade ago, we never imagined measuring our blood pressure and heart rate without visiting a clinic. In this chapter, you'll be introduced to today's industry and how it evolves over the period. You'll also learn about Internet of Things (IoT) and Industrial Internet of Things (IIoT).

Before this book delves into the world of IoT and the use of IoT in various industries, this chapter provides some background information regarding industries and IoT, including the following:

- An explanation of the historical approach to Industry 4.0

- The building blocks of Industry 4.0 and how they are related to IoT

- Benefits and challenges of Industry 4.0

Historical Perspective: Setting the Stage for IIoT

Speaking of revolutions, we have had revolutions in the technology industry, as shown in Figure 1-1. These revolutions occurred when we changed any one or all factors from among the place, the path, or the pace, to produce goods from raw materials.

© Nirnay Bansal 2020
N. Bansal, *Designing Internet of Things Solutions with Microsoft Azure*,
https://doi.org/10.1007/978-1-4842-6041-8_1

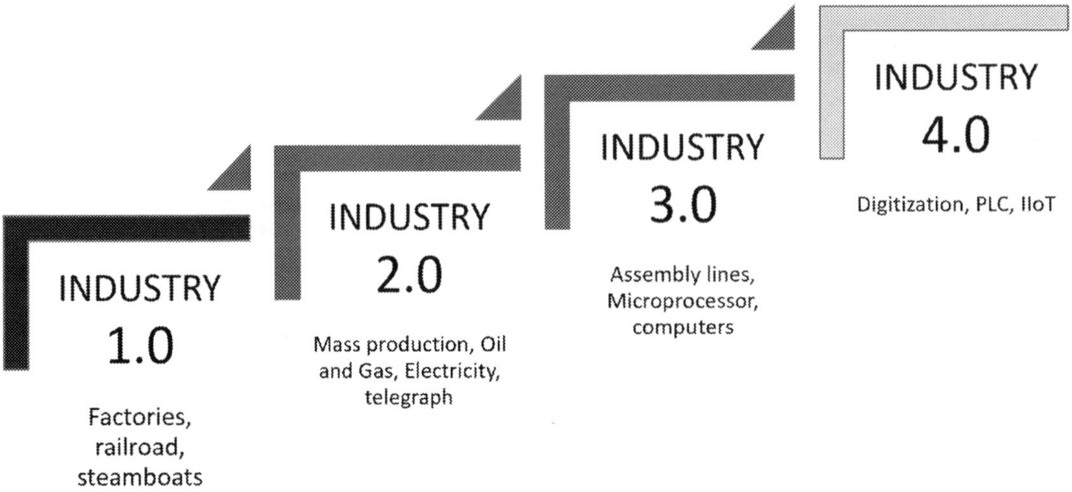

Figure 1-1. *The four industrial revolutions*

The First Industrial Revolution: Version 1.0

Humans have been manufacturing goods for and by themselves for ages. At first, they were mostly engaged in farming. Later they started exchanging farming products for other goods they needed. The first Industrial Revolution picked up in 1760. During this revolution, place, path, and pace all changed. The place changed from home in a village to a factory in town. The path changed from horse, walking, or boat to railroad or steamboats. Pace of production changed to mass production due to mechanization in factories. Here we started using machines. The first generation ran to the end of the eighteenth century, and then matured from Europe to the United States. In this period, factories were powered by steam and water and much focus was on manufacturing of textiles.

The Second Industrial Revolution: Version 2.0

The first Industrial Revolution ran for a century and then humankind saw another big shift. We called it the second Industrial Revolution. This time path and pace changed. The path changed to oil and gas. During this time the two big innovations were the introduction of electricity and aviation. Pace changed multifold due to communication advances like the telegraph. The introduction of steel helped in making engines and machines, and the introduction of chemicals helped in making dyes and fertilizers during this phase.

The Third Industrial Revolution: Version 3.0

Another century passed after the second Industrial Revolution and humankind saw another big shift, the third Industrial Revolution. This time again path and pace changed. The path moved to nuclear energy. Pace changed again multifold due to communication by transistor and microprocessor. This period of advancement considerably improved the efficiency of assembly lines. During this time, early computers were introduced with limited computing power and exceptionally large physical size. This laid the foundation for today's computer systems. This revolution gave us an era of high-level automation in manufacturing. Due to information technology (IT) this revolution has also been called the digital revolution.

The Fourth Industrial Revolution (Industry 4.0): Version 4.0

We are currently in the fourth Industrial Revolution, an era of automation with advanced programmable logic controllers (PLCs) that started between 2011 and 2015. We are still using the same place (i.e., factories) and the same path (i.e., power source and communication systems) of the third Industrial Revolution, but this time industries moved more toward digitization, including new technologies like artificial intelligence, cloud computing, robotics, 3D printing, the IoT, and 5G wireless technologies. Although we didn't change the power source, we actually added renewable power sources like solar farming and wind energy. These new power sources reduced the rate of carbon emissions, making the earth greener. Digitization led to a change in the pace, or production efficiency. Industry 4.0 started when industries started increasing automation, introducing smart machines and proactive monitoring.

IT systems were always collecting data. We were good at taking backups and storing huge amounts of data. Recent advancements, though, started converting these data into meaningful information and thus helped users make meaningful decisions.

The Internet connected humans, and was therefore known as the Internet of Humans (IoH). When devices like thermostats, light bulbs, fitness bands, microwaves, and doorbells were connected, it became known as the IoT. When sensors, instruments, and devices started interconnecting with the Internet to change, improve, or optimize industrial processes, this became known as the IIoT. Some people also call it the Internet of Industrial Things (IoIT).

The introduction of smart industries helped employees to focus more on customers and less on monitoring and processes. One key thing that helped in achieving this was sensors. Factories started using the IoT for example systems to monitor, analyze, and make decisions to improve working conditions. Throughout this book, you will be introduced to the different possible uses of IIoT and how IIoT is an industry-agnostic concept. Various countries promote different environments of research and standards for Industry 4.0. The United States has the Smart Manufacturing Leadership Coalition (SMLC), a nonprofit organization working to provide easy and affordable smart manufacturing platforms. Throughout this book, you will learn how every type of industry can and should take advantage of the IIoT to save operational costs, optimize productivity, and proactively detect failures.

Bonus Read

Do you realize it has been just about a decade we have been in the fourth Industrial Revolution, but we are already moving toward the fifth Industrial Revolution? There is a blurry line between Industry 4.0 and Industry 5.0. Most of the place (i.e., factories), path (i.e., power source), and technology remain the same, but pace will again be enhanced multifold in manufacturing and production systems. It is just a natural and obvious upgrade to Industry 4.0. The main thing that would change is the relationship between human and machine. The decision is now datacentric. There was always a line between where machine ends and where human takes over; we never worked together. In Industry 5.0, though, we work side by side. With Industry 4.0 nothing is impossible, but with Industry 5.0, technology will alter our behaviors and relationships, and become a more integral part of our physical and social spaces. For example, robotics, IoT, drones, AI, and machine learning will make most of the decisions: Genetically modified seeds reduce the use of pesticides in farming, autonomous vehicles will run on roads, avoiding accidents, and wearable devices will take care of health in real time.

Building Blocks

It is important to understand the basic building blocks of Industry 4.0 and how it all works together. Figure 1-2 shows the following four Industry 4.0:building blocks:

- IIoT
- Cloud technology
- Data analytics
- Security

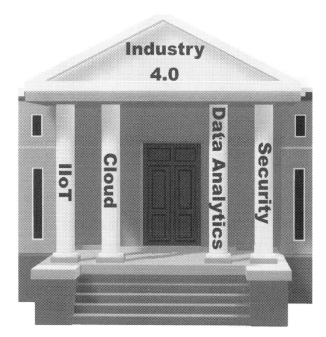

Figure 1-2. *Building blocks of Industry 4.0*

Industrial Internet of Things

The first building block of Industry 4.0 is sensors and devices. Sensors are the hardware that detects and measures a physical property of some kind; for example, pressure sensors measure pressure on an object. Assume your machine is getting large amount of pressure from gas accumulating in pipes. What would happen when you don't have a pressure sensor? Your machine breaks down, production stops, and a new pipe could take hours, if not days, to arrive. Are sensors new in the business? No. They have been available for some time, but we converted sensors and devices into smart sensors and smart devices in Industry 4.0. These smart sensors and smart devices are collectively referred to as Things.

These Things not only detect and measure a physical property, but record an infinite volume of data and store it on a network via an available communication channel like Wi-Fi, Internet, Bluetooth, and so on. With new emerging technologies, these Things can process these data using embedded intelligence and can react to it; for example, they might trigger some event and communication with other Things. Technically, these Things allow a wide variety of functions over the same or different communication channels.

Most of these sensors have been available for years, but mass production and availability have improved the affordability of such Things. With growing needs and high demand, we are developing new Things that are easy to use, and can also perform analysis, draw conclusions, and trigger action.

Note   We will be talking about various type of sensors in the next chapter.

Cloud Technology

The next important building block of Industry 4.0 comes from the solution to where we store the infinite abundance of data generated from smart Things. We have created more data in the last two years than was created in thousands of years of human existence. The question is what we should do with it. How can we analyze and use it?

Data have always been a problem. For the first three generations of industry, the absence of data was a problem. Now, with Industry 4.0, the abundance of data is a problem. We realized this and developed devices and the infrastructure to store data in hard drives and developed the knowledge and skills to analyze these data. Sharing this huge amount of data was an issue, too. We also realized that and we moved to the cloud.

Cloud platforms are the future due to the introduction of new capabilities and technologies. It is very complex and not cost-effective to keep such a large data infrastructure in house. The performance of cloud technologies made it easy to share and mine these data.

Industry 4.0 has become a success because it is not reserved for large corporations. It can help any organization, from startups to medium-sized businesses, in addition to large corporations. The cloud made this emerging technology and infrastructure affordable to all types and sizes of organization.

Speed (i.e., reaction time) is another challenge with thousands of sensors and terabytes of data. Moving such a large volume with low latency can be achieved by the cloud. For example, streaming a video feed to detect a face in a crowd or find a tool on the floor requires sufficient processing power and speed.

> **Note**   In-depth discussion of data analysis and machine learning is outside the scope of this book. I highly recommend reading *Machine Learning with Microsoft Technologies* by Leila Etaati (Apress, 2nd ed. edition (November 27, 2019)), and *The Decision Maker's Handbook to Data Science* by S. Kampakis (Apress, 1st ed. edition (June 13, 2019)).

Data Analytics

Industry 4.0 is supported by a third building block, data analytics. I remember my first database class in graduate school, when the professor asked what the difference is between data and information. Raw and unorganized facts are data. The knowledge you gain after processing those data are called information. Smart sensors and devices generate data, but not information.

It is true that it is important that we understand and learn how to analyze data, but it is equally true that we need to make conclusions and take action based on those data. Thus, Industry 4.0 needs a workforce who can analyze real-time data, make meaningful conclusions about the patterns and relationships, and finally provide the necessary actions to managers.

When you analyze data for predictive maintenance, it is called predictive analysis; for example, a temperature sensor shows that the temperature in a machine room is increasing. When you analyze data to find the root cause of an issue it is called diagnostic analysis; for example, analyzing a pressure sensor to find out why the shaft broke in a boiler. When you analyze existing data to predict the future, this is called prescriptive analysis. Industry 4.0 is based on prescriptive analysis. AI and machine learning are the most learned technologies in the last few years.

Maximizing profit and increased competitiveness are among the top goals of management. IoT helps in maximizing production efficiency and increasing productivity and better decision making via prescriptive analysis on the data.

Security

Industry 4.0 is about increased competitiveness; thus, security is categorized into two components.

- Threat to information
- Threat to assets

Securing information means securing design documents, proprietary processes, intellectual property, financial documents, and client information. Securing assets means protecting the platform, equipment, and machines.

If the security of information is compromised, then a company's competitive advantage is jeopardized. If the security of assets is compromised, then machine breakdowns, accident, or a total shutdown could happen. In today's world, each device and network is a vulnerability. When sensors and devices are connected and communicating over a network about the environment and taking actions, they need to be secure.

Each company should choose vendors with security credentials and purchase hardware only after validating security. Also, IoT sensors and devices should be segregated from the main network. Security should be a shared responsibility between the IT team and managers.

Industry 4.0 poses potential dangers. Therefore, our goal is to have a security-first culture in every industry.

Benefits and Challenges

The benefits of Industry 4.0 are significant due to the use of the latest technologies. The following are some of the most important benefits.

- *Increased productivity:* Production lines can produce more and do it faster. Machines experience less downtime because of enhanced machine monitoring and real-time decision making.

- *Increased profitability:* The mantra of increased profitability is simple: higher revenues and reduced costs. Industry 4.0 technologies enable organizations to produce higher quality with higher productivity.

- *Faster decision making:* With feedback and data analysis, managers can make faster and more accurate decisions for managing existing products and in launching new products.

- *Increased competitiveness:* With online inventory management solutions and tracing of real-time demand and supply, managers can better forecast demand.

Despite the benefits, the adoption of Industry 4.0 presents several challenges, including those listed here.

- *Lack of in-house talent:* Developing solutions using any new technology is complex and draws on many different types of skills and experiences. IoT is no different. The skills gap is perceived as a major challenge, especially because it requires all three critical skill sets: hardware expertise, device programming, and the derivation of useful information using AI and machine learning. There are, however, some proactive steps organizations can take, like training in-house employees, giving incentives to take on new challenges, and hiring part-time or contract employees.

- *Increasing operating expenditures:* Full IoT project implementation could require hundreds of devices and sensors. For most large-scale environments, this number can grow into the thousands. Managers need to provide proof of value to show whether these IoT investments can either save costs or increase revenue and get the required executive approval. In most cases it is hard to get these answers due to lack of expertise and confidence among business executives and board members.

- *Lack of IT reliability:* Information infrastructure includes information management systems, data communications networks, and storage and computation capacity. For an IoT solution to work, information infrastructure must have the high degree of connectivity, compatibility, and ease of use that already characterizes traditional physical infrastructure. Currently communication networks are a challenge in hard-to-reach areas like offshore oil rigs, electricity towers in mountains and forests, and ships sailing in deep oceans. Satellite communication can bridge some of these gaps, and 5G will help bridge the gap further.

- *Lack of IoT standards:* In Chapter 2 you will learn about different type of protocols supported by IoT device manufacturers, cloud providers, and software development kits (SDKs). We also cover various communication media used by the heterogeneous family of connected Things. Due to a lack of standards, manufacturers and IoT solution providers are building solutions using unlimited possible combinations of these technologies. Some cheap products don't follow all security guidelines and have serious security vulnerabilities, making them a threat. Many standardization organizations and government organizations are creating IoT standards and regulations to overcome this issue. Chapter 14 includes a list of current IoT standards and regulations.

- *Security concerns:* Although I identify security as a challenge in all the industry-specific chapters in this book, I dedicate a full chapter to it. Chapter 14 provides a more detailed discussion of the problem and recommends solutions so that readers can access advanced security issues without having to make notes in each chapter separately.

Summary

This chapter provided theoretical information about the generations of industry, past and present. It discussed how industry has evolved and what it took to make the industry of the present, Industry 4.0. I pointed out several benefits of the current era that managers can leverage and challenges they must tackle.

This discussion sets the stage for the introduction of IoT, which managers hardly think of when talking about process improvement, increasing production, and optimizing cost and waste reduction. The next chapter discusses how IoT can be your partner at each stage to achieve this.

CHAPTER 2

Basic IoT Concepts

All computer systems are a combination of different hardware and software components. IoT is the concept that combines the physical environment with hardware and software, creating a new generation of systems that can take input from the physical world and use this to make decisions to work under influence of those environmental parameters.

This chapter provides an overview of exciting and relevant technical areas essential to managers and professionals in any industry. Although this book lists specific industries using IoT, its primary focus is the methodology for creating a secure and useful environment of devices and sensors to improve industrial goals.

In describing the IoT in detail, this chapter covers the following topics.

- Theoretical concepts of IoT

- Concepts, hardware, and platforms of an IoT solution available on the market

- Defining high-level ideas about IoT in industry

Introducing the Internet of Things

The name of the IoT comes from two common terms: Internet and Things. The **Internet** is the global network connection we all are familiar with, and the **Things** are sensors and devices that can communicate over a given communication channel.

I introduced Things in Chapter 1, but now we can drill down on this term to learn about the available options. Things could be anything, for example, from small sensors like temperature and humidity sensors, to medium devices like smartphones and cameras, and larger objects like buildings and vehicles, or even an entire city. When these elements connect to the Internet and send and receive data over the communication network, they become smart and form the IoT.

© Nirnay Bansal 2020

N. Bansal, *Designing Internet of Things Solutions with Microsoft Azure,*
https://doi.org/10.1007/978-1-4842-6041-8_2

Often, IoT devices are not full computer systems, or do not have any full-size displays. Instead, IoT devices have several common electronic components with one or more specialized sensors soldered on a small board. These boards have either an open socket to connect it to the network with wire (local area network [LAN], wide area network [WAN]) or an additional chip to connect it to the network wirelessly (Bluetooth, Wi-Fi).

Building Blocks

Now that you understand the Internet and Things, let's look at the IoT layer by layer. The effectiveness and applicability of any system is directly proportionate to the performance of its building blocks. As shown in Figure 2-1, IoT has three building blocks that determine the way IoT interacts to accomplish more.

Figure 2-1. *Building blocks of IoT*

Things

Things is the first endpoint of IoT but the second most important building block. It consists of core basic hardware, or a combination of one of more sensors that can gather data and transfer these data over the network. Some optional capabilities of Things are communicating with other Things, analyzing data, and performing actions; for example, making the decision to start an air conditioner when the room temperature goes above 70°F.

Your old smartphone is one of the cheapest Things that supports Internet Protocol version 6 (IPv6) and contains various sensors to sense the external environment, memory to store data generated from the sensors, a processor to analyze the stored data, and various communication channels to transfer the raw data and results from the analysis. In this book, I provide a couple of labs that use a smartphone instead of any custom hardware. You will see how smartphones can be cost- and time-effective IoT devices. They can work as a remote control or security device and connect home, car, and fitness devices.

A Thing is an abstract object and can be customized to use in any vertical industry (health care, manufacturing, home security, etc.). The question is if Things are such important objects, why they can't come with the machines themselves. Things do come with modern machines, but in most older industries, machines were procured in a previous generation. Replacing those machines using shareholders' money is neither a cost-effective solution nor a good managerial decision. We know that Things add intelligence to manual processes, so we can use this Thing externally with the existing machines.

I am endorsing some magic number provided by researchers about an expected 50 billion connected devices by 2020, or 75 billion by 2025, or 500 billion by 2030, but I strongly believe that only those businesses that learn to use data generated by Things will survive and thrive in the future. Every company, in every industry, of any size, needs to invest in IoT and make it a priority for their business strategy. Different type of available sensors and how we can use them are discussed later in this chapter.

Cloud

Data that are gathered from the Things need to be stored and processed. As I said earlier, not all Things are capable of analyzing the data, nor do they have enough memory capacity to store data. The cloud solves the problem of both storage and processing power. The cloud is the third building block of IoT.

My clock shows 8 a.m. daily, but until I link an action item like ringing an alarm if the clock is capable, or link a manual action for me like starting for the office, this clock is useless, consuming battery power and taking up space on my bedside table. Similarly, once these data land on the cloud, the challenge is to properly use them.

Within the next five years, more than 90 percent of all IoT data will be stored on the cloud. In other words, we can say the cloud is needed to provide network connectivity to Things and is capable of receiving and storing the enormous amounts of data they generate. Its job would not be finished, though, until the given cloud platform is capable of processing these data and results are used for meaningful decision making and action items.

This building block also includes device management and data management.

Device Manager

A device manager is responsible for the following areas.

Device Registration

Every device must have a unique ID; smartphones, for example, have International Mobile Equipment Identity (IMEI). Once the device attaches with a network, it has a unique IP address. The unique device number with a unique IP address helps establish the identity of a device and separate it from untrusted devices. It helps the device manager keep real-time status information for the device.

Note   IPv6 is a natural and necessary replacement of IPv4. I highly recommend all managers and readers of this book invest in only Things capable of IPv6, not because it has 340 undecillion (340 trillion trillion trillion) addresses, but because IPv6 is bundled with various security features.

Controlling Device

Device manager also controls devices and sets configurations to determine how it behaves in the environment, such as activating and deactivating a device. If a Thing is capable of analyzing and taking actions, then the device manager defines and configures clear standard situations and actions for all possible conditions. There could be many actions defined for one situation, as well as the same action is defined for multiple situations.

If a Thing is capable of communicating with other Things on a network, then the device manager defines and configures clear standards and restrictions. A Thing might be able to communicate to only one Thing on the network, or a Thing might be able to communicate with multiple or all Things on the network.

Data Manager

This building block also includes data management. The data manager is responsible for several functions.

Data Definition

Data definition indicates clearly which data a connected Thing can send. One big challenge in managing data definition is data drift or schema drift. When manufacturers upgrade firmware, data coming from systems can change. It is important that your cloud data management solution is able to handle such data drift without interrupting.

Data Filtration

Data need to be filtered before they are moved to actual storage. This includes removing duplicate data and erroneous records.

Data Storage

First, our storage must be able to store structured and unstructured data. Second, it should provide a complete solution for high availability and disaster recovery. Third, because an immense amount of data is generated, it must be stored such that it supports real-time analytics. Finally, it should also be able to enrich the data before storing, to save time in preparing the data for analytics and machine learning.

Often, companies experiment with their IoT strategy before they launch full-scale efforts. A proof of concept (POC) is a low-cost, low-risk approach that can help you refine your strategy. However, many enterprises that have implemented a successful IoT POC or pilot study are surprised as they shift into production. Difficulties arise as the project scales up. The data streaming from a few connected devices might be manageable, but storage can become an issue as more devices come online. The data management solution should also provide alerts in case any issues arise during the process.

Security

Talking about security last doesn't seem right. It is not the last building block, but the first building block of IoT. Data gathered from IoT poses potential dangers related to intellectual property, privacy, and liability. Therefore, our goal is to have a security-first culture in every industry and built-in security at every level of planning and implementation. This is critical to secure an industry, as threats are an undisputed justification to invest in security at both the planning and implementation levels.

The most common type of attack to steal data is a phishing attack, but when securing our IoT, we should take an outside-in approach, because such an approach most closely explains the adversary's view. Let's explore the possible threats in turn.

Fake Devices

As mentioned earlier, sensors are the first entry point in any IoT system. It is possible for an attacker to introduce a new device on a network.

Device Manipulation

Devices are the building blocks for IoT and an attacker might try to modify and manipulate the data coming from these devices. This could lead to bad decisions and wrong actions.

Trust Level

The trust level defines the action privilege(s) that devices have. A breach in trust level could stop a device from taking meaningful actions or cause it to start taking actions that the device is not allowed to perform.

Chief information security officers (CISOs) need to understand all possible types of attacks and build policies to prevent them and mitigate the effects when they do happen without affecting the company's reputation and value chain.

Using IPv6 means that some of your security items are already covered. With IPv4, it is easy for an attacker to redirect traffic and manipulate the conversation, but IPv6 encryption and integrity checking is the new standard, which makes it very difficult for attackers to bypass. Most managers are unaware of which version of IP is running in devices used in their company, but it is important for them to enforce adaptation of IPv6 in their technology vision.

Design Principles

Referring to the challenges of Industry 4.0 in Chapter 1, when you implement the IoT project in your industry, it should overcome as many of those challenges as possible. The IoT project shouldn't be an aesthetic design, but it can be a frumpy design with emphasis on a broad system, like how all of the different elements will interact with each other. A design principle that treats an IoT project as a single device is inefficient; therefore the IoT should treat a device as an element in an operating ecosystem. Figure 2-2 shows the design principles that will aid in implementing a strong IoT project in any industry.

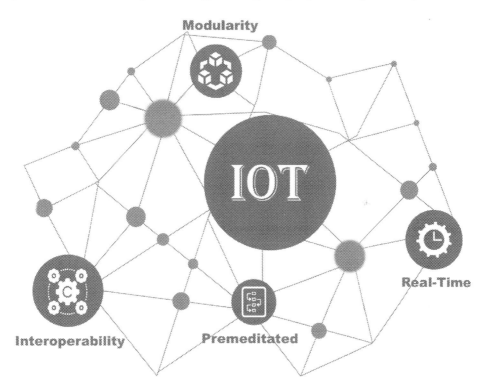

Figure 2-2. *Design principles of IoT*

Modularity

Modularity is required at the hardware level as well as at the software level. As technology is changing every day and new devices and sensors are available, your IoT project must be able to adapt fast and smoothly to these changes and industry needs. All sensors in the project should be independent and interchangeable, such that changing one will not require other devices or sensors to change.

One of the main goals of IoT is facilitating communication between devices. Communication between devices must not be tightly coupled and interaction should be allowed only through well-defined common interfaces.

It is difficult to expand your IoT project because different sensor manufacturers support different protocols and different interfaces. Sometime a sensor from different vendor needs to be added using different connectivity options. As a system grows to a large-scale IoT application, a custom design reduces the ability to stick to one standard, and there are trade-offs with cost by developing a diverse solution from multiple platforms or operating environments. As a solution architect practitioner, I always identify the theoretical advantages of modular design, like decreased complexity and reduction of redundancy when exploiting data ontology and Thing ontology. As a manager, creating such a solution often demands a reimagining of the hardware procurement and modular design approach to facilitate that convergence.

Interoperability

With the introduction of hundreds (if not thousands) of new IoT devices to the market, today we are experiencing a revolution in connecting via smart devices and a revolution in our industrial processes to produce customer-centric products. Unfortunately, interoperability is the missing piece. It is common for manufacturers to develop devices using their own specifications and communication protocols. This issue is becoming more critical with the lack of a consortium framework from big companies.

Devices and sensors need to be able to communicate with humans. At the end of the day, our IoT project requires interoperability to create seamless programming and connectivity of the devices and sensors. The exchange of data or passing an action via message between different things should be handled fluidly. This means we need standards that dictate communicable, operable, and programmable interactions across devices, regardless of make, model, manufacturer, or industry.

Usually an IoT project is considered a calm designed system: It doesn't constantly require attention, but it should not be a forgotten system, either. Each manufacturer provides its own data format, application programming interface (API), and control system, leading to more interoperability issues. Such interoperability issues are the cause of problems for managers, such as vendor lock-in, fewer IoT platforms to choose from, and implementing an IoT project in the future at a large scale.

Although Cloud IoT platform vendors bridge this gap via their application layer, making it more generic, and via working directly with manufacturers to preconfigure their platform with their hardware needs. Interoperability is the key for all cloud providers to develop and offer competitive solutions. The agreement on one standard is essential for manufacturers, which could interact with each other. Still, though, there is no clear standard defined by any formal body. Therefore, it is the job of a manager to design and procure hardware and a platform that supports IoT interoperability.

Real Time

All devices and sensors collect data in real time. Similarly, the design of an IoT project should support real-time data storage and analysis to make decisions fast. Real time doesn't mean when the data reaches the network or is in the computer system to process, but as soon as a sensor measures the data.

Real time in industries like agriculture and fleet tracking is not as important, but for industries like medical, smart vehicle, and aerospace, this is a core requirement. I will leave it to you to classify if stock analysis, social media trend analysis, online advertising, CO_2 detection, and motion detection could be categorized as real-time or near real-time processing.

This design principle challenges the second building block of IoT, the cloud. The cloud is not low latency (latency refers to the delay between the time data are sent by one party and received by another). Isn't the cloud already designed for low-latency usage, with the help of Content Delivery Network (CDN) and having a datacenter in your geographical region closer to your site? Yes, the answer is confusing. Think about low latency as relative: If you compare it with the latency of on-premises servers, then cloud latency is significant.

AI and machine learning require large historic data sets. For timely decision making and action, the cloud platform provides analytics tools such as complex event processing (CEP) to analyze data on a real-time or a near-real-time scale. CEP is important, if not mandatory, in some industries like manufacturing, where managers invest in IoT due to its parallel processing capability to recognize patterns and either trigger automated action or an alarm for human intervention.

Examples of industries in which we might need near-real-time analysis are those that use cognitive technologies. These services are able to perform tasks that only humans used to be able to do, like computer vision, natural-language processing, and speech recognition

---

Note   Because the speed at which data can travel over the network is limited by the speed of light, it adds a minimum of 1 ms with every 186 miles.

A possible solution could be placing data at the edge of the network, called fog networking, or with smaller cloud providers available near your worksite. Fog is a network architecture for a decentralized infrastructure where data storage and data computation stay as close as possible to the device that is generating those data. Conventionally due to the size of the data and processing capacity required, we prefer centralized cloud technology, which additionally controls, configures, and manages device security. Fog is bringing these all capabilities and functionalities to the device itself. Recently we started using fog networks with Edge computing. Readers should note that fog computing is not replacing cloud computing, but it is empowering those devices where response time is critical, a reliable network is not available, or cost is not a factor.

Premeditated

This is my personal favorite. I believe that not just IoT projects but any software design should follow a premeditated design pattern as compared with an impulsive design pattern. The definition of completion for an IoT project is the ability to predict, adapt to situations, and take action. For example, the smart thermostat learns from our temperature pattern and adjusts itself intelligently over time.

Usually security features are premeditated, but an IoT project shouldn't restrict premeditated design to just security; it should be implemented at every level of the project. Traditional working conditions will certainly be disrupted, but the employees need to trust that their IoT system is designed to avoid failures, correct issues, take appropriate actions.

Additionally, when designing an IoT system, managers need to think about cross-department collaboration. Other departments like legal, security, and finance, as well as external partners like vendor and sales representatives also need to trust the system. Do you make appointments with manufacturers to fix machines that are not yet broken? For example, if the IoT system is flagging a machine to break down in the next two months, finance needs to trust the system and either start the process to approve and generate a purchase order for a new machine or make an appointment with the manufacturer to fix the machine you have.

Do you increase production and invest in raw materials because system predicts demand will increase in the next quarter? Do you drive a car that can control any possibility of collision? Do you purchase a house knowing the energy radiation level from a cellular base station (cell site or cell tower) is high? Think about these questions. These are the most essential principles that truly make an IoT an IIoT.

IoT Devices and Sensors

A sensor is a device that is able to detect changes in an environment and record its physical properties. It can then display them, transmit them, or process them to make a decision to adjust other physical conditions. Because of lack of standardization on sensors, not all sensors generate the same type of data. Sensors can be analog or digital. Analog sensors additionally require an analog-to-digital converter to store or transmit the data. Some sensors provide low-level data (i.e., in bits and bytes) and some sensors provide data in human-readable format like Extensible Markup Language (XML) or JavaScript Object Notation (JSON). By using various type of sensors, I helped my clients to efficiently make decisions for their business's products and services.

The following list describes the key sensors being used extensively in the IoT and IIoT world.

- *Temperature sensors:* Temperature sensors (from the family of thermal sensors) measure the temperature of any physical object including air (air has mass and takes up physical space; therefore, air is a physical object). I believe the temperature sensor is one of oldest sensors in this family. You can find them in your thermostat, air conditioner, oven, and furnace.

- *Pressure sensors:* Pressure sensors measure the physical or atmospheric pressure. They are used to detect the pressure in gas chambers, pipes, boilers, and other sealed systems. You can find them in modern digital weight machines, in your car as a tire pressure monitoring system, and your smartphone when you squeeze it.

- *Impedance sensors:* Impedance sensors are contactless sensors that measure the impedance between voltage and current, for example, to measure nanometric displacement. You can find them in heart rate monitors and glucose monitors.

- *Humidity sensors:* Humidity sensors measure the amount of water vapor in air, usually in parts per million (PPM). I have this feature in a clock in my bathroom.

- *Magnetic sensors:* Magnetic sensors detect the presence of a magnetic field and measure flux, strength, rotation, and direction of any changes and disturbances in the magnetic field. You can sometimes find them in navigation devices.

- *Motion sensors:* Motion sensors detect any physical movement around a permissible limit of the sensor. Passive infrared sensors are commonly used to detect low-level radiation emitted by a warm body. Other technologies are microwave and ultrasonic detection. You can find them at work in your favorite store doors.

- *pH sensors:* pH sensors measure acidity or alkalinity of water-based solutions. The value displayed is actually the voltage between two electrodes. It is often used in detecting acidity or alkalinity levels in swimming pools, municipal water supplies, wine, beer, and soil.

- *Level sensors:* Level sensors measures the level of a liquid relative to a benchmark normal value. You can find them in your vehicle's fuel gauges and they notably indicate when the fuel level of your tank is close to empty.

- *Image sensors:* Image sensors function to capture images to be digitally stored for processing. This is one of the most important sensors used in Industry 4.0 on production lines to detect the quality of a product or the product itself, and in wireless cameras on manufacturing shop floors to find tools.

- *Proximity sensors:* Proximity sensors detect the existence of a nearby object without physical contact. There are many different types of technology used to build these sensors, like capacitive, inductive, ultrasonic, magnetic, and photoelectric.

- *Water quality sensors:* We discussed pH sensors already. Water quality sensors measure different parameter of water quality. In addition to pH level, they can also measure chemical presence and electric conductivity. With an increasing demand for organic food and growing such food using hydroponics and aquaponics technology, these sensors are increasingly important.

- *Strain sensors:* Strain gauges measure the strain or a force on an object. Its value measures are actually a force, pressure, tension, and load. These sensors are used in various industries for process monitoring, quality control like threads, safety equipment, and so on.

- *Chemical sensors:* Chemical sensors are an extension of water quality sensors and measure changes in liquid or to measure air chemical changes. This is one of the most important sensors for human life. They are used in industries, cities, and nuclear plants to detect harmful chemicals.

- *Acoustic sensors:* Acoustic sensors measure sound via different audio technologies like microphones. They are used in industry to identify and diagnose faults in machinery without any physical contact with the machine; that is, they are contactless sensors. It also has important military uses, as in submarines.

- *Gas sensors:* Gas sensors are similar to chemical sensors. They measure changes in air quality or detect various gases in the air. Gas sensors detect and measure natural gases. There are various sensing technologies available, including electrochemical, photoionization, and semiconductor.

- *Smoke sensors:* Smoke sensors are an extension of gas sensors and measure gases related to smoke and particles in the in air. Sensing technologies include optical sensors or ionization detection. You can find smoke sensors in your home, HVAC systems, or offices as smoke detectors.

- *Infrared (IR) sensors:* IR sensors measure the heat of an object. Technically they measure IR radiation because anything that emits heat gives off IR radiation. IR sensors are invisible to the human eye. You can find them in your remotes, computer mouse, night vision devices (like security cameras), and telescopes. There is another type of IR sensor available that can detect people, sometimes referred to as a passive infrared (PIR) sensor.

- *Acceleration sensors:* Acceleration sensors (from the family of seismic sensors) measure orientation of an object like tilt, motion, positioning, shock, or vibration. The word *acceleration* came from physics and is defined as the rate of change of velocity of the object per unit of time. In industry, acceleration sensors are used to measure vibration in machines. They are also used in building maintenance to measure inclination. You can find them in your smartphone, GPS devices, and modern cars.

- *Gyroscopic sensors:* Gyroscopic sensors are extension of acceleration measure the rotation of an object using a three-axis system. It is used for navigation and measurement of angular and rotational velocity in three-axis directions. You can find them in your smartphone, game controller and drones.

- *Optical sensors:* Optical sensors measure physical quantity of light. They can measure units as small as a photon up to a high-powered laser. You can find them in your smartphones when it adjusts screen brightness for you.

- *Fingerprint sensors:* Fingerprint sensors are the most familiar biometric sensors, used in smartphones and home security devices. Optical sensing and capacitive sensing technology are available today and both measure the fingerprint or impression using light.

- *Radiation sensors:* Radiation sensors are also known by different names based on the technology they use in detecting radiation levels; examples are Geiger Muller detectors, scintillation detectors, and gamma counters. Today there is lot of anxiety about radiation levels in populations living near nuclear power plants or cellular base stations. You can find these sensors in some wearable devices like dosimeters and wall-mounted devices used in waste management areas, radioactive contamination zones, and cargo areas.

- Global Positioning System (GPS) sensors: GPS sensors measure geolocation using the time a signal takes to travel between satellites and ground stations on Earth. For better accuracy, GPS measures distance from three or more satellites. Although it is used in a large set of devices, GPS sensors are commonly used in smartphones, some new models of cars, and smart watches.

IoT Platforms

Connecting one device to a service on your computer is quite easy. However, when an industry starts an IIoT project, it requires one solution for hundreds (if not thousands) of devices. We require a full-stack platform to connect, build, manage, and monitor the system. Figure 2-3 shows a few well-known IoT platforms.

Figure 2-3. *Cloud IoT platforms*

Microsoft Azure IoT

The Microsoft Azure IoT is an IoT cloud platform. It is a collection of Microsoft-managed cloud services that connect, monitor, and control IoT devices to transform business processes. These cloud services are then further divided into software-as-a-service (SaaS) and platform-as-a-service (PaaS) solutions with trade-offs for technical abstraction, level of customization, and time to market.

- *IoT Central* is a SaaS solution that comes with easy-to-use and preconfigured templates to start quickly with your IoT project.

- *IoT Solution Accelerators* is an open source PaaS solution that has multiple prebuilt solutions. These solutions are provided to accelerate your development and later allow you to customize the solution to meet your needs.

- *IoT Hub* is a PaaS solution and technical foundational of the preceding offerings. It supports bidirectional communication; for example, it can command and control communications from the cloud back to the devices. IoT Hub also supports Android Things via Java SDK.

- *IoT Edge* is neither a PaaS nor an SaaS solution. It technically lets you run cloud intelligence, data analysis, and custom logic directly on IoT devices; when combined with Edge processing, this can offer faster processing with low latency and reduce the time and cost of data travel to the cloud servers.

Microsoft Azure IoT provides SDKs in C, C#, Java, Python, and Node.js to build, manage, and monitor devices with IoT Hub. It supports Linux, Windows, and real-time operating systems.

Microsoft Azure IoT also supports the following protocols:

- *HTTPS*: HTTP/HTTPS is a request/response Web messaging protocol. HTTP uses connection-oriented Transmission Control Protocol (TCP) as a transport protocol and Transport Layer Security/Secure Sockets Layer (TLS/SSL) for security. The default port is 80/443 (TLS/SSL).

- *Advanced Message Queuing Protocol (AMQP):* AMQP is a request/response and publish/subscribe-based messaging protocol designed for lightweight machine-to-machine (M2M) communications with reliability, security, provisioning, and interoperability. AMQP uses connection-oriented TCP as a transport protocol and TLS/SSL and Simple Authentication and Security Layer (SASL) for security. It is the preferred protocol to address applications requiring fast and reliable business transactions. The default port is 5671 (TLS/SSL) or 5672.

- *AMQP over WebSocket:* This protocol has the capabilities of AMQP defined previously but allows clients to connect over HTTPS standardized protocol using port 443.

- *Message Queuing Telemetry Transport Protocol (MQTT):* MQTT is a very basic publish/subscribe-based messaging protocol designed for lightweight M2M communications in large networks of various small devices that need to be monitored or controlled from a back-end server on the Internet. MQTT client publishes messages to an MQTT broker, which is subscribed to by other clients. MQTT uses connection-oriented TCP as a transport protocol and TLS/SSL for security. It guarantees reliable delivery of messages. It does not support device-to-device communication. The default port is 1883/8883 (TLS/SSL).

- *MQTT over WebSocket:* MQTT over WebSocket has the capabilities of MQTT previously defined, but allows clients to connect over HTTPS standardized protocol using port 443.

Amazon AWS IoT

The AWS IoT is an IoT cloud platform from Amazon. It is a fully managed platform providing IoT services backed with a number of AWS cloud computing features, from cloud storage to an extensive set of developer tools. You have probably heard about iRobot (or own one); this is the best example of an IoT device that uses the AWS IoT platform. It uses a broad range of AWS products for IoT, including mobile services analytics, storage, databases, platform management, and networking activities.

- *AWS IoT Core* is a technical foundational platform that enables devices to connect, process, and act on device data sent to AWS Services.

- *Amazon FreeRTOS* is an open source microcontroller real-time operating system (RTOS) that provides easy programming and management of small, low-power Edge devices. It can connect with AWS IoT Core to use other cloud services.

- *AWS IoT Greengrass* provides security and intelligence to the device to run machine learning programs using AWS Lambda functions and Docker containers locally. It provides devices the capability to run everything locally in near real time and offline, and sync data with AWS as and when needed.

- *AWS IoT 1-Click* is a service that enables simple devices to trigger AWS Lambda functions that can execute an action.

AWS IoT provides various interfaces to build and manage an IoT project:

- AWS CLI

- IoT API

- SDKs

AWS IoT provides Mobile SDKs for iOS and Android, Arduino SDK and Device SDK in Embedded C, C++, Java, JavaScript, and Python. AWS IoT supports the following protocols:

- HTTPS

- MQTT

- WebSocket

Note   You can integrate Alexa Voice Service (AVS) in any connected device without cost and complexity of computation, memory, and audio interface, therefore enabling consumers to talk directly to Alexa from your device.

Google Cloud IoT

The Google Cloud IoT is an IoT cloud platform from Google. It is a fully managed pay-as-you-go cloud service that works with number of Google Cloud Platform (GCP) services like InfluxDB storage, advanced analytics, and machine learning with Cloud Machine Learning Engine. The following are the key features.

- *Cloud IoT Core* is also a device-agnostic service that allows users to connect, store data, and manage devices in the cloud. It forwards data to a multiple cloud Pub/Sub (Publisher-Subscriber) topic to perform streaming analysis.

- *Edge TPU* is a new hardware chip designed to run with *Cloud IoT Edge* to bring AI and machine learning capability to gateways and connected devices. Edge TPU helps with low-latency and real-time intelligent decisions locally on the device through the Lite version on TensorFlow.

Google Cloud IoT provides a Device SDK in Embedded C. Cloud IoT supports Android Things operating systems and Linux-based operating systems. Google Cloud IoT supports industry-standard HTTP and MQTT protocols.

There are some other notable Cloud IoT providers:

- Cisco IoT Cloud Connect

- IBM Watson IoT

- Oracle IoT

- Cumulocity IoT

Industrial IoT

When IoT combines with industry to bridge the gap between the physical world and cyber ecosystem to create immense opportunities for managers to improve process, increase productivity, and optimize cost, then that industry enters into Industry 4.0 or IIoT.

IIoT provides channels for Things to communicate with humans about the physical environment, monitor production processes to help meaningful real-time decisions based on past or present data, and harvest historic data to propose data points at which managers could optimize costs. IIoT includes applications used in industries for better efficiency and reliability in their operations, therefore it is an industry-agnostic term.

With IIoT, it is now possible to gather data about events that were invisible in the past and also hard to measure. Machines are now empowered to make near-perfect decisions and automate actions that previous industrial revolutions could not handle. Therefore, when we think of IIoT we actually think about a smart factory. IIoT is not just a digital transformation, but a requirement of managers to make fast, accurate decisions to compete in a crowded market.

Although IIoT particularly interests the manufacturing, retail, and transport industries, there are other industries in which we need to make processes more efficient, intelligent, and customer-centric. Let's look into those industries that have already rolled out IoT initiatives.

- Manufacturing is covered in Chapter 5.

- Agriculture is covered in Chapter 6.

- Energy is covered in Chapter 7

- Home automation and smart homes are covered in Chapter 8.

- Supply chain is covered in Chapter 9.

- Financial services are covered in Chapter 10.

- Health care is covered in Chapter 11.

- Retail is covered in Chapter 12.

- Transportation is covered in Chapter 13.

There are some other notable applications in smart city applications.

- Monitoring of availability of parking spaces in the city.

- Intelligent highways with warnings and diversions according to climate conditions and unexpected events like accidents.

- Intelligent and weather adaptive streetlights.

Other than wearable gadgets available today, my personal favorite IIoT features that have made significant difference in my life are as follows.

- Measurement of the energy radiated by cell stations and Wi-Fi routers near me.

- Sound level monitoring in neighborhoods and at community events.

- Detection of toxic gas leakages and levels of hazardous gases in the air.

- Monitoring of ozone levels.

Summary

In this chapter, we have learned about different types of sensors available. It is possible to use these sensors as stand-alone devices or with other sensors on the same board. Once you know how to read data from these sensors, you have endless possibilities, and you're ready to explore IoT. You can use data from sensors by storing them in the cloud and using those data later to create dashboards.

You could be thinking about the knowledge you acquired by reading this chapter by thinking about the sensors that are already present in your industry, as well as the ones that are new to you and could be added or proposed to your organization.

Finally, you learned about different IoT platforms available. Now, you are ready to move technical parts of the book. Throughout this book and during the labs provided, I assume you are using the best sensors with no errors in readings.

CHAPTER 3

Microsoft Azure IoT Platform

As we learned in the previous chapter, the cloud is the one of the main building blocks of IoT. Its jobs are to connect, manage, and secure Things, as well as provide meaningful insight on the data generated by them. Among the many IoT cloud providers available, Microsoft Azure provides end-to-end services and solutions, presenting itself as a complete IoT platform to enable digital transformation for your organization. Although this book lists specific industries using IoT, Microsoft Azure IoT services are industry agnostic.

This chapter provides an overview of relevant services and solutions essential to run a successful IoT project in your industry. We will soon understand an IoT project life cycle, then we will work on creating an IoT Hub. We will also be looking at pricing models to help you in creating a budget forecast. This will help us in build momentum for future chapters to understand how the IoT Hub endpoints work.

This chapter covers the following topics.

- Introduction to Azure IoT

- Azure IoT services and solutions

- Architecture

Introduction to Azure IoT

The Microsoft IoT platform is called Azure IoT because Microsoft Azure is its core foundation. Azure IoT represents a set of fully managed services and solutions specifically for IoT, including IoT Hub, IoT Edge, and IoT Central applications, as well as offerings from Azure like storage, stream analytics, Azure data lake, and Azure machine learning. Using Azure core offerings, we can harness the full power of the cloud.

© Nirnay Bansal 2020
N. Bansal, *Designing Internet of Things Solutions with Microsoft Azure,*
https://doi.org/10.1007/978-1-4842-6041-8_3

Together with services and built-in solutions, Azure will help you implement an IoT strategy quickly and efficiently. If you are a startup or a large corporation, creating proof of concept with just one device to start your IoT journey up to thousands of devices (if not millions), then Microsoft offers global autoscaling for you.

Note   Azure IoT supports bidirectional communication between devices and the cloud (in the standard pricing tier only); that is, device-to-cloud communication when a device sends telemetry data to the cloud and cloud-to-device communication when the cloud sends actions and commands to the device.

Azure IoT Services and Solutions

Azure IoT offerings are divided into two categories: SaaS and PaaS, as shown in Figure 3-1. On the one end services are customizable and can be used as per the needs of your organization, and on the other end the solutions are developed with common scenarios you see in your industry (e.g., physical environment monitoring).

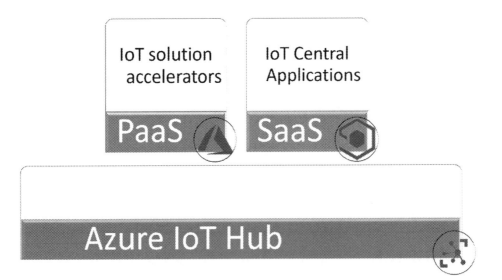

Figure 3-1. *Categories of Azure IoT Hub service offering*

As a manager and developer, you can start building custom solutions using IoT Hub or use templates. We will be talking about templates in detail shortly. Azure Portal itself is a PaaS service, so no matter which solution you choose, Azure Portal will help you get started. Let's investigate each category.

SaaS

IoT Central is a fully managed SaaS solution. It simplifies the initial setup to connect, monitor, and manage your Things and removes the need for cloud solution expertise, thus drastically reducing initial costs and the burden of developing and maintaining the project. Most small clients benefit from this offering due to low time-to-market (TTM) to launch a minimum viable product (MVP) for market testing and early trials. If you are looking to accelerate development and don't require deep levels of service customization, Azure IoT Central is a great place to start. It can also simulate test data, so that you can immediately test your selected device. At the time of writing, various IoT Central applications templates for common vertical industry scenarios like retail, health, energy, and government were available.

All IoT Central applications support IoT devices and IoT Edge devices; additionally, preconfigured IoT Plug-and-Play devices from certified manufacturers are also available as device templates. A device template contains a capability model that specifies the telemetry, properties, and commands that the device implements, cloud properties like last serviced, any customized device properties, and UI dashboards to monitor and manage the devices.

IoT Central applications allow you to export data and customize user roles and permissions. This is very important if you are a solution provider and need multitenancy in your application to support multiple partners but still separate them from one another for security purposes. Multitenancy allows customers and organizations globally across regions to use your solution without knowing the actual implementation of it. You can build IoT Central applications from Azure Portal as well as from `https://apps.azureiotcentral.com/`.

Note   Azure continues to invest in IoT Central and I am always excited to learn about new announcements at the IoT Solutions World Congress and similar conferences.

IoT Central has three tiers to choose from: Free, Standard 1, and Standard 2. The cost is low compared with other competitors, as well as with any custom solution you can build using IoT Hub.

The Free tier is only free for seven days with the first five devices free. Additional devices cost less than $1 per month and an additional 1 million messages cost $15 per month for a standard message size of 4 KB.

PaaS

IoT solution accelerators are a complete set of cloud-based services that implement a common IoT scenario like remote monitoring, connected factory, predictive maintenance, and device simulation. It is open source code that allows you to customize the solution accelerators for your use case. I started my learning of end-to-end solution development from these accelerators. Solution accelerators are not available on Azure Portal but are available at `AzureIoTSolutions.com`. The portal contains four accelerators from Microsoft I listed earlier, and couple of accelerators from Microsoft's partners. Unlike an IoT Central application, which doesn't spin any IoT Hub in your subscription, solution accelerators spin the IoT Hub as well as VM, storage, CosmosDB, Logic app, KeyVault, and several more services.

Accelerators build on .NET and Java and you have the option to choose which technology you are comfortable with and have in-house resources for in case you want to further customize it. I will show both these options and will encourage you to use CLI to build an accelerator.

Note   You can't select Tier (SKU) if you build solution accelerators from Azure Portal, but it is available if you use CLI.

IoT Hub is a PaaS solution. It is called hub because it is a central unit for all of the messages supporting bidirectional communication between device and cloud; that is, it is the cloud gateway. It manages billions of IoT devices and provides reliable and secure communication between IoT devices and the cloud; all data are encrypted. If you want to easily provision millions of devices rapidly, rather than provisioning them one by one, you need to enable the Device Provisioning Service while creating your hub.

There are two tiers available in IoT Hub: Basic and Standard. The only advantage of Standard over Basic is that Standard allows IoT Edge, streaming, and cloud-to-device communication. If you are not looking for these features, the Basic tier would be very cost effective. You can upgrade it at any time, without any service interruption. Costs as of this writing are shown in Tables 3-1 and 3-2.

Table 3-1. *Basic Tier Pricing*

Edition Type	Price Per IoT Hub Unit (Per Month)	Total Number of Messages/ Day Per IoT Hub Unit	Message Meter Size
B1	$10	400,000	4 KB
B2	$50	6,000,000	4 KB
B3	$500	300,000,000	4 KB

Table 3-2. *Standard Tier Pricing*

Edition Type	Price Per IoT Hub Unit (Per Month)	Total Number of Messages/ Day Per IoT Hub Unit	Message Meter Size
Free	Free	8,000	0.5 KB
S1	$25	400,000	4 KB
S2	$250	6,000,000	4 KB
S3	$2,500	300,000,000	4 KB

As you will notice, it is flat cost per device. This is good because there is no catch and you know the cost of your IoT project in advance. Also, it is easily calculated. On the negative side, you pay this price whether you use it or not. Here I would say other IoT platform providers have an edge because they offer pay per use.

IoT provides two SDKs for working with IoT Hub, the Device SDK and Service SDK. Both SDKs are provided in C, C#, Java, Python, and Node.js, with the Service SDK also provided in iOS.

> **Note**   For all Kafka lovers, you can use it with IoT Hub.
>
> I extolled the advantages of using IPv6 in Chapter 2. Unfortunately, IPv6 is currently not supported on IoT Hub.

Digital Twins is a PaaS service. This service represents the next generation of IoT, which models the world of devices in physical space. For example, it can maintain a graph of people and devices, so when a lot of people walk in a corner of the floor that no one had previously been in that day, the cooler or heater will start in that section of the floor.

Unfortunately, you cannot create Digital Twins from Azure Portal, but you need to use a management API to configure and use it.

I introduced *IoT Edge* briefly in Chapter 2. The fundamental problem of the cloud is latency. Although the cloud is powerful for storage and processing, it creates delays. By bringing computing capabilities to local devices, IoT Edge computing can process data in real time and prevent security breaches. If you want to make analysis and decisions based on the device, without first moving data to the cloud, then IoT Edge is what you are looking for. You have a runtime that facilitates communication between the device and the cloud, one or more modules that enable deployment of both custom logic and cloud logic on IoT Edge devices, and enable you to install workloads and finally interface for monitoring and management.

IoT Edge is available on the Basic tier also (that contradicts my first statement), but technically speaking it is only available for testing.

The custom code is not a complete rewrite of your cloud service code. Because IoT Edge supports both Linux and Windows, it also supports the same programming languages (i.e., Java, .NET Core 2.0, Node.js, C, and Python). The source code of IoT Edge itself is open source, bringing flexibility and creativity from the programming community. The container on the module is a full standard Docker container. Because you can have one more module, you can feed the output of one module into another, creating a value chain and data flow story. The icing on the cake is that you don't need to deploy everything every time. You can only deploy updates to just one module.

Let's talk about AI and machine learning on IoT Edge. IoT Edge is not complete if it won't fulfill Microsoft's vision of the intelligent cloud. Microsoft has made it easy to run machine learning models by allowing developers to import AutoML models in a module. For example, a developer can deploy a web service app that is wrapped around a machine learning model into a Docker container to a module. Machine learning and AI models built using known algorithms or advance algorithm directly, running these models on IoT edge devices enables AI capabilities to be handled directly on a device.

Azure IoT Hub Setup

In this section, I will show you how to set up Azure IoT Hub with Azure Portal and Azure command-line interface (CLI). Let's start with Azure Portal. I assume you have an active subscription, or you can get a free account from `https://azure.microsoft.com/en-us/free/` with $200 credit for one month and more than 25 services free for 12 months. Most of my examples will be using free services. Let's get started.

1. Log in to Azure Portal at `https://portal.azure.com`.

2. Click Create A Resource, as shown in Figure 3-2.

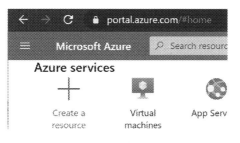

Figure 3-2. *Creating a resource*

3. Type iot and select IoT Hub from the drop-down list, as shown in Figure 3-3.

Figure 3-3. *Selecting a IoT Hub*

4. Click Create, as shown in Figure 3-4.

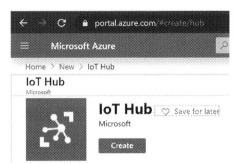

Figure 3-4. *Creating a new Hub*

5. On the Basics tab under Resource Group, click Create New, as shown in Figure 3-5. Enter the appropriate name and click OK.

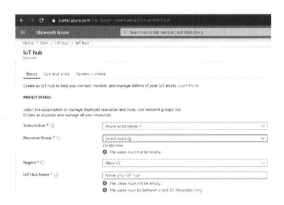

Figure 3-5. *Naming a new resource group*

6. Enter a value for the IoT Hub Name.

7. On the Size and scale tab, select F1: Free tier. If you miss this step, the default is S1: Standard tier, and it will cost you $25 per device per month.

8. Click Review + Create.

9. Click Create.

10. Wait until the Your Deployment Is Underway message is gone. Once done, click Go To Resource. Congratulations! Your first IoT Hub is ready.

Let's do the same step with CLI. But why CLI? It is not about just being comfortable with the command line. One of the main advantages of using CLI is the ability to script and automate deployment of the same environment later. It is easy to read as compared with Azure Resource Manager (ARM) templates and code reviews are easy.

1. Log in to Azure Portal (`https://portal.azure.com/#home`).

2. Click the Cloud Shell icon.

3. Select PowerShell. If you don't have storage set up, you need to create it.

You need to add the Azure IoT extension to the cloud shell instance to enable IoT-specific additional functionality.

```
PS Azure:\> az extension add --name azure-cli-iot-ext
```

Create a resource group to manage all the resources

```
PS Azure:\> az group create --name rgIot --location westus2
```

```
PS Azure:\> az iot hub create --resource-group rgIot --name myfirstiothub --sku F1 --partition-count 2
```

Wait the command to run. Congratulations! Your IoT Hub is ready.

Did you notice how easy and quick this is using the CLI as compared with using Azure Portal UX? I will leave the choice up to you.

Note   If you already created an IoT Hub using Azure Portal UX steps I provided earlier, then you will get error message:

```
Max number of Iot Hubs exceeded for SKU = Free, Max Allowed = 1
```

To correct this error, delete the IoT Hub and rerun the same command.

There can exist only one IoT hub name in the world. If your name is already taken you will see error message:

```
IoT Hub name 'myfirstiothub' is not available
```

To override this error, change the IoT Hub name and rerun the same command.

Let's now create the IoT Central application.

1. This time go to Home. Type iot and select IoT Central Application.

2. Click Create.

3. Enter the appropriate resource name.

4. Enter a value for Application URL (this should be unique globally).

5. Select an existing resource group.

6. The only pricing plan available is Paid Application, but don't worry; IoT Central is valid for seven days as a free trial for up to five devices.

7. Select from the 12 industry-focused templates (Retail, Energy, Government, and Healthcare) or Custom Preview Application.

8. Click Create.

You can create an IoT Central application from `https://apps.azureiotcentral.com/`. Alternatively, you can do using this CLI command:

```
PS Azure:\> az iotcentral app create --resource-group rgIot --name
"iotcentralapp2020" --subdomain "iotcentralapp2020" --sku S1 --template
"iotc-default@1.0.0" --display-name "My readers have IoT Central
Application"

--template defines which industry-focused template you would like to create.
```

Congratulations! Your first IoT Central application is ready.

Let's now create IoT Solution Accelerator. As discussed previously you cannot create IoT solution Accelerator from Azure portal. To create please open AzureIoTSolutions. com using same credentials you used to login on Azure Portal as shown in Figure 3-6.

Figure 3-6. *IoT Solution Accelerator portal*

1. Click the Device Simulation template.

2. Click Try Now.

3. Enter and appropriate deployment name.

4. Select the Use Existing IoT Hub option.

5. Select a location close to your region.

6. Click Create. At this point, you might want to relax and have a cup of coffee because it will take close to 20 minutes to create the IoT Solution Accelerator.

Remember I said you need to use CLI if you want to choose a Tier. It is now time to build the IoT Solution Accelerator using CLI. Unfortunately, PowerShell commands are not available and only the bash shell (sh) command is available.

Switch your Cloud shell to Bash and run the following commands.

```
user@Azure:~$ npm install iot-solutions -g
user@Azure:~$ pcs login
user@Azure:~$ pcs -t remotemonitoring -s basic -r dotnet
```

Alternatively, you can use -s standard and -r java options to change the tier and technology of your deployment.

In any case, the command will ask for more details and you need to enter resource name, VM login credentials, and other information to complete the command.

Congratulations! Your first IoT Solution Accelerator is ready.

Azure IoT Architecture

Before we start our industry-based use cases, let's understand the last piece in this three-part theory-based chapter, the IoT architecture. So far, we have learned that the IoT ecosystem starts with a sensor, reading environmental physical properties into digital values. These data flow through given communication channels to the cloud or to available storage. This process is repeated hundreds and thousands of time a day. Now, multiply this whole flow by thousands or millions of sensors. Finally, these data are used for analysis and meaningful decision making through events or machine learning.

As an IASA certified solution architect, I must design an architecture that is scalable, secure, maintainable, usable, reliable, and available. The data we keep should work seamlessly with other internal or external parts to be used without compromising performance.

This part of the chapter is intended for those in technology roles, such as chief technology officers (CTOs), architects, and developers. In comparison with the architecture of projects you have created in the past, the IoT architecture is bit more complex because it uses disparate technologies and complex services that are either new, not yet mature, or not designed specifically for IoT.

Different sensors and devices choosing different communication protocols is another challenge. Some devices also require bidirectional communication. These devices securely connect with the cloud and deliver critical business value. Do we need fog computing to analyze data close to where they are generated to avoid security security issues? As you can see, we have many moving pieces and no one technology or answer can meet our requirements.

The architecture shown in Figure 3-7 is divided into five distinct logical layers to build a complete IoT project.

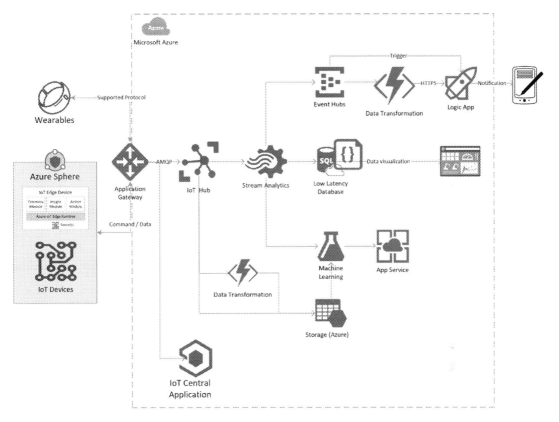

Figure 3-7. *Azure IoT architecture*

The Producer

In our case is the producers are sensors, devices, and IoT Edge devices. For IoT Edge devices, deploying Azure Stream Analytics enables near-real-time intelligence closer to IoT devices. Remember that security comes first. Therefore, we need security at the device level as well. In our architecture, all IoT hardware is secured by Azure Sphere. We will be talking about Azure Sphere in Chapter 14.

IoT Hub or IoT Central

This layer is used to register these producers and keep their state. The reliability and ordering guarantees provided by this tunnel are on par with TCP. The application gateway simply passes communications between the devices and IoT Hub. The gateway understands the protocol on both sides and translate it. The devices are unaware that they are communicating with the cloud via a gateway, and a user interacting with the devices in IoT Hub is unaware of the intermediate gateway device. Security at this layer is powered by configuring IoT Hubs to only allow connections using TLS version 1.2. If you are using an IoT Edge device, you can additionally configure the Cipher suite with various available bit encryptions.

Storage

IoT applications can ingest large amounts of data, which might require continuous processing over the stream of messages. We selected storage to ensure that these discrete data are transmitted, processed, and consumed securely, while being stored durably. Therefore, our architecture chooses multiple storage options, from cheap blob storage to low-latency CosmosDB for flexible data models with reliable performance and automatic scaling of throughput capacity. You can also choose Azure SQL instead of CosmosDB if you are planning for more relational system. I couldn't think of any scenario of relational database management systems (RDBMS) here though.

Data Transformation and Analytics

This layer is used to analyze the data. The primary goal of implementing an IoT project in industry is prediction and visualization. We need a stream analytics engine so that we get responses more quickly on the physical environment and act based on telemetry. We can make informed decisions about new and existing products and make processes more efficient.

To achieve this important goal, we need an analytics service that provides varying views on our data, different analytics workflow, and real-time metrics. Azure Stream Analysis (ASA) connects to IoT Hub securely on TLS 1.2 and data are encrypted. It is a fully managed, serverless PaaS cloud offering. It processes data in real time and aggregates complex data structures. The output can be stored in any storage option so that it can be used by business intelligence (BI) applications like Power BI.

Another egress (output) of ASA in our architecture is further feeding into Event Hub. Here the consumer is Azure Function, and it triggers a logic app for real-time notification about the events, results, and decisions to the actors.

The last egress of ASA in our architecture is feeding data to Azure Machine Learning (ML). Some example of using Azure ML are fraud detection, identity-theft protection, and optimizing resources based on learned information.

Time and sequence are important when critical data arrive at rest. The Azure Time Series Insights service is good option for analytics, storage, and visualization of such data. You can easily find hidden trends and anomaly detection.

Raw data can be fed directly to Azure Function. Azure Functions are small pieces of code based on a single responsibility principal. Azure Function is designed to massage data or to solve a specific problem. The output then is stored to the storage of choice.

The Consumer

The consumer is, for example, a smartphone, telemetry portal, or BI website. For example, Microsoft Power BI is used for presenting and visualization of the processed data and offers options to share these data with others and collaborate. You can use natural language commands to query data. With time-series analysis you can use Grafana or Kibana, professional data visualization and analytics tools. For example, you can build a complex custom dashboard, for hardware health monitoring, and sending alerts and notifications based on time-series insight.

Summary

This chapter explored some of the fundamentals of the Azure IoT Platform. You might have noticed that some of the decisions, like choosing between PaaS or SaaS solutions, are very easy if you consider your requirements. The biggest points to consider are your in-house capability and TTM.

We then focused on building IoT Hub, and IoT Central and Accelerator solutions via Azure Portal and CLI commands. Now that you've gone through the process of creating these services, which is required to start any IoT project, take a step forward and think about how you can use this IoT core service, which devices you have to connect with them, and how you want to visualize the data.

Finally, we learned about the IoT architecture that covers the most common cases. You have the opportunity to use additional components and tools for handling your operations. You might require other Azure or non-Azure services that allow you to monitor and perform long-term analysis on top of device data. Your IoT architecture should drive rich analytics capabilities across vast areas of crucial enterprise functions, such as operations, customer care, finance, sales, and marketing.

CHAPTER 4

Streaming IoT Data to Microsoft Azure

In Chapter 3, we learned how to create Azure IoT Hub, another PaaS offering IoT Solution Accelerators, and another SaaS offering IoT Central Applications, but no devices were registered. This chapter is a natural extension of the previous chapter. Here, I start from scratch and guide you through the capabilities of IoT Hub:

- Device management
- Sending telemetry data, device to cloud (D2C)
- Querying data from IoT Hub
- Sending responses to devices, cloud to device (C2D)
- Storing data
- Analyzing data

Managing IoT Hub

We created IoT Hub with Azure Portal and Azure CLI. Let's first review Figure 4-1 for all the available parameters associated with IoT Hub from Azure Portal. Additionally, you can also view the Hub's activity logs, although in our case it should have no logs. Let's go through the important menu options we are going to use in this and future chapters.

© Nirnay Bansal 2020
N. Bansal, *Designing Internet of Things Solutions with Microsoft Azure*,
https://doi.org/10.1007/978-1-4842-6041-8_4

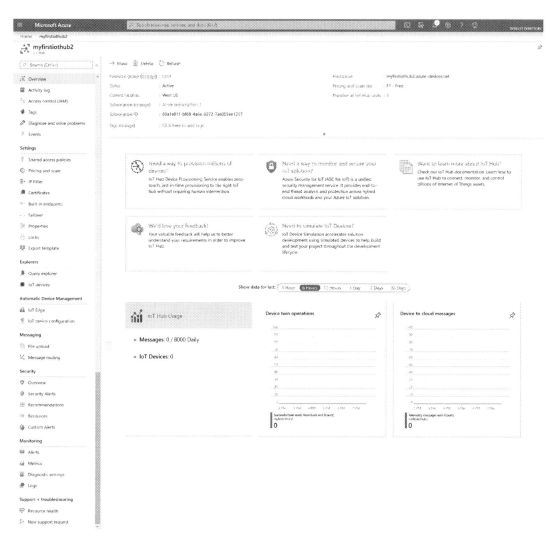

Figure 4-1. *Azure IoT Hub Overview page*

Overview

The IoT Hub Overview page gives you a quick summary about the resource group and region under which you created the IoT Hub, hostname, and a DNS endpoint you will use to connect from an SDK and configure in sensors, the pricing tier you selected, number of devices you registered, and number of messages you consumed. It also includes charts showing you message patterns.

Shared Access Policies

Under Shared Access Policies, you can grant any combination of permissions to access the endpoints. By default, the policy `iothubowner` has Admin-level rights. You can perform actions related to devices as well as messages, whereas with `service` and `device` you can only perform actions related to messages and devices, respectively. There are two more policies, `registryRead` and `registryReadWrite`. The device management component uses the `registryReadWrite` policy.

Actions related to messages include receiving device-to-cloud messages, sending cloud-to-device messages, retrieving the corresponding delivery acknowledgments, delivery acknowledgments for file uploads, and communication and monitoring endpoints.

Actions related to devices include sending device-to-cloud messages and receiving cloud-to-device messages, performing file uploads from a device, and monitoring device-facing endpoints.

Note   Security is most important thing. I highly encourage you to use **IP Filter** to specify valid IP address ranges that the IoT Hub will accept.

Built-In Endpoints

Each IoT hub comes with a built-in Event hub to store system and device messages with a default retention period of one day. You can only change this retention period to the maximum of seven days at the time of creating IoT Hub. You can use the given connection string to read messages from the Event hub from your favorite tool. Once you create any custom endpoint from the Message Routing menu option under Messaging, messages are only delivered to the built-in endpoint if they don't match any query.

Query Explorer

We use Query Explorer to retrieve information regarding device twins and jobs, as well as message routing via query languages like SQL.

IoT Devices

We use IoT devices to view, create, delete, and update devices in your IoT Hub. This was not available initially when IoT Hub launched. The only option to register a device is via an SDK. This is a helpful tool for managers not familiar with coding who still would like to manage devices.

File Upload

When a device is sending unstructured data like large files with images or videos, you first need to enable file upload notifications and configure the storage from this menu option.

Message Routing

Referring back to our architecture diagram in Chapter 3, message routing becomes very important when you have multiple data destinations for the telemetry data generated from your IoT devices. If you have multiple data channels like Event Hub, Service Bus Queue, and Service Bus Topic, and would like different message to go to different Azure services, then you can configure that here. The message to the Azure service endpoint is many-to-many; that is, a message can reach one or more Azure services for further processing or storage. If you don't define any message route, then messages are sent to the default endpoint (i.e., Event Hub).

The maximum message size supported is 256 KB, but the messages are metered in 4 KB blocks; for example, a message of 15 KB will count as four messages. In our case we created IoT Hub under the Free tier, so the messages are metered in 0.5 KB blocks; for example, a message of 15 KB will count as 29 Messages. Up to 10 custom endpoints and 100 routes can be created per IoT Hub.

Device Management

A device cannot connect to a hub unless it has an entry in the identity registry. As shown in Figure 4-2, registering device is easy from Azure Portal. Under Explorer, click IoT Devices, and then select New.

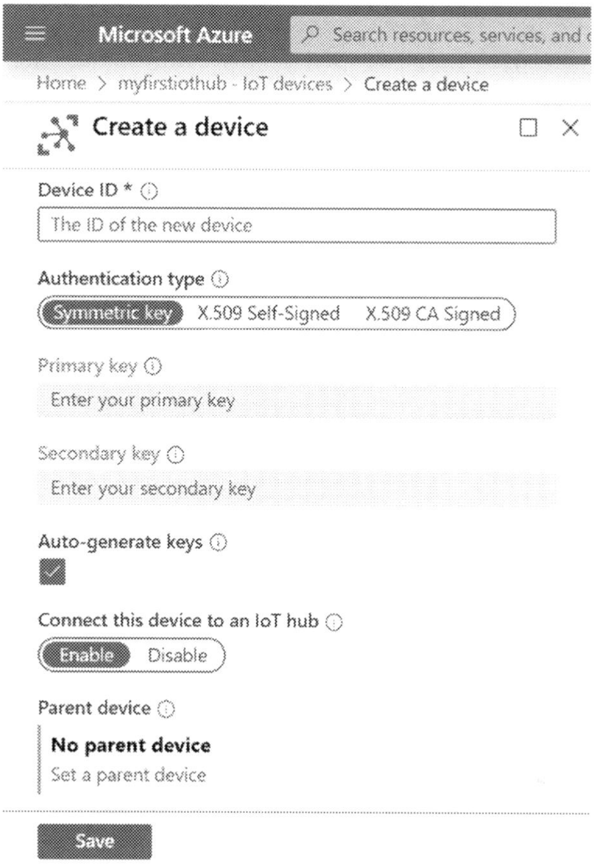

Figure 4-2. *Registering a new device*

To create a device on this screen, enter a Device ID value, a case-sensitive alphanumeric string (up to 128 characters long) that can contain certain special characters like - . + % _ # * ? ! ( ) , = @ $ and '. Click Save to create a device identity for your IoT Hub. The primary and secondary keys are created for you. Under Explorer, return to IoT Devices, then select the device you just created. You will see a symmetric key and connection string for that device.

Let's register a new device with CLI. Open Cloud Shell, select PowerShell (discussed in Chapter 3), and execute the following command:

```
PS Azure:\> az iot hub device-identity create -n myfirstiothub -d
mySecondDevice
```

Wait for the command to run. Congratulations! Your second device is registered.

Let's perform the same action from an SDK. No matter which SDK you choose, the steps will be same. To get the IoT Hub connection string go to shared access policies, click `iothubowner`. As shown in Figure 4-3, the Shared Access Policies page, copy the Connection String—Primary Key.

If you copy the connection string from the `service` or `device` policy, the code when executed will give you following error at runtime:

`"Message":"ErrorCode:IotHubUnauthorizedAccess;Unauthorized".`

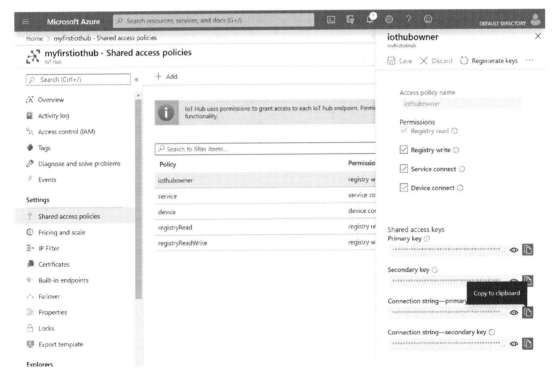

Figure 4-3. *Copying the connection string from the shared access keys*

In Microsoft Visual Studio, create a new console (.Net Core) project called IoTProject. To register a device using Azure IoT Hub Service SDK for .NET, you need to install `Microsoft.Azure.Devices` nuget.

Add the following `using` statements at the top of the `Program.cs`:

```
using Microsoft.Azure.Devices;
using System.Threading.Tasks;
```

In Program, copy the following code and execute it.

```
private static string connectionString = "<Connection stringhere>";
private static string deviceId = "<device id>";

private async static Task AddDeviceAsync()
{
    //Creates a RegistryManager from the Iot Hub connection string.
    var registryManager = RegistryManager.CreateFromConnectionString(co
    nnectionString);

    //Register a new device with the system
    var device = await registryManager.AddDeviceAsync(new
    Device(deviceId));

    Console.WriteLine("Generated Symmetric Key for Authentication:
    {0}", device.Authentication.SymmetricKey.PrimaryKey);
}
```

Simply call this method from Main:

```
static void Main(string[] args)
{
    AddDeviceAsync().Wait();

    Console.ReadKey();
}
```

Execute and go back to Azure Portal. Under Explorer, click the IoT Devices menu option. Congratulations! Your device is registered.

Note   This is a simple demo, but security should be our priority; therefore, the connection string of the iothubowner is not to be shared inside your client apps. Save it in Azure KeyVault and access the string from KeyVault in your program.

Sending Telemetry Data Device to Cloud (D2C)

Stream Structural Data

We have a registered device in our IoT Hub; now let's send a D2C message to the IoT Hub. All we need is this simple code example. For this action, we need the Device SDK for Azure IoT Hub. Install the Microsoft.Azure.Devices.Client nuget. You can use any connection string from shared access policy.

Add the following using statements at the top of the Program.cs:

```
using Newtonsoft.Json;
using Microsoft.Azure.Devices.Clients;
```

In Program.cs, copy the following code and execute it:

```
private async static Task SendSensorData()
{
    var telemetryDataPoint = new
    {
        deviceId = deviceId,
        temperature = 30.3,
    };

    var messageString = JsonConvert.SerializeObject(telemetryDataPoint);
    var message = new Message(Encoding.ASCII.GetBytes(messageString));

    var deviceClient = DeviceClient.CreateFromConnectionString(connection
    String, deviceId, TransportType.Http1);
    await deviceClient.SendEventAsync(message);
}
```

Simply call this method from Main:

```
static void Main(string[] args)
{
    SendSensorData().Wait();

    Console.ReadKey();
}
```

Allow the code to execute. Congratulations! You sent D2C structured telemetry data to your IoT Hub.

I chose `http1`, but with .Net SDK you can choose any transport protocol from `Amqp`, `Amqp_Tcp_Only`, `Amqp_WebSocket_Only`, `Mqtt`, `Mqtt_Tcp_Only,` and `Mqtt_WebSocket_Only`. If you created a Project Type UWP (Universal Windows Platform) app, then currently `Amqp` and `Mqtt` are not supported. If you are using another SDK like Java or Python, then choose the transport protocol accordingly.

Stream Nonstructural Data

Working on unstructured data is different than sending a structured D2C message. In the case of unstructured data like images and video, Azure cannot easily map the data your devices send in the relatively small D2C messages. To send large files with images or videos, you need to configure a storage container and enable file notification from the File Upload menu option under Messaging in IoT Hub as shown in Figure 4-4.

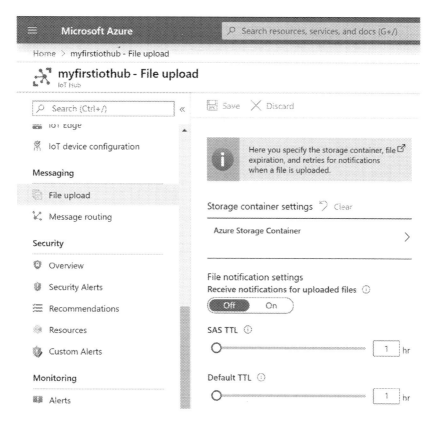

Figure 4-4. *Enabling File Upload configuration*

Add the following using statement at the top of `Program.cs`:

```
using System.IO;
```

In Program.cs, copy the following code and execute it:

```
private static async Task SendUnstructuredDataAsync()
{
    string fileName = "color.png";

    var deviceClient = DeviceClient.CreateFromConnectionString(connection
    String, deviceId,
        TransportType.http1);

    using (var sourceData = new FileStream(fileName, FileMode.Open))
    {
        await deviceClient.UploadToBlobAsync(fileName, sourceData);
    }
}:
```

Again, I chose `http1`.
Simply call this method from `Main`:

```
static void Main(string[] args)
{
    SendUnstructuredDataAsync().Wait();

    Console.ReadKey();
}
```

Wait for the code to run. Congratulations! You sent D2C unstructured data to your IoT Hub.

Let's send a D2C message with CLI. Open Cloud Shell and select PowerShell (discussed in Chapter 3), and execute the following command:

```
PS Azure:\> az iot device send-d2c-message -n myfirstiothub -d
mySecondDevice --data 'temperature=30.3'
```

Wait for the command to run.

To upload an unstructured file like a large file with images, execute the following command:

```
PS Azure:\> az iot device upload-file --hub-name myfirstiothub2 --device-id
mySecondDevice --content-type 'image/jpeg' --file-path '{file path here}'
```

Wait for the command to finish. Depending on the file size, this can take few seconds. Congratulations! You sent D2C structured and unstructured data to your IoT Hub from a registered device.

IoT Hub Query Explorer

The IoT Hub Query Explorer menu option provides an SQL-like language to query devices and jobs. All commands are executed on the device registry with FROM clause on `devices`. This is the table name (aka collection name) in IoT Hub. You can use a regular WHERE clause on `deviceid`, as well as tags you configured for that device.

Select Query Explorer under your IoT Hub. Type the following queries in the execution window and output will appear in the result window. By default, Device Twin is selected under the Collections drop-down list. To query jobs, change the selection to Jobs. Device twin is the name of document that keeps device state information; for example, metadata, configurations, and conditions. Azure IoT Hub internally maintains a device twin document for each device. Jobs is another collection inside the device twin JSON document that contains the information of the operations executed on the device. When you select Jobs from the Collections drop-down list, the query runs on `device.jobs`.

The following are some sample queries demonstrating the power of the Query Explorer.

Here is a simple query to select all devices registered in IoT Hub. This query uses the Device Twin collection.

```
SELECT * FROM devices
```

Notice some elements that the system maintains and allows you to query on, like `status`, `connectionState`, `lastActivityTime`, `capabilities.iotEdge`, and `cloudToDeviceMessageCount`.

Filtering data over these elements is easy.

```
SELECT LastActivityTime FROM devices WHERE status = 'enabled'
```

Grouping and aggregations are also supported.

```
SELECT COUNT() AS numberOfDevices FROM devices
```

So far, we have only executed queries in Query Explorer, but SDKs allow us to do the same in a programming way. All we need is this simple code example. For this action, we need Services SDK for Azure IoT Hub. Install the `Microsoft.Azure.Devices` nuget. You can use any connection string from shared access policy.

Add the following using statements at the top of the Program.cs:

```
using Microsoft.Azure.Devices;
```

In Program.cs copy the following code and execute it:

```
private static async Task QueryAsync()
{
    //Creates a RegistryManager from the Iot Hub connection string.
    var registryManager = RegistryManager.CreateFromConnectionString
    (connectionString);

    //Define the query to be executed
    var query = registryManager.CreateQuery("SELECT * FROM devices", 10);

    while (query.HasMoreResults)
    {
        // Retrieves the next paged result
        var page = await query.GetNextAsTwinAsync();
        foreach (var device in page)
        {
            Console.WriteLine(device.DeviceId);
        }
    }
}
```

The second parameter in `CreateQuery` is page size, and it is of type `nullable int`. Notice that I am passing 10 here. I recommend always giving some small number (1–100) in case you have hundreds of devices. `GetNextAsTwinAsync` is designed and capable of retrieving any remaining result set.

Simply call this method from Main:

```
static void Main(string[] args)
{
    QueryAsync().Wait();

    Console.ReadKey();
}
```

Send Response to Device, Cloud to Device

When your temperature device senses a value greater than 75°, you need to invoke the start method in your air conditioner over the HTTP protocol. IoT Hub provides fully managed bidirectional communication between solutions and devices. C2D messages are important for any IoT device, which are waiting for some action or for maintenance of devices like firmware updates or configuration management. Such messages are also known as command and control messages.

The C2D message goes to a device-specific endpoint and an acknowledgment is sent by the device to the cloud. C2D is available on all protocols.

Add the following using statements at the top of Program.cs:

```
using Microsoft.Azure.Devices;
```

In Program.cs, copy the following code and execute it:

```
private async static Task SendC2DMessageAsync()
{
    var serviceClient = ServiceClient.CreateFromConnectionString(connection
    String);
    var commandMessage = new Message(Encoding.ASCII.GetBytes("Cloud to
    device message."));
    await serviceClient.SendAsync(deviceId, commandMessage);
}
```

Simply call this method from Main:

```
static void Main(string[] args)
{
```

```
        SendC2DMessageAsync().Wait();

        Console.ReadKey();
    }
```

Wait for the code to run. Congratulations! You sent C2D structured telemetry data to your IoT Hub.

Was this message actually delivered? Once the IoT device has received the message and taken appropriate action, it needs to respond back to the IoT Hub. To get an acknowledgment back from the device you need to modify the code. Add the following line in the `SendC2DMessageAsync()` function:

```
commandMessage.Ack = DeliveryAcknowledgement.Full;
```

Add another method to receive a feedback acknowledgment for the message you sent:

```
using System.Linq;

private async static void ReceiveFeedbackAsync()
{
    var serviceClient = ServiceClient.CreateFromConnectionString(connection
    String);
    var feedbackReceiver = serviceClient.GetFeedbackReceiver();

    while (true)
    {
        var ack = await feedbackReceiver.ReceiveAsync();
        if (ack == null) continue;

        Console.WriteLine($"Received acknowledgement: {0}", string.Join(", ",
        ack.Records.Select(f => f.StatusCode)));
        await ack.CompleteAsync(feedbackBatch);
    }
}
```

There is another communication option available when talking about C2D messages, direct messages. This option is available using MQTT or AMQP only. You use a direct method to invoke a method on a device.

```
public static async Task<CloudToDeviceMethodResult>
InvokeDirectMethodOnDevice()
{
    var serviceClient = ServiceClient.CreateFromConnectionString(connection
    String);

    var methodInvocation = new CloudToDeviceMethod("WriteToMessage") {
    ResponseTimeout = TimeSpan.FromSeconds(300) };
    methodInvocation.SetPayloadJson("{\"newdevicesequenece\":78}");

    var response = await serviceClient.InvokeDeviceMethodAsync(deviceId,
    methodInvocation);

    return response;
}
```

Storing Data

By default, messages are stored in the built-in Event Hub that comes with IoT Hub. In addition, IoT Hub exposes the messages and events built-in endpoint for your back-end services to read the D2C messages. Depending on your retention policy, messages can be stored in the built-in Event Hub for further processing from one day to a maximum of seven days. Technically speaking, the built-in Event Hub is compatible with any Azure services like Azure Function, Stream Analytics, Apache Storm and Spark, and Azure Databricks. Additionally, you can create custom endpoints to route messages.

As shown in Figure 4-5, along with the built-in Event Hub, IoT Hub currently supports Azure Storage containers, Event Hubs, Service Bus queues, and Service Bus topics. (Following our architecture in Chapter 3, we will be configuring a storage container to store our messages as blobs.)

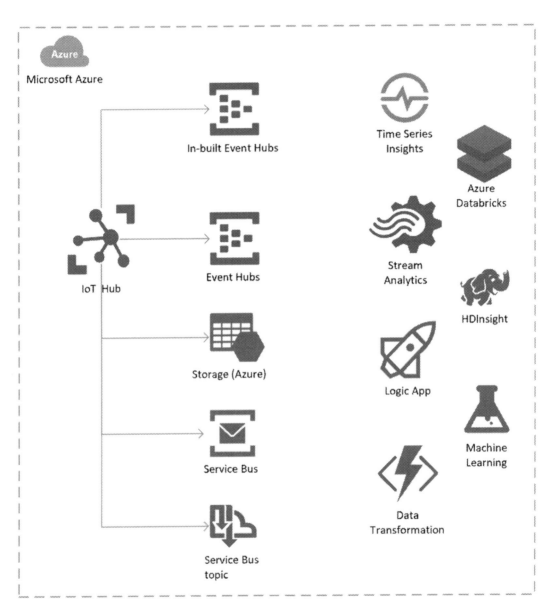

Figure 4-5. *Message and event storage and processing architecture*

IoT Hub comes with a built-in Event Hub, but you might need to route your messages to multiple Event Hubs for further processing. The built-in Event Hub is not from other Azure services like the Logic app (discussed in the next section). Routing messages to customer endpoints like Event Hub is handy to customize retention policy, route messages to multiple event hubs, and process them separately based on business logic.

Azure Service Bus acts as a messaging backbone that connects any devices, applications, or services running to any other applications or services in the cloud and transfers data between them. Queues work based on a one-to-one communication model. Topics in Service Bus work as a one-to-many communication model. Each queue acts as a broker that stores the sent messages until they are collected by the receiver. Subscribers of the topic can apply filters to get only targeted messages. Depending on your retention period requirements, Message Replay and Time to Live of the message Service Bus could be a good choice.

Microsoft Azure offers Azure Storage, which provides storage that is highly available, secure, durable, scalable, and redundant. There is no physical limitation on storage capacity. For example, Azure Blob storage can store large amounts of nonstructured data, and Blob storage can be used to present data publicly or to store data privately. Storage was the most liked endpoint type for message routing because it makes it super simple to build a cold-path analytics pipeline. for example, Azure Data Lake Storage Gen v2 provides a robust and cost-effective way to store massive amounts of data on the existing Azure Blob storage platform and is fully compatible with numerous analytic platforms, such as Hadoop, Azure Databricks, and Azure SQL Data Warehouse.

Analyzing Data

Now that we have data coming from our registered devices and landing in the Azure cloud, it is time to explore possible options for processing and analyzing those data. My goal here is to explore all the possible options from a bird's-eye view. You should get insight into how to deploy them. In upcoming chapters, we will be exploring some of these services in depth and learning how we can use them in our IoT project.

As data coming from IoT devices could be structured as well as unstructured streams, we need to explore services based on data type. Let's start with the most commonly used streaming service, Azure Stream Analytics.

Azure Stream Analytics

Azure Stream Analytics is a fully managed serverless (PaaS) in-memory and real-time data analytics and event processing engine. It is designed to run transformation queries against streaming data coming from multiple sources like IoT Hubs, Event Hubs, and Azure Blob storage. Azure Stream Analytics can be deployed in Azure or at the edge in containers deployed to devices.

As shown in Figure 4-6, you can set up one or more input sources to extract knowledge structures from devices, sensor data from IoT Hub, credit payment feeds from Event Hub, and telemetry's big data stored in Blob storage. Due to the capability of real-time processing, this is best suited for organizations that need critical information with high throughput and low latency. These kinds of organizations cannot simply keep the data coming in cold storage blob with no answers for a long time. Therefore, they need stream processing, which can handle millions of events per second.

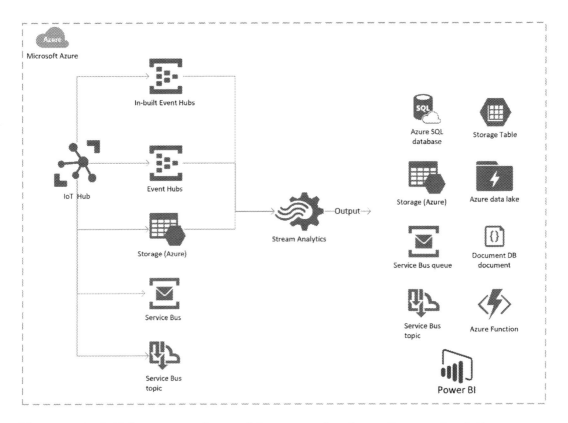

Figure 4-6. *IoT data processing architecture usign Azure Stream Analytics*

Note   At the time of writing, Reference data can come only from Blob storage. Reference data are any data you need to correlate, look up, and expand data with a basis like converting IDs into meaningful names.

The primary job of Azure Stream Analytics is to correlate data from multiple sources, filter out bad data or data of no use, transfer data, aggregate the data, and finally analyze the data to generate meaningful results for further triggers or actions. All transformation is written in SQL-like language.

The final result is call output, and Azure Stream Analytics can output results with ultra-low latencies to various Azure services; it can store output in SQL Database and Cosmos DB, can store output in Azure Storage and Azure Data Lake Gen1 Storage, can feed output for further processing to Service Bus Topic/Queue and Azure functions, or simply create a data source for a real-time dashboard in Power BI. Each of the outputs is strategically provided for every kind of organizational need.

Azure Stream Analytics is billed by streaming unit, which is a blend of computing, memory, and throughput.

Azure Time Series Insights

One of the main goals of implementing an IoT project in your industry is to convert data into actionable insights like improving operation efficiency, spotting anomalies, and finding hidden trends for fast decision making. To help achieve this, Microsoft provides Azure Time Series Insights (TSI) for real-time data insights. TSI (see Figure 4-7) is a fully managed offering, primarily developed for data generated from IoT devices. It guarantees the sequential order of data arrival. TSI calls input event sources, and the only options available as event sources are IoT Hub and Event Hub. TSI stores, aggregates, and visualizes telemetry and trends in graphical format without writing any code. It stores data into solid-state drive (SSD), allows you to query on-demand, and provides visualization through the Time Series Insights explorer.

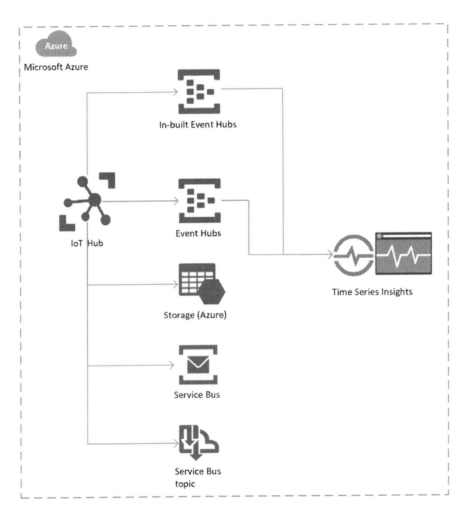

Figure 4-7. *IoT data processing architecture using Azure Time Series Insights*

There is always a point of discussion that TSI is used to look back, for root cause analysis, to detect anomalies, or to flag low and high values. Technically, though, you predict the future and perform model forecasting. You can apply perspective views and discern patterns when performing root cause analysis. Manufacturers are using the TSI analytical system for device monitoring and predictive maintenance.

This is different from Stream Analytics, first, because it doesn't require any coding knowledge, like writing scripts and functions in SQL-like language. Second, you don't always need to transform and preprocess data before visualization. Due to that second difference, a third difference is the cost. Finally, the time you can store data ranges from from 1 to 400 days in warm storage and up to 120 days in cold storage.

TSI recently introduced a new pricing model, whereby the customer is billed by the amount of data processed (i.e., cost per data processing unit). TSI still supports previous Tier S1 and S2 for 1 million and 10 million events per day per instance, respectively. Customers can also configure tiers with higher capacity.

Logic App and Function App

Both the Logic app and Function app are part of serverless computing. Serverless means no infrastructure is maintained by the user. Both Azure platform services are different and useful for different requirements, but their interaction with IoT Hub is the same, as shown in Figure 4-8.

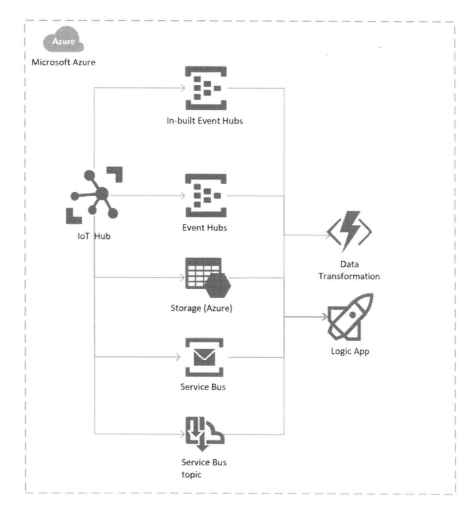

Figure 4-8. *IoT data processing architecture using Logic app and Function app*

Logic app is a logic workflow consisting of activities. To normal users it looks like a data flow diagram in Microsoft Visio with bunches of boxes connected with each other, called actions. Logic app has only one entry point and can be triggered via HTTP request. It can be scheduled like a service to execute at predefined intervals. Another advantage of Logic app is scaling. When the number of requests increases above a set threshold, Logic app instances will increase. It provides a run history to examine specific runs in full detail.

Function app requires developer skills, and code is deployed as a small piece of meaningful and reusable methods. Azure functions are microservices based on the single responsibility principle, which can be easily shared across services. You can choose any language from .Net Core, Node.js, Python, Java, or PowerShell commands. You can see an execution history from a monitor tab. Consider using Logic app first until your requirements can be met, but if your requirement is to write your own code with much flexibility, then use Azure Function. Please note that the more code you write, the more responsibility you have.

Both Logic app and Azure Function use consumption-based billing and there is no upfront cost. Additionally, Function app can run on the App Service plan.

Power BI

Power BI is a business analytics service by Microsoft that aggregates, analyzes, and visualizes data. Users can share data, reports, and dashboards with other users directly through e-mail. PowerBI is powered with built-in charts, graphs, and various types of business visualization managers need day to day. Users can use custom R and Python scripts and ArcGIS maps for custom visualization.

Unfortunately, PowerBI cannot use IoT Hub directly for real-time visualization. You need another Azure service like Stream Analytics, Azure Function, CosmosDB, Table Storage, SQL Database, and others. The only possible option to connect PowerBI to IoT Hub directly is via Azure.

Azure Machine Learning and Cognitive Services

I include Machine Learning and Cognitive Services due to their capability to work with semistructured data. In the case of IoT Edge devices or IoT devices generating semistructured data like audio and images, they can process information using AI models. Azure Machine Learning is a cloud predictive analytics PaaS offering used to train, deploy, and manage machine learning models. Similarly, you can build custom image classifiers and deploy them using Custom Vision Service.

Both of these services encompass a tremendous range of industrial applications, such as predictive maintenance and anomaly detection. Custom Vision can be used for functions like visual inspection of machine parts, identifying tools on a manufacturing floor, and detecting parts on an assembly line. Similarly, Machine Learning can detect anomalies and indicate predictive maintenance for an engine based on audio signals.

In previous chapters we talked about Edge devices. IoT Edge brings computing capabilities to devices locally to process data in real time and prevent security breaches. Microsoft has made it easy to run machine learning models by allowing developers to import Azure Machine Learning models in a module. For example, Custom Vision Service can be used to train a model and deploy it over IoT Edge.

Summary

This chapter has explored some of the fundamental methods of Azure IoT Hub. To start with, we registered devices using various methods. Later in this chapter we focused on sending D2C and C2D messages. Now that you've gone through the process of sending messages, think about how you can use this, which type of data (structured or semistructured) you need, and how you want to analyze it.

Finally, at the end of this chapter, I provided the various IoT architectures for processing and analyzing data generated from the devices. In the next chapters, we will look at examples of each of them to build a full end-to-end solution for your industry.

Now, you have the opportunity to configure Stream Analytics, Time Series Insight, Logic app, and Function app in your Azure subscription. You might require other Azure or non-Azure services that allow you to monitor and perform long-term analysis on top of device data. Your IoT architecture should drive rich analytics capabilities across vast areas of crucial enterprise functions, such as operations, customer care, finance, sales, and marketing.

CHAPTER 5

IoT Applications in Manufacturing

Detroit, a city in Michigan, was known for adopting the second Industrial Revolution early and thus were at the forefront to adopt the fourth Industrial Revolution before others. Auto companies big or small, use technology to make their production lines more reliable and sustainable. I am calling it technology because most of the workforce in these companies are experienced employees, and they might not know technological terms like AI or IoT. In this chapter, I provide applications of IoT using by these employees unknowingly on a day-to-day basis, to detect and predict mechanical failures on the manufacturing line.

This chapter provides use cases for managers to explain to unions, to make them understand how helping workers adapt to new technologies will reduce layoffs and provide workers the opportunity to survive and even thrive using these technologies. IoT is set to revolutionize the manufacturing industry in terms of its operational efficiencies through predictive maintenance and optimized production lines.

When things broke down, you would go out and fix them; this is called reactive maintenance. Predictive maintenance is one of the areas that benefited most in the manufacturing industry using machine learning algorithms. It focuses on how to predict when certain conditions are going to occur and when machines will fail. Later this chapter covers the application of IoT in exploring the capabilities of Azure IoT predictive maintenance. We discussed IoT Central in Chapter 3, and I will be using a preconfigured solution that comes with IoT Central.

Later we will discuss predictive maintenance, one of many IoT use cases that managers have had difficulty integrating into their existing operational technology and legacy machinery. Finally, we will also cover the benefits of doing so.

© Nirnay Bansal 2020
N. Bansal, *Designing Internet of Things Solutions with Microsoft Azure*,
https://doi.org/10.1007/978-1-4842-6041-8_5

Manufacturing

How do you motivate hardworking, loyal employees with years of experience in manufacturing to use new technology? Companies are aware of these challenges, and to implement technology at the enterprise level, they started slowly with awareness, training and showcasing the capability of one good product at a time. Let's take the example of an everyday worker on a shop floor. He digs through an unorganized mess of tools laying all over the floor. He then sets out on a walk around the shop floor, searching workstations for the tool and interrupting other team members to ask if they've seen it. As a manager in your company, would you go and explain machine learning and AI to those working on the production floor? No, but what if you were to go with an augmented-reality-enabled wearable device and help that worker search for that part he was looking for? This will remove anxiety and fear about machine learning, AI, and these advanced IoT technologies.

I remember in 2001, one of my internship projects in a multiproduct company was to design and automate a process to sort emails and assign customer complaints to the relevant department. At that point, this job was done by two people manually. There was no popular email provider and the company had its own email server set up in-house. I got access to the directory (MAPIFolder) where each incoming email was dropped as a file. I designed and implemented a simple system in Visual Basic 6, with a file reader (InboxItems), reading the body of the email using Mailobject, and searching for product names in content. Based on the product name matched in the email body, I assigned the mail to a respective department. The database I used was Microsoft Access. I did it to eliminate repetitive work using a custom algorithm. As a manager, your task is the same: getting rid of repetitive work, proving the advantages of technology, and allaying the fears of your workers. In manufacturing, there are repetitive tasks that can be easily automated.

We use these advanced IoT technologies not only because we need increase profit, but also to meet strict quality management standards. Think about food factories, following strict food safety guidelines. Using paper or multiple spreadsheets is a labor-intensive process and creates risk. This industry must rely on the cloud and AI cognitive services to meet guidelines and gain the confidence of its customers with zero error tolerance. Tetra Pak, the largest supplier of food packaging, produces 600 data points per piece of equipment with high frequency. That's too much data for any human to analyze in real time.

Blurring geographical boundaries to take advantage of time differences and competitive workforces is another reason we need IoT. Senior executives need to oversee and monitor the manufacture of pipeline seating in the Pacific Northwest of the United States, although the actual manufacturing line is in Shanghai, China, some 5,700 miles away. The need to view real-time information and insights is crucial, for both the headquarters as well as for plant managers in Shanghai. Without any IoT implementation, data need to be fed into spreadsheets. By the time this information reaches the executives, the data are old and not always actionable. With monitoring of machines, process and production managers now look for patterns, relationships, and causality across the plant with greater speed, accuracy, and efficiency to develop better solutions for building products and improving yields.

Another pushback we saw from employees and unions was in regard to job security. The *Wall Street Journal* reported that technological change sweeping the auto manufacturing industry was forcing job cuts. Any kind of automation always got a slight reprieve from the accusations that it has been the key driver in job losses, in the United States and in other countries as well. I certainly agree that no company fires a worker for fun. Sometimes we introduce automation into a task that no one really wanted in the first place. Companies first try to train the talent they have, upgrade their knowledge, and then move them to different department. If nothing works out, the final option is job loss. Of course, embracing robotics allows companies to reduce costs, but it actually frees the employees to do something that cannot be done by robotics, perhaps opening new opportunities. Technology might help create new job categories. Humans are not replaceable with automation. You should stop thinking about whether technology led to a loss of jobs, and instead focus on how to facilitate the transition of your employees into new job opportunities.

Today, every industry makes worker safety its highest priority. Did you notice how many employers either allowed their workers to work from home or closed locations completely during the 2020 COVID-19 outbreak? Similarly, managers keep a close eye on dangerous jobs, machines, and locations listed as red flags. Their top priority is to have zero accidents. Often the reasoning behind implementing robots is a desire to replace human laborers performing dangerous tasks. Working with high-speed machines, being in the presence of poisonous gases, and moving forklifts are all safety challenges. Think about a company that frequently has major accidents and another company with no major accidents in the last year. Which one would you join? Safety attracts good talent, and helps in retaining talent. In the current world, customers are conscious, too. They would like to purchase goods and services (do business) from a company that is moral and socially responsible.

Applications

Some of the common applications of IoT in manufacturing are predictive maintenance, asset tracking, and energy management. The IIoT platform has proven its importance in uncovering process and workflow inefficiencies in industry. The most common feature we learned about is data analysis and usability, but the most important feature is security, including access management, security patch updates, and device authorization. These are the most prominent applications of IoT in manufacturing to directly improve shop floor productivity.

We will be covering logistics and supply chains in detail in Chapter 9. I will not discuss further the obvious advantages of IoT in manufacturing, which you already know about, like increasing productivity and efficiency and gaining a deeper insight into customers' behavior patterns and needs. The following are other essential use cases to help explain the applications of IoT in manufacturing plants.

Use Case 1: Unlocking Innovation

In the introduction to this chapter, I proposed that technology might help create new job categories and automating repetitive tasks could free up employees to think about product innovations. Many companies invest in events like hackathons (or hackdays, hackfests), a design sprint-like event where all employees are asked to think differently. This concept started in the IT industry with computer programmers, but it has crossed industrial boundaries. By the end of an event, a team comes up with new product idea, existing product improvement, patentable technology, or solution to any existing small or big problem in their department. Companies benefit from these events and therefore reward winning teams with incentives.

Recent innovations using IoT have occurred in the mining industry. RTVis™ (Rio Tinto Visualization) is a trademarked information system used to automate every aspect of mining. The mining engineers and technicians are seated in a control center complex in Perth, Australia, remotely guiding the mining operations of an iron ore mining site in Pilbara, Australia. The control center is connected to driverless trucks and trains, autonomous drill machines, and guiding loading and unloading of the ore from the mining site. The system controls multiple drills using sophisticated algorithms. The biggest advantage is managing controlled blasts using data from sensors and deep learning from past blasts.

There have also been innovations in human–machine collaboration. For example, retail warehousers like Amazon and Alibaba have added robots in their warehouses to help with the logistics of locating products and bringing them to workers, rather than having employees go to the shelves to hunt for products. In this case, people work along with the army of robots to cut operating costs.

Use Case 2: Subscription Economy

You pay monthly for Netflix and Spotify subscriptions because they align with your phone and Internet utilities, which you pay for monthly. Customer now, however, also like to subscribe for goods for which they think they know the consumption cycle, like soap, shampoo, or milk. When you subscribe, these things will get delivered at your configured preset intervals. This type of shopping is different than traditional retail, and is known as a subscription economy. Taking it to the next level, for a flat $1,500 monthly fee, a Cadillac customer can swap out his or her car up to 18 times per year. The fee covers all registration, maintenance, and scheduled repairs. Now let's talk about the manufacturing industry in this growing subscription economy:

Kaeser Kompressoren, a German manufacturer of air pumps, compressed air dryers, and filters, is now offering IoT digital twins: product and services. The company has added sensors with their products, which send data back to the company's data center in real time. These data are then used to offer predictive maintenance. The company calls it Air-as-a-Service (AaaS). Customers are happy because they are saving money in unnecessary visits from Kaeser maintenance team, and they receive productive visits when compressors are actually about to shut down. Any shutdown is bad for business. Caterpillar is similarly adding sensors to its heavy equipment to suggest when parts need replacing, including air filters. The company is making good amount of money from this offering and dispatching original equipment manufacturer (OEM) parts.

For airlines, Rolls Royce is now charging its customers by the hour instead of an upfront capital cost. Customers pay by the hours an engine runs in an arrangment called engine as a service. This is generating a continuous revenue stream for the company, and small customers are happy. More than 25 sensors track engine health data and fuel usage to uncover data insights that will enable airlines to improve operational performance and fuel efficiency. Along with this, Rolls Royce added a maintenance as a service offering: They would take over all the upkeep and life cycle management of the engines. Again, customers are getting the advantages of not keeping records of scheduled maintenance and also having maintenance done at any locationoffered by Rolls Royce. This reduces operating costs, slashes engine downtime, and lengthens the average life of its jet engines. A key driver of competitive advantage for Rolls Royce in the IoT-enabled engine industry is the first-mover advantage associated with collecting and using customer data to optimize its other products and services. For example, the company is rolling out the same service for its luxury cars connected with IoT data capabilities, which is different then the current car leasing business model.

Use Case 3: Predictive Maintenance

Predictive maintenance is a popular application of predictive analytics that can help businesses in several industries achieve high asset utilization and savings in operational costs. The most visible concept of predictive maintenance is using connected sensors to monitor maintenance needs in the manufacturing industry. Companies traditionally used manual logs, past experience, and manufacturer recommendations. Under that model, sometimes parts were replaced even though they were working fine and still had life left. On the other hand, sometimes parts broke down before expected, shutting down production. The IIoT takes networked sensors and intelligent devices and puts those technologies to use directly on the manufacturing floor, collecting data to drive three levels of maturity.

> *Level 1:* Sensors help in reactive maintenance. If a machine goes down, connected sensors automatically pinpoint where the issue is occurring.

> *Level 2:* Predictive analytics.

> *Level 3:* The next level is autonomous self-healing.

Predictive maintenance has several benefits, including these:

- Reduce maintenance costs

- Avoid unexpected failures

- Improve repair and overhaul time

- Optimize spare parts inventory

- Increase in uptime

We discuss more about this use case using implementation in the lab section of this chapter using Azure IoT Solution Accelerator. Common predictive elements a manager needs to know are the following:

- *Life:* Time the equipment has left until it fails.

- *Probability:* Probability of failure.

- *Breakdown point:* Likely component of a given failure.

- *Risk level:* Equipment risk ranking.

- *Maintenance recommendation:* Given a certain error code and other conditions, maintenance steps, tips, and manufacturer's recommended solution.

We are not using any real device here, because there is no easy way to plug your customer sensor or device into this preconfigured solution accelerator.

Lab: Predictive Maintenance

Modern aircraft engines are equipped with highly sophisticated sensors to track their functioning. By combining the data from these sensors with advanced analytics, it is possible to both monitor the aircraft in real time, as well as predict the remaining useful life of an engine component so that maintenance can be scheduled in a timely manner to prevent mechanical failures.

We also need a visualization dashboard, so that aircraft technicians can monitor the sensor data from an airplane or across the fleet in real time and use visualizations to schedule engine maintenance.

In this lab I am using a prebuilt solution that can be provisioned from the Azure Solution Accelerator portal by navigating to `https://www.azureiotsolutions.com/`. Log in and click My Solutions, then click Create A New Solution. Select the Predictive Maintenance solution box and use the wizard to set the solution. We went through this in detail in Chapter 3. Enter a solution name (I chose PredictMyMaintenance), select Subscription, select a region, and click Create. The Create button launches a workflow that will deploy an instance of the solution within a resource group in the Azure subscription you specify. The next screen, shown in Figure 5-1, will show you the resources this solution is provisioning.

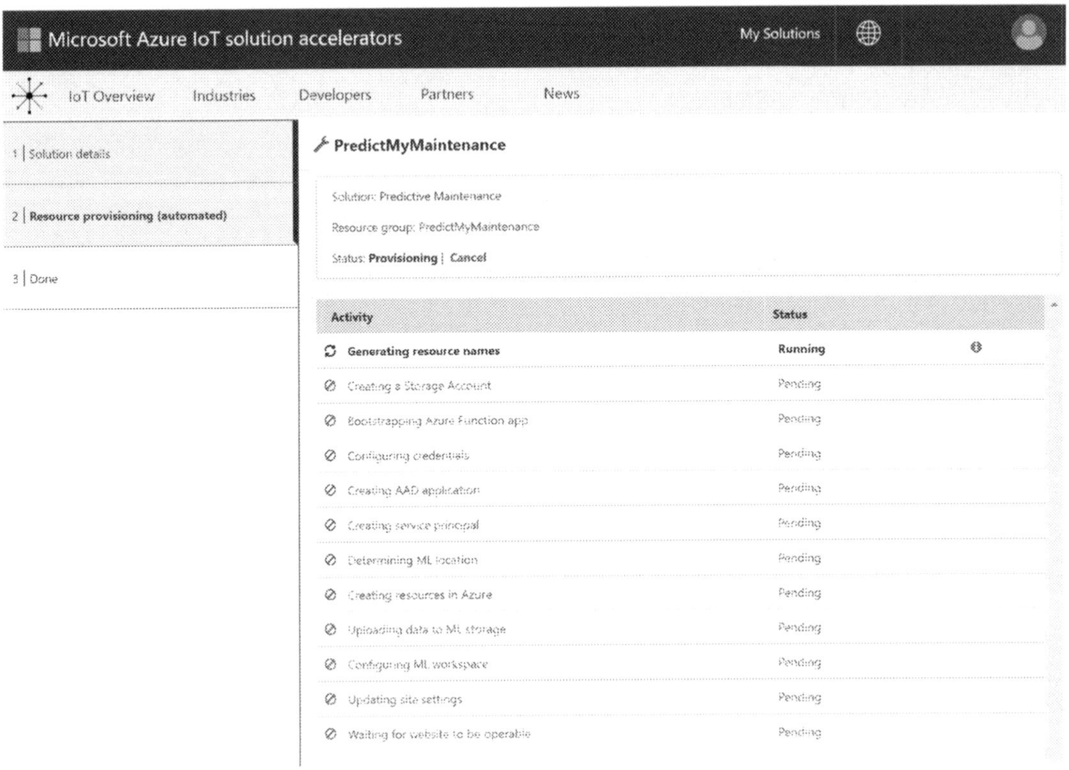

Figure 5-1. *Provisioning Predictive Maintenance solution accelerator resources*

When the deployment to your Azure subscription is complete, you will see a green checkmark and Ready on the solution tile. You can now sign into your Predictive Maintenance solution accelerator dashboard. The data source of this solution is comprised of an emulated data set stored in a `.csv` file in Azure Blob storage.

Azure Resources

As shown in Figure 5-1, the Predictive Maintenance solution accelerator is provisioning these resources.

Storage Account

This is a multipurpose storage account. It stores data for predictive experiment files to manage partitions of the Event Hub processor, keeps telemetry data from the devices, and keeps device simulation data (these are temporary data if a project goes live and is connected with real devices) and data to visualize on the dashboard generated from webjob and Stream Analytics.

80

Along with this storage account, creating resources in Azure also creates two storage accounts. The first storage account contains two containers: `simulatordata` and `<yoursolutionname><random alphanumeric>`. The simulator container is dedicated to storing training data sets, test data sets, and experimental outputs. The same container also has four tables. Azure Table is the fastest, cheapest, most queryable (in this scenario) solution.

- *DeviceList:* Contains registered devices.

- *Devicemlresult:* Contains result data that come out of the Machine Learning job.

- *Devicetelemetry:* Contains all the device data that are coming in through IoT Hub. It is populated from the Stream Analytics job.

- *Simulatorstate:* Contains the state changes of the simulators, which is read by the Web app.

The second container's name is matched with the eventhub name and contains eventhub's data.

Functions App

This contains several functions to be called from the next stages of the deployment, as shown in Figure 5-1; for example, to perform a microtask, such as `createAADApplication`, `createServicePrincipal`, `generatePassword`, `getMLStorageLocation`, `setupMLWorkspace`, and `uploadFileToStorage`. The output of all these functions is stored to the storage account created previously.

Azure Resources

This next step will create several Azure resources, as shown in Figure 5-2. It deployed two app service plans: `<yoursolutionname>-plan` and `<yoursolutionname>-jobsplan`.

Note   By default, systems deploy them with a P1 plan. This is a costly plan—around $200 per month. The first thing you need to do is open it, click Scale up, and change it to the F1 Free plan or D1 shared plan. Similarly, do this for the Functions app, too.

∧ Deployment details (Download)

Resource	Type	Sta...	Operation details
⊘ PredictMyMaintenancejafjq-jobhost/Appsettings	Microsoft.Web/sites/config	OK	Operation details
⊘ PredictMyMaintenancejafjq-jobhost/MSDeploy	Microsoft.Web/sites/extensions	OK	Operation details
⊘ PredictMyMaintenancejafjq-jobhost	Microsoft.Web/sites	OK	Operation details
⊘ PredictMyMaintenancejafjq-jobsplan	Microsoft.Web/serverfarms	OK	Operation details
⊘ PredictMyMaintenancejafjq/Appsettings	Microsoft.Web/sites/config	OK	Operation details
⊘ PredictMyMaintenancejafjq/MSDeploy	Microsoft.Web/sites/extensions	OK	Operation details
⊘ PredictMyMaintenancejafjq	Microsoft.Web/sites	OK	Operation details
⊘ PredictMyMaintenancejafjq-Telemetry	Microsoft.StreamAnalytics/streamingjobs	OK	Operation details
⊘ PredictMyMaintenancejafjq-plan	Microsoft.Web/serverfarms	OK	Operation details
⊘ iothub-jafjq/events/telemetrycg	Microsoft.Devices/Iothubs/eventhubEndpoints/ConsumerGroups	OK	Operation details
⊘ iothub-jafjq/iothubowner	Microsoft.Devices/Iothubs/iothubkeys	OK	Operation details
⊘ mlPredictMyMaintenancejafjq	Microsoft.MachineLearning/workspaces	OK	Operation details
⊘ mlPredictMyMaintenancejafjq	Microsoft.MachineLearning/workspaces	OK	Operation details
⊘ mlPredictMyMaintenancejafjq	Microsoft.MachineLearning/workspaces	OK	Operation details
⊘ PredictMyMaintenancejafjq-eventhub/PredictMyMaintenancejafjq-ehdata	Microsoft.Eventhub/namespaces/eventHubs	OK	Operation details
⊘ PredictMyMaintenancejafjq-eventhub/RootManageSharedAccesskey	Microsoft.Eventhub/namespaces/authorizationRules	OK	Operation details
⊘ storagejafjq	Microsoft.Storage/storageAccounts	OK	Operation details
⊘ storagejafjq	Microsoft.Storage/storageAccounts	OK	Operation details
⊘ mljafjq	Microsoft.Storage/storageAccounts	OK	Operation details
⊘ PredictMyMaintenancejafjq-eventhub	Microsoft.Eventhub/namespaces	OK	Operation details
⊘ iothub-jafjq	Microsoft.Devices/Iothubs	OK	Operation details
⊘ storagejafjq	Microsoft.Storage/storageAccounts	OK	Operation details
⊘ mljafjq	Microsoft.Storage/storageAccounts	OK	Operation details

Figure 5-2. Resources deployed in creating resources in Azure stage

It will give you a warning that the Always On feature is not allowed in the target compute mode. Open App Service, navigate to Configuration, click General, and toggle Always On to Off.

Event Hub

The Event Hub is internal to the solution, used to manage data queues. It collects, rapidly transforms, and processes large amounts of information, and uses partitions, which define how many concurrent consumers and producers can access the data pipeline. Similarly, in this solution Event Hub receives preprocessed telemetry data, processes it, and saves it back to storage. When you are working with high volumes of data that just cannot get lost, this is essential.

IoT Hub

IoT Hub is the ingestion point where the data from the simulated plane come into the system. It receives the actual raw data from devices. All device management tasks are facilitated by IoT Hub. Similarly, in this solution IoT Hub has four devices registered. To see the registered devices, open IoT Hub and click IoT Devices under Explorers.

Stream Analytics

By now you know Stream Analytics is a real-time cloud stream processing offering, designed to analyze incoming data to get real insight on the process being monitored. Similarly, in this solution, the stream analytics is provisioned with the name `<yoursolutionname>-Telemetry`. To analyze the different steps in this, open it and click Job Diagram under Support + Troubleshooting.

As shown in Figure 5-3, the Stream Analytics job has one input, `IoTHubStream,` and two outputs `Telemetry` in Azure Table Storage and `TelemetrySummary` in Event Hub. The analytics job queries the data stream from the IoT Hub to extract sensor data, which are subsequently stored in the Telemetry data table. Additionally, the Stream job calculates the average sensor data using a sliding window and then passes the resulting summary data to the Event Hub.

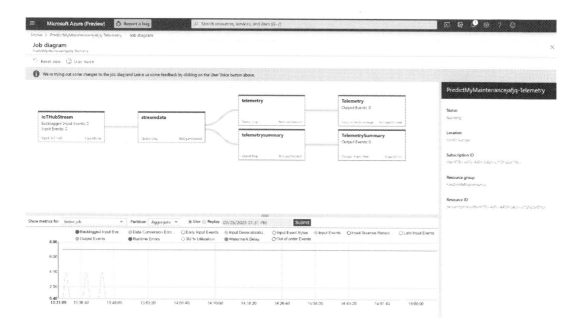

Figure 5-3. *Job diagram of Stream Analytics*

Use the following query to calculate the summary with a sliding window.

```
SELECT
    DeviceId,
    Cycle,
    AVG(Sensor9) AS Sensor9,
    AVG(Sensor11) AS Sensor11,
    AVG(Sensor14) AS Sensor14,
    AVG(Sensor15) AS Sensor15
INTO [TelemetrySummary]
FROM [StreamData]
GROUP BY
    DeviceId,
    Cycle,
    SLIDINGWINDOW(minute, 2)
HAVING SUM(EndOfCycle) = 2
```

The query of `telemetrySummary` as shown here calculates the average of sensor data within a specific period of time and engine cycle. There are three types of windows available.

- *Tumbling window:* This uses a fixed size, nonoverlapping series of events.

- *Hopping window:* This uses a fixed size but overlapping series of events.

- *Sliding window:* This outputs a series of events only when the values within the window actually change, enter, or leave the time window.

Machine Learning Studio Workspace

Azure Machine Learning is used to make predictions on the remaining useful life (RUL) of aircraft engines given the inputs received. To see your ML Workspace, you must go back to your solution. Navigate back to `https://www.azureiotsolutions.com/`, and click My Solutions, then click the solution you created. You will see a link to your ML Workspace. This will take you an Azure ML portal at `https://studio.azureml.net`.

Every Machine Learning model has these steps common, having a training set, test set, and actual data to be evaluated. These three inputs are shown in Figure 5-4. These data are preprocessed using R-Script for removing bad data, creating metadata. You can see these scripts by clicking these boxes. Once the data are preprocessed, they are used to train two machine learning regression models: decision forest regression and boosted decision tree egression. Subsequently, the models are scored and evaluated using the test data. The training data set is used to train two models, which are then evaluated and used to predict RUL.r

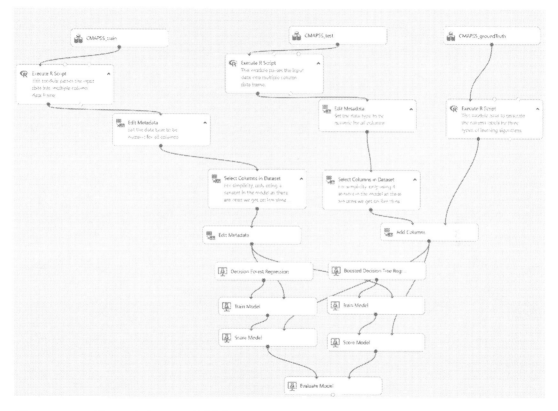

Figure 5-4. *Remaining useful life engines experiment at Machine Learning Studio (classic) workspace*

There exists another experiment, Remaining Useful Life [Predictive Exp.]. This is the actual web service that performs the remaining steps of the first experiment model (i.e., score model) and contains web service input and web service output nodes. You can call this web service manually with data to see the output score of the trained model. To see the test data, you can use the properties window or enter data manually.

Solution Dashboard

You can open your solution dashboard by navigating back to `https://www.azureiotsolutions.com/`. Click My Solutions and then click the solution you created. You will a Go To Your Solution Accelerator link. This will display the dashboard shown in Figure 5-5.

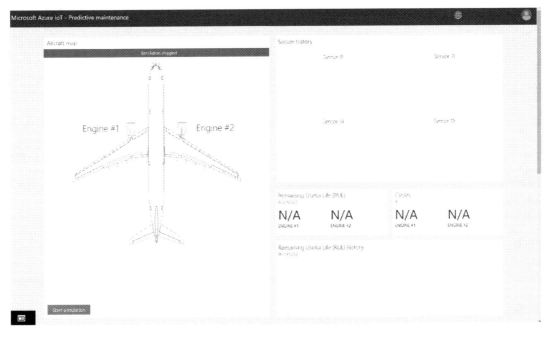

Figure 5-5. *Solution Acclerator dashboard*

Notice the aircraft design with two engines on the left half of the page and various telemetry data from sensors on the right side of the page. The RUL comes from the Machine Learning model, which uses simulated sensor data to calculate when engines are expected to fail.

On this dashboard, there are two sensors installed in each engine. They are labeled sensor 9, sensor 11, sensor 14, and sensor 15. Sensor readings are captured every half-hour during each flight, which lasts from two to ten hours. The total flight duration is denoted as the cycles. We can see data coming from the engines directly in the Azure storage.

The full simulation takes about 35 minutes. The 160 RUL threshold is met for the first time at around five minutes and both engines hit the threshold at around eight minutes. The simulation runs through the complete data set for 148 cycles and settles on final RUL and cycle values. You can stop the simulation at any point, but clicking Start Simulation replays the simulation from the start of the data set.

Now it is time to see some data and overall, the solution working. Click the blue Start Simulation button. You will see "Starting" for couple of minutes, as the system is cold booting before you see sensor readings and the calculated RUL as shown in Figure 5-6. To see the warning, you need keep the solution running for about half an hour, the time engine data takes to reach to the critical stage.

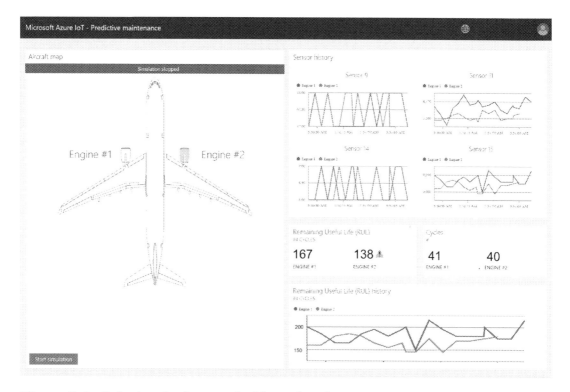

Figure 5-6. *Solution Acclerator dashboard with warning sign and calculated remaining useful life (RUL) from the Machine Learning model*

When RUL is less than 160, the telemetry section displays a warning symbol next to the RUL display. The solution portal also highlights the aircraft engine in yellow. Notice how the RUL values have a general downward trend overall but tend to bounce up and down. This behavior results from the varying cycle lengths and the model accuracy.

You can stop the simulation at any point, but clicking Start Simulation replays the simulation from the start of the data set.

Note   If you haven't scaled down your app service plan, then delete the resources. Your free credit will be used within 24 hours. If you no longer need the solution accelerator, delete it from the Provisioned Solutions page by selecting it and then clicking Delete Solution.

For advanced readers, skilled in programming, Microsoft also provides the full source of this solution on the GitHub repo at `https://github.com/Azure/azure-iot-predictive-maintenance`. Going through the code is outside the scope of this book.

Benefits of Using IoT in Manufacturing

Manufacturers and industrialists in every sector have a significant opportunity at hand, where they can not only monitor but also automate many complex process. Although there have been systems that can track progress in the plant, IIoT technology provides far more intricate details to managers. The following list highlights a few key benefits.

- *Increased safety:* By implementing AI in machines using IIoT, a data analytics system can inform employees immediately of issues. By analyzing data over an extended period of time, long-term exposure can be calculated, and potentially hazardous conditions can be detected in advance. Monitoring the number of injuries, illness rates, near misses, short- and long-term absences, vehicle incidents, and property damage or loss during daily operations ensures better safety and working conditions.

- *Reduced costs:* Managers are aware of the potential to save money and increase profit through the adoption of IoT, but how and where is always a challenge. The answer lies in cost savings in repairs, number of breakdowns, and total labor cost saved from manual checks. I agree that not all machines require sensors. You have to do a cost–revenue analysis. Hence, start with one machine and a few sensors and build the enterprise-level project based on learning and your company specific key performance indicators (KPIs).

- *24/7 production:* By using autonomous processes, you can reach 24/7 production with limited human oversight. Self-dependent systems provide resilience to industries and help them to achieve a faster time to market. Faster and more efficient manufacturing and supply chain operations allow for reduced product cycle times. This shorter time to market gives you an edge over competitors and first market advantage.

Challenges of Using IoT in Manufacturing

The toughest challenges enterprises face in starting IoT-enabled digital transformation initiatives include uncertainty about the return on investment (ROI), data security and privacy issues, the lack of qualified employees, and integration with the legacy systems. Let's look into the key challenges.

- *Large investment needs and uncertainty about the ROI:* IoT initiatives incur several investments like procuring hardware, adding connectivity, adding cloud storage, and technical support. Business managers need to know how quickly they can roll out new solutions and how quickly a solution will start generating revenue. Large hardware costs sometimes bring down quarterly results and convincing shareholders to undertake such an infrastructure expense is difficult without taking a hit on share price.

- *Data security issues:* IIoT adopters believe IIoT is increasing the risk of cyberattacks. We talked about this in detail in the first few chapters.

- *Lack of qualified employees:* It is a hard truth that businesses have a shortage of people at the management level with experience in IoT. They were running businesses traditionally for decades and don't want to invest the time to learn about new technologies due to their busy schedules. Lack of skilled employees is another side of the same issue. Specific skills that are lacking in employees include data analytics, experience in big data, IoT sensors and devices, IT security, and AI.

- *Integration with legacy systems:* The difficulty of rolling out IoT solutions in manufacturing ecosystems is integrating information technology (IT) and operational technology (OT) without data losses and security inconsistencies. Ensuring seamless convergence between IT and OT is difficult because in the past, the systems had different objectives, so they were built based on different technologies and networks.

Exercise

You can practice other preconfigured solutions from the same portal; for example, deploy Connected Factory. This solution is my favorite because it is directly related to manufacturing. This solution includes industrial device interoperability, remote management, and Azure Time Series Insights. Benefits of this solution include the following:

- *Visibility across your manufacturing operations:* Make more informed decisions with a real-time picture of operational status.

- *Improved utilization:* Maximize asset performance and uptime with the visibility required for central monitoring and management.

- *Reduced waste:* Take faster action to reduce or prevent certain forms of waste, thanks to insight on key production metrics.

- *Targeted cost savings:* Benchmark resource usage and identify inefficiencies to support operational improvements.

- *Improved quality:* Detect and prevent quality problems by finding and addressing equipment issues sooner.

For advanced users, the code for this solution is available at `https://github.com/Azure/azure-iot-connected-factory`.

Summary

In the 2016 presidential election, automation and robotics got a slight reprieve from accusations that it has been the key driver in job losses in the United States. We discussed the other side of this accusation and why it is important to automate repetitive and dangerous tasks. Investments in education and training by both employers and employees helps retain valued employees and use their experience in new roles, innovating new products and services and thus generating new revenue streams.

We discussed various use cases that are different from traditional use cases in the manufacturing industry. We discussed how investment in hackathons can unlock new opportunities. We also discussed the subscription economy.

Finally, we explored the capability of Azure IoT Solution Accelerator using predictive maintenance preconfigured solutions. Predictive maintenance is the algorithm to determine unscheduled equipment downtime in the future. I started by creating a solution, and then I analyzed its components and Azure resources like Storage, Stream Analytics, and Event Hub, which are all offered by Azure. Finally, I explained how telemetry data is generated by the simulator serverless webjob. We also explored various sections of the dashboard.

CHAPTER 6

IoT Applications in Agriculture

The Bengal Famine, one of the world's worst food disasters, occurred in 1943 in British-ruled India. An estimated 4 million people died of hunger that year in India. After gaining independence in 1947, it took India 20 years to realize necessity of food security and it started working on a Green Revolution in 1967. Using high-yield variety seeds, machines like tractors, irrigation facilities, pesticides, and good fertilizers resulted in a 30 percent increase in crop yield by 1979. Since then India has continuously expanded its farming areas, doubled crops on the existing farmland, and used more genetics-improved seeds.

We sometimes joke, "Hey! This will not solve the world's hunger problem," but according to the Food and Agriculture Organization of the United Nations, it is a real problem: The world will need to produce 70 percent more food in 2050. Shrinking agricultural lands and depletion of finite natural resources are increasing the need to enhance farm yield. One of the most critical natural resources for agriculture, fresh water, aggravates the problem. Global warming adds its own flavor to this problem of unpredictable weather: unusual rain patterns, hailstorms in warmer parts of the world, and other extreme weather events. Due to not having too much profit from agriculture for these same reasons, farmers are moving into jobs or other businesses, which exacerbates the problem. Now we have several problems to solve.

We need the next round of Green Revolution, and this time we need it in every part of the world. In this chapter, we discuss application of IIoT to increase agricultural production at lower cost. This industry is still immature, which leaves the door wide open for IoT engineers to invent or discover smart farming solutions and for managers to design offerings for each level of farmers. This chapter provides a comprehensive overview of the impact IoT could make on agriculture, explaining some key aspects in detail through use cases. I tried to provide use cases to enhance understanding of the

© Nirnay Bansal 2020
N. Bansal, *Designing Internet of Things Solutions with Microsoft Azure*,
https://doi.org/10.1007/978-1-4842-6041-8_6

design models and the extent to which the implementation is accurate and realistic. Moreover, use cases that need further improvement are pointed out. Finally, the chapter is summarized, and an exercise is proposed for you to brainstorm.

Agriculture

By the 1970s, new genetically modified seeds, better chemical fertilizers, stronger pesticides, and improved irrigation had helped farmers in developing countries. By the 1990s, almost 75 percent of the area under rice cultivation in Asia was growing new varieties that yield better results. Overall, a very large percentage of farmers in the developing world were using Green Revolution seeds, in addition to the better use of natural and chemical resources. Agriculture is changing rapidly, and preparing to fight problems such as droughts, fires, natural disasters, and other issues linked to global warming.

When we look at the fourth-generation revolution in manufacturing, health, and security, we look at the possibility of revolution in agriculture to keep up with the growing demand for food, and look for the technologies that can be used in agriculture. It now seems logical that devices, sensors, and automation need to find applications in agriculture, with smart farming and precision farming. Actually, they are related but different.

- *Smart farming:* The use of technology to improve efforts in raising livestock and growing crops by making processes predictable and improving their efficiency. Other goals of any IoT including agriculture are to reduce waste, enhance productivity, optimize resources, and reduce costs. The focus is based on collection of data and the application of these data; for example, determining how the collected information can be used in a smart way.

- *Precision farming:* Agriculture or livestock get the precise treatment they need based on the data and predictions determined by devices and sensors with great accuracy. The key point here is optimization. Instead of applying an equal amount of fertilizer over an entire field, based on data, precision farming finds the areas of greatest need and apply the fertilizer accordingly. Instead of giving the same dose of medicine to all livestock, precision farming pinpoints the reason for the illness and initiates recommendations to separate these livestock from the others.

Note   Did you know a drones can spray fertilizer 40 to 60 times faster than doing so by hand?

Smart farming and precision farming can be implemented in three simple stages: awareness, implementation, and action.

Awareness

Farmers need to be aware of what kind of data can be collected by smart agriculture sensors and devices. Technically we can sense all physical properties of the environment that fall under various categories. For example, we can monitor weather conditions, soil quality like pH level and various mineral levels, plant growth progress, cattle health, livestock movement, and more. Probably the most popular smart agriculture device is the weather station that helps to map climate conditions. Another common use is sprinkler controllers that manage irrigation systems that can work independently or can be combined with weather stations to make meaningful decisions. The last example use is crop monitoring. This is difficult to implement, and needs to be combined with AI using edge computing or cloud computing. Examples include monitoring anomalies in crop growth, color of leaves, and yield to effectively prevent any diseases or infestations that can harm yield.

We need to be aware of actions we need to perform after sensing these data, like automating multiple processes across the production cycle (e.g., irrigation, fertilizing, or pest control). For example, data collected can be used to map the real-time climate conditions in the field and take the required measurements to improve their capacity and avoid loss.

Awareness about livestock management using IoT is another related topic. Just like crops can be monitored using technology, wireless sensors can be attached to animals to monitor their health and movement. Farm owners need to know how to use IoT to collect data regarding the location, well-being, and health of their cattle. This information helps to prevent the spread of disease and also lowers labor costs. Going beyond general monitoring, special sensors can monitor temperature, health, activity, and nutrition insights for each individual farm animal.

Implementation

To build an IIoT solution for your agriculture needs, you need to choose the sensors, depending on the types of information you want to collect and the goal of your solution. These sensors collect data and these data are then stored in one place so that farmers can easily check them and analyze them to make the right decision. Therefore, we need a data analytics engine capable of applying predictive algorithms and machine learning and providing actionable insights and recommendations. With timely implementation to generate these data and automation, farmers will be better able to nurture, harvest, and replenish their crops. For example, in the fall, immediately after the harvesting, farmers need data on soil conditions so they can replenish fields. This is a challenging step, and we will address challenges later in this chapter.

Action

The core of the IoT is the data generated by sensors and devices. The use of sensors in every step of the farming process can determine things like how much time and resources a seed takes to become a fully grown vegetable. Once you install IoT devices and data start reaching storage, you can start analyzing or making sense of data, either manually using your prior experience or in an automated fashion using some machine learning algorithm. This observation comes from data about crops, livestock, the soil, or weather, but diagnostics come from predefined decision rules and prior experiences. You can either choose an AI algorithm or manually observe and decide on a diagnostic; both methods enable farmers to quickly react to emerging issues and changes in ambient conditions. Once you make a decision, the final step is to make the actual treatment your farm needs to yield meaningful results. As a result, all these factors can eventually lead to higher yield and higher revenue.

Unmanned aerial vehicles like drones play an important role in this process. Before I start, let me present the advantages of drones. Drones are used in crop health assessment, irrigation, crop monitoring for illness and deficiency, fertilizer spraying, and soil and field analysis. Drones do all these things using multispectral, thermal, and visual imagery data they collect using aerial analysis. Using these data, a good algorithm could determine plant health indexes, plant counting, yield prediction, stockpile measuring, water clogging and drainage mapping, weed presence, and so on. Still drones are not a one-size-fits-all solution. We still need different sensors that measure the environmental parameters according to the plant requirements.

Other IoT devices that help in smart farming are RFID tags, cameras, and robots. It is easy to keep an eye on plants and livestock using low-cost RFID tags and cameras. RFID-chipped ear tags monitor livestock and provide information about where they like to feed and relax. A collar tag with sensors can deliver temperature, health, and activity reports on each individual animal. Understanding animal behavior is very important for yield, by determine what the animals prefer. Robots are simple machines that are used in harvesting, irrigation, and fertilizer spraying. Robots also increase food safety and provide around-the-clock efficiency as compared with human labor. We think about robots as clumsy and bulky, but actually robots in this context are gentle and are commonly used in fruit picking and weed pulling. These robots are trained to use a special vision system to detect when some fruit is ripe and then pluck it or to spot weeds and pull them. Such technology is important where health hazards are high and there is a long-term labor shortage.

You might already know about hydroponics and aquaponics, two of my recent favorites. Connected agriculture spaces such as hydroponics and aeroponics are on the rise. We are now applying machine learning algorithms like neural networks and Bayesian networks to control growth of hydroponic plants like tomatoes and lettuce. The intelligent system provides appropriate control actions based on the data gathered by the sensors. We explore this technology further in the case study later in this chapter.

Applications

There are many types of IoT sensors available for agriculture. The agriculture industry should rely heavily on innovative ideas because of the steadily growing demand for food. I will be giving examples of the top two use cases of IoT in agriculture, but here is a quick list of applications I can think of using IIoT.

- *Wine quality enhancing:* Producing wine is not just an agricultural undertaking, it is an art. To master this art you need to know lot of things at every cycle. One of them is monitoring the moisture level of soil to control grapevine health. Another important factor is the trunk diameter in vineyards to control the amount of sugar in grapes.

- *Greenhouses:* IoT sensors allow farmers to collect various data points on critical microclimate factors including temperature, humidity, light exposure, and carbon dioxide across the greenhouse. Controlling these microclimate conditions can maximize the production of fruits and vegetables and their quality.

- *Golf courses:* Keeping golf courses green is a challenge as well as a requirement for the best experience. Getting information on dry zones to perform selective irrigation reduces the water resources required.

- *Meteorological station network:* The study of weather conditions in fields to forecast ice formation, rain, drought, snow, or wind changes is very useful for any crop loss mitigation.

- *Composting:* Different levels of humidity and temperature are required to make compost from alfalfa, hay, straw, and so on. Controlling these parameters will also prevent fungus and other microbial contaminants.

- *Offspring care:* By knowing eating patterns and places animals like to eat, farmers can grow animal edibles. Monitoring the health of the offspring ensures healthy and productive livestock. Doing so reduces the numbers of lives lost due to variable factors.

- *Toxic gas levels:* Detection of ventilation and air quality problems in farms that might result from incompetent or failing ventilation systems and alert of harmful gases from excrement can help preserve the health of farm workers.

Let's move to the top two use cases.

Use Case 1: Livestock Monitoring

There's a lot of manual work involved in livestock monitoring, including driving out to the pasture several times a day to check on, herd, and feed livestock. Ranches with livestock, particularly large-scale agricultural operations, provide one of the best use cases to leverage new technology that uses IoT. Livestock monitoring or simply animal tracking is a process to record location. It can also be used for pattern identification of animals grazing in open pastures or location in big stables. Each year, farmers lose significant amounts of profit due to animal illnesses. There are many ways that IoT-enabled livestock management solutions allow farmers to promote better livestock health.

- *Livestock wearables:* Monitoring heart rate, respiratory rate, blood pressure, temperature, digestion level, and other vital signs can help farmers know a cattle's health levels in advance. The livestock wearables connected to a gateway for a low-cost, low-bandwidth technology to stream data to the cloud. For example, a cow's temperature could rise enough to trigger an alert well before the farmer notices a change in behavior.

- *Livestock reproductive cycles:* Observing an animal's reproductive cycle traditionally is tedious, but with the help of IoT-based monitoring, it can be simplified. For instance, a connected IoT device can help to monitor and measure a cow when it goes into heat, as cows can be in heat for around eight hours. When the cow goes into labor, an IoT sensor can send an alert to the farmer, making the calving process safer and eliminating the need for the farmer to continually check on the cow to see if she has started calving.

- *Livestock location tracking:* This is helpful in locating sick animals as well as establishing and optimizing grazing patterns. Often, farmers face a tough task locating separated livestock. Moreover, the sensors integrated into the IoT device can notify the farmer when a cattle's behavior appears to be changing.

Use Case 2: Hydroponics

The trick behind hydroponics is to control the exact conditions of plants grown in water to get the highest crop efficiency. This type of agriculture could be high yielding if monitored and controlled efficiently. Hydroponics starts with small or large space, shaded or open, equipped with sensors that monitor temperature, moisture, carbon dioxide, air current, fertilizer flow, and the pH of the water. The data gathered from these sensors are uploaded to the cloud, allowing teams of engineers to monitor and take action. It's the IoT in a completely antiseptic space.

Hydroponics is very important in countries with two types of climate conditions: low levels of rainfall and extreme cold. In these types of countries, where you have to feed people year-round and have limited space, like the Middle East and northern countries, this system can solve the problem quickly and effectively.

Why would consumers pay three times the price for hydroponically grows versus traditionally grown produce? First, hydroponics doesn't use soil; it uses water. Second, most hydroponics operations don't use direct sunlight; they use growing light. Sterilization with ultraviolet rays means produce is protected from outside contamination and no soil means less (to no) fertilizer.

I provide more details about how to use sensors using Raspberry Pi in the lab later in this chapter. Whether we need one sensor or multiple sensors, the method remains the same. Raspberry Pi is a minicomputer the size of a credit card. Despite having small dimensions, Raspberry Pi can be used to do many things, like a personal computer, and can be used for IoT projects like monitoring hydroponics sensors. With the wireless capabilities of Raspberry Pi, an IoT system with the needed sensors can simplify the process of getting up and running with significantly less technical effort, while lowering the overall time required to sustain a successful crop.

Note   Fujitsu produces between 2,500 and 3,000 heads of a low-potassium, low-nitrogen organic lettuce a day grown with no pesticides and no sunlight in a controlled environment. This lettuce sells for ¥400 to ¥500, more than three times the normal price of ¥150 to ¥250. Such a large number of crops within one year at these higher prices could grow a farmer's earnings and thus make the farming business profitable.

Lab: Working with Sensors Using Raspberry Pi

In this lab we are setting up Raspberry Pi 3+ with Microsoft Windows 10 IoT Core. Many of you know about open source support of Raspberry Pi 3, like Python and Java. Installing Windows 10 IoT Core and using UWP app or simply a C# application is also easy, using your existing knowledge of Microsoft technology.

Windows 10 IoT Core is not Windows 10 as you know it from PCs. It is another branch of Microsoft's ubiquitous operating system (OS) designed to be run on low-power devices. This is a slimmed-down version of the OS aimed at IoT devices. It can be downloaded and installed on IoT hardware for free. Currently it supports Rasberry Pi, MinnowBoard, NXP devices, DragonBoard, and Qualcomm devices.

Windows 10 IoT Core doesn't support running traditional Win32 apps or even boot into the desktop. The IoT allows you to run a single UWP app at a time and the real purpose of the OS on Raspberry Pi is to run small applications, which are designed for a diminutive computer board.

Installing Windows 10 IoT Core on Raspberry Pi

The following are the hardware prerequisites.

- A PC running Windows 10 version 10.0.10240 or higher.

- Raspberry Pi 3+. I am not using Raspberry Pi 4 because Microsoft no longer supports Windows 10 IoT Core for new devices. The next nearest supported hardware is NXP devices. For the sake of simplicity for first-timers, though, I am using the well-known Raspberry Pi hardware.

- 5V 2.5A Micro USB power supply (AC adapter). For some older models 2A works, but for stable Raspberry Pi 3+ with lot of sensors connected to it, I recommend the 2.5A adapter. Pi will only draw as much current as it needs.

- 16 GB MicroSD card class 10 or better.

- HDMI cable.

- Ethernet cable (if Wi-Fi is unavailable).

- Any other peripherals (e.g., mouse, keyboard, etc.).

Microsoft offers an official build of Windows 10 IoT for the Raspberry Pi. Here's the procedure to install Windows 10 IoT Core on the Raspberry Pi 3.

1. Go to the Windows 10 Developer Center at `https://docs.microsoft.com/en-us/windows/iot-core/downloads`.

2. Click Download the Windows 10 IoT Core Dashboard to download the application.

3. Install the application and open it.

4. Select Set Up A New Device from menu on the left.

    As shown in Figure 6-1, select Raspberry Pi 2 & 3, select the
    correct drive for your MicroSD card, and give your device a name
    and admin password.

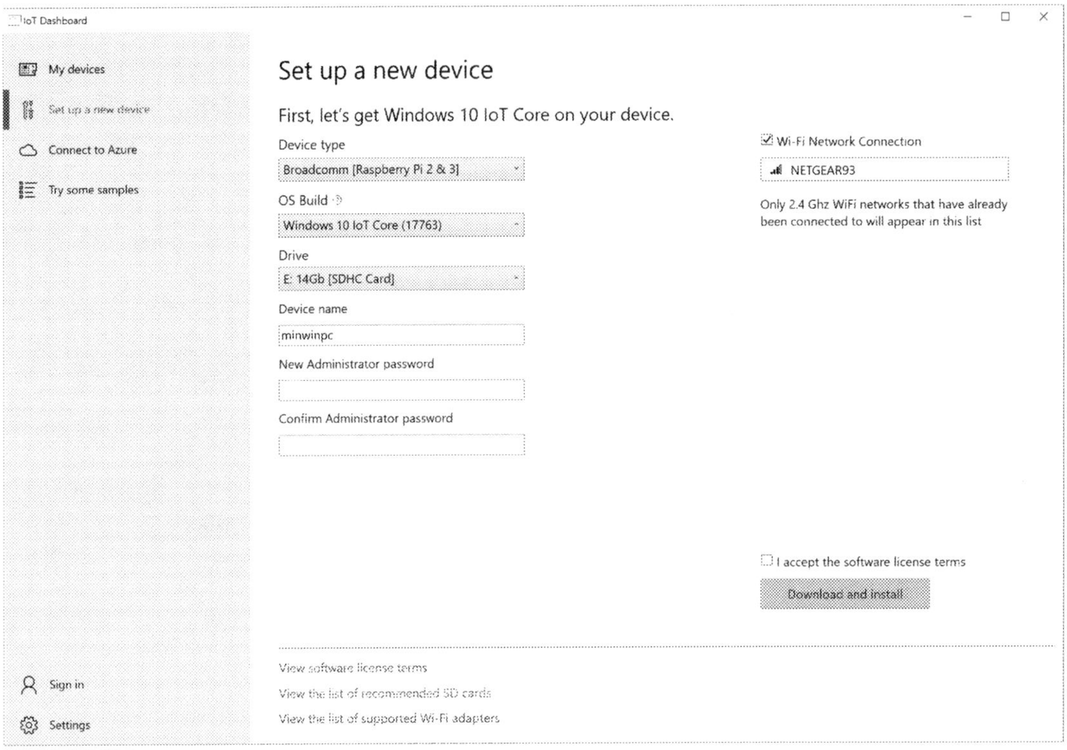

Figure 6-1. *Set up a new device using Windows 10 IoT Core Dashboard
application*

5. Select the Wi-Fi network connection you want your Raspberry Pi
    to connect to, if required. Only networks your PC connects to will
    be shown.

6. Click Download And Install.

The application will now download the necessary files from Microsoft and flash them
to your MicroSD card. It will take some time. As shown in Figure the 6-2, the dashboard
will show you the progress.

While this is installing, sign in to your Live, Outlook, or Hotmail account by clicking
Sign In on the left menu, as shown in Figure 6-2.

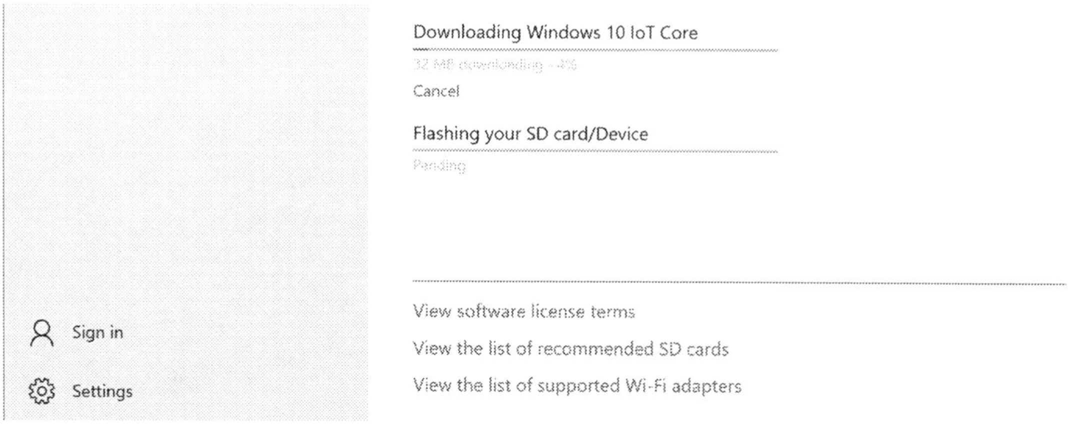

Downloading Windows 10 IoT Core

32 MB downloading - 2%

Cancel

Flashing your SD card/Device

Pending

View software license terms

View the list of recommended SD cards

View the list of supported Wi-Fi adapters

   Sign in

   Settings

Figure 6-2. *Download and installation progress on Flash drive*

Let's assemble our hardware in four easy steps.

1. Connect the micro USB power supply.

2. Connect an HDMI cable to your display.

3. Once the image has been installed on the MicroSD card, eject it from your PC and insert the MicroSD card into the slot on your Raspberry Pi.

4. Power up.

The first boot will be slow and might reboot multiple times to finish the OS installation. You'll be asked to choose a language. If you would like to use Wi-Fi, you'll need to provide the Wi-Fi network credentials to connect to the Web. Currently it only supports 2.5 Gz Wi-Fi networks.

Welcome to the first screen of your Windows 10 IoT Core, as shown in Figure 6-3. Go to Sign In and use the same credentials you used for the Windows 10 IoT Core Dashboard earlier.

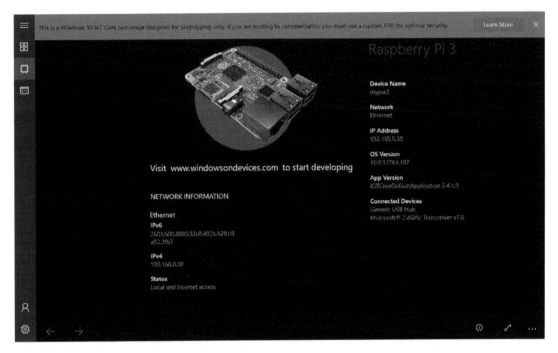

Figure 6-3. *Home page of Raspberry Pi 3+ with system information*

This will display your device in the Windows 10 IoT Core Dashboard application under My Devices automatically. You can use the Windows Device Portal to connect your device through a web browser. The device portal makes valuable configuration and device management capabilities available.

Running Hello World! Application

Let's validate everything is set up correctly using the Hello World! sample provided with the Windows 10 IoT Core Dashboard application as shown in Figure 6-4. Open the IoT Core Dashboard and select Try Some Samples. Select the Hello World program and select your device in the Device drop-down list. Enter your device credentials. Click Deploy And Run. Once done, you can see all the running applications over the device and the portal. Click Click Me. Congratulations! Your Raspberry Pi is now ready.

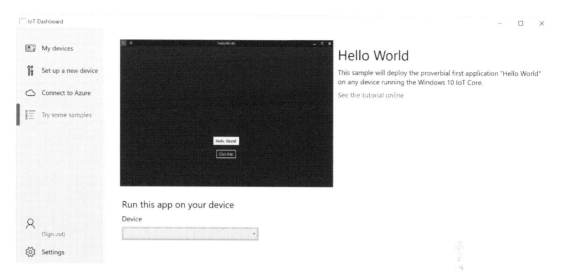

Figure 6-4. *The classic Hello World sample application comes with the Windows 10 IoT Core Dashboard*

Working with Analog-to-Digital Sensors

Now it is time to use real sensors. To start with, I choose an analog-to-digital sensor. These are the most complicated sensors because they don't provide any direct access to the data. We must read raw analog signals and need to convert bytes into meaningful results.

In this example, I am using a Thermistor sensor to read room temperature using PC8591 connected to GPIO on a breadboard. A large number of raw sensors can be used with this method. Working on this exercise will create a good base to work with other sensors.

As shown in Figure 6-5, connect the Serial Data Line (SDA), Serial Clock Line (SCL), and Ground (GND) of PCF8591 to Raspberry Pi. Connect Drain supply (VDD) to a 3.3V power supply. Finally connect a 10K resister with Thermistor on AIN0 (AIN denotes an analog input). You can use the same setting to connect other sensors like a photoresister also known as light dependent resistors (LDRs). Not every pin on a microcontroller has the ability to do analog-to-digital conversions. On the PCF8591 board, these pins have an AIN in front of their label (AIN0–AIN3) to indicate these pins can read analog voltages. To start, we need to define the pin as an input. To match the circuit diagram in Figure 6-5 we will use AIN0.

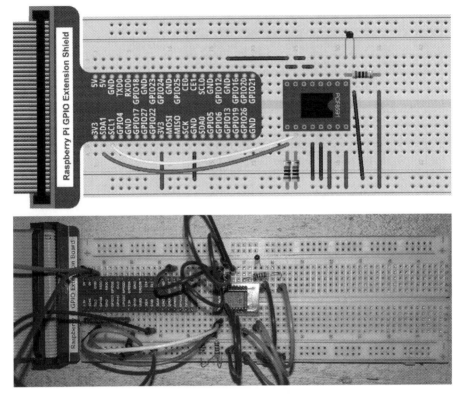

Figure 6-5. *Thermistor sensor connected with PCF8591 using GPIO*

As you might have noticed in Figure 6-3, my Raspberry Pi has version 10.0.17763. I downloaded and installed the same version of the Windows SDK from `https://developer.microsoft.com/en-us/windows/downloads/sdk-archive/`. It's time to write some code using Visual Studio 2017.

1. Open Visual Studio and create a new project with File | New Project.

2. Select the template Blank App (Windows Universal).

3. Add a reference to the Windows IoT extension SDK by right-clicking the References entry under the project. Select Add Reference, then navigate in the resulting dialog box to Universal Windows ➤ Extensions ➤ Windows IoT Extensions for the UWP, select the check box, and click OK.

4. Add the following code in `MainPage.xaml`:

```xml
<Grid Background="{ThemeResource
ApplicationPageBackgroundThemeBrush}">
    <TextBox x:Name="TempReadingBox" HorizontalAlignment="Left"
    Margin="431,405,0,0" Text="TextBox" VerticalAlignment="Top"
    Height="95" Width="406" FontSize="36"/>
</Grid>
```

We now need to work in `MainPage.xaml.cs`.

First, import the library for I2C bus communication and the device library that allows access to device properties as well as additional properties specified during device enumeration. The I2C library provides a communications channel to a device on an interintegrated circuit

```csharp
using Windows.Devices.Enumeration;
using Windows.Devices.I2c;
```

Now define some variables. The first variable contains the address of the I2C bus, and the second variable contains the address of the first analog input pin.

```csharp
// PCF8591 address; The address has 127 bits, so 0x90 >> 1 = 0x48
private const byte I2C_ADDR_PCF8591 = (0x90 >> 1);
I2cDevice i2cPCF8591 = null;
```

Next, we've made an initialization call to search for an I2C device. It creates a new instance of the `I2cConnectionSettings` class for an interintegrated circuit device with the specified bus address.

```csharp
string deviceSelector = I2cDevice.GetDeviceSelector();
var i2cDC = await DeviceInformation.FindAllAsync(deviceSelector);

var i2cSettings = new I2cConnectionSettings(I2C_ADDR_PCF8591);
i2cSettings.BusSpeed = I2cBusSpeed.StandardMode;
i2cPCF8591 = await I2cDevice.FromIdAsync(i2cDC [0].Id, i2cSettings);
```

Call write to select the DA and read the bytes from the AIN0 channel. The following three lines of code reads the analog value–such a simple and neat code.

```
i2cPCF8591.Write(new byte[1] { 0x40 });
byte[] tempData = new byte[2];
i2cPCF8591.Read(tempData);
```

Finally, perform arithmetic operations to calculate temperature. The full source code will look like this.

```
public sealed partial class MainPage : Page
{
    // PCF8591 address has 127 bits, so 0x90 >> 1 = 0x48
    private const byte I2C_ADDR_PCF8591 = (0x90 >> 1);
    I2cDevice i2cPCF8591 = null;

    public MainPage()
    {
        this.InitializeComponent();
        InitI2C();
    }

    private async void InitI2C()
    {
        // Initialization I2C - device with RPI2
        string deviceSelector = I2cDevice.GetDeviceSelector();
        var i2cDC = await DeviceInformation.FindAllAsync(deviceSelector);
        if (i2cDC.Count == 0)
        {
            TempReadingBox.Text = "DeviceInformation objects is null";
            return;
        }

        //Settings for PCF8591
        var i2cSettings = new I2cConnectionSettings(I2C_ADDR_PCF8591);
        i2cSettings.BusSpeed = I2cBusSpeed.StandardMode;
        i2cPCF8591 = await I2cDevice.FromIdAsync(i2cDC [0].Id,
        i2cSettings);
```

```csharp
    if (i2cPCF8591 == null)
    {
        TempReadingBox.Text = "I2cDevice object is null";
        return;
    }

    var temperature = await GetTemperatureAsync();
    TempReadingBox.Text = temperature.ToString();
}

public async Task<double> GetTemperatureAsync()
{
    //A0 = 0x40 is for function register to select DA
    byte[] tempCommand = new byte[1] { 0x40 };
    i2cPCF8591.Write(tempCommand);

    // Per datasheet 14-bit temperature needs 10.8 msec
    await Task.Delay(50);

    byte[] tempData = new byte[2];
    i2cPCF8591.Read(tempData);

    // Combine bytes
    var rawReading = tempData[0] << 8 | tempData[1];

    //calculate voltage
    var voltage = rawReading / 255.0 * 3.3;

    //calculate resistance value of thermistor
    var Rt = 10 * voltage / (3.3 - voltage);

    //calculate temperature (Kelvin)
    var tempK = 1 / (1 / (273.15 + 25) + Math.Log(Rt / 10) / 3950.0);

    //calculate temperature (Celsius)
    var tempC = tempK - 273.15;

    return tempC;
}
```

Make sure the app builds correctly. For Raspberry Pi 2 or 3, select ARM. Select Remote Machine as shown in Figure 6-6.

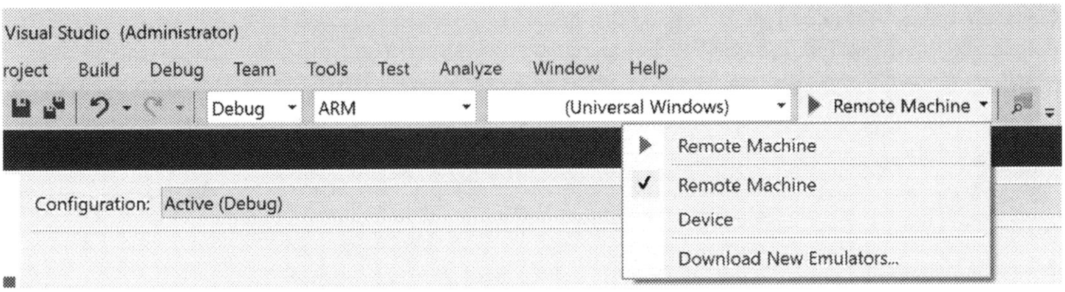

Figure 6-6. *Build and Debug settings*

As shown in Figure 6-7, Visual Studio will present the Remote Connections dialog box. Put the IP address (in this example, we're using 192.168.0.30) or name of your IoT Core device (in this example, we're using mypie3) and select Universal (Unencrypted Protocol) for Authentication Mode. Then click Select.

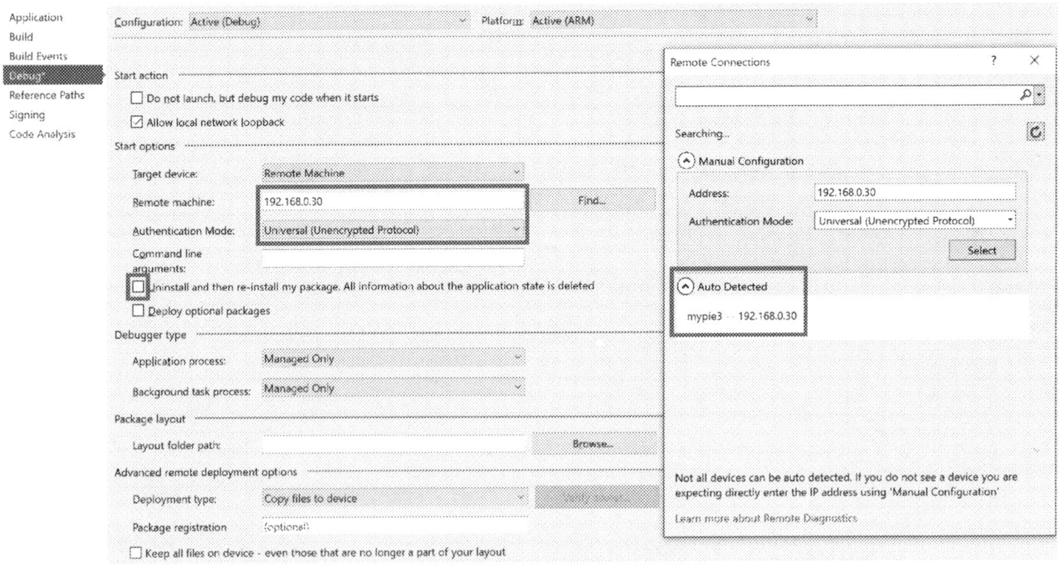

Figure 6-7. *Project properties to deploy application on Raspberry Pi*

Deploy the app to your Windows IoT Core device. If you see a DEP6957 error, the quick way to deploy your application is by building an `.appx` file and deploy it using the IoT dashboard portal.

Create an .appx file using MakeAppx.exe, which comes with Windows SDK.

```
MakeAppx pack /d "<your local path>\bin\ARM\Debug" /p "<your local path>\
outpout\Temp_I2C" /h SHA256
```

Generate a certificate as shown in Figure 6-8. Run the following command to sign your .appx file with the certificate you generated.

```
signtool sign /a /v /fd SHA256 /f "<your local path>\TemporaryKey.pfx"
"<your local path>\outpout\Temp_I2C.appx"
```

Both commands need to be executed in x86_x64 Cross Tools Command Prompt for VS 2017, found on your Start menu under the Visual Studio 2017 folder (and not your regular command prompt).

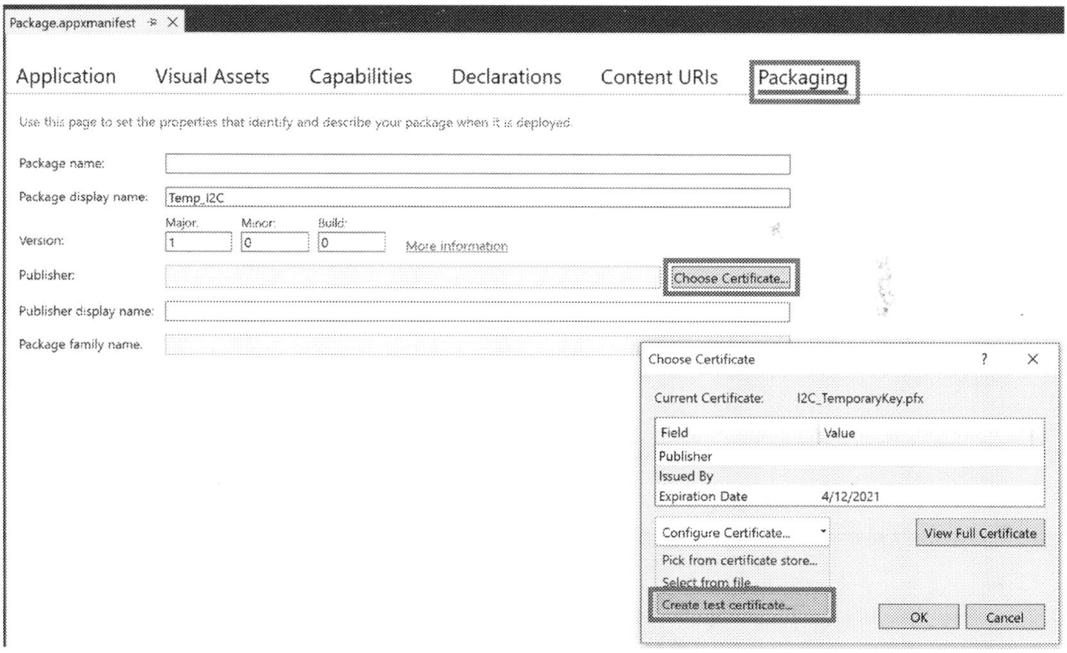

Figure 6-8. *Generate a certificate to sign assembly*

Finally upload the .appx file using the portal as shown in Figure 6-9. Wait for deployment to finish. Once it is done, select Start from the drop-down menu against the Temp_I2C app. Wait until you see an application screen with the current room temperature in the box.

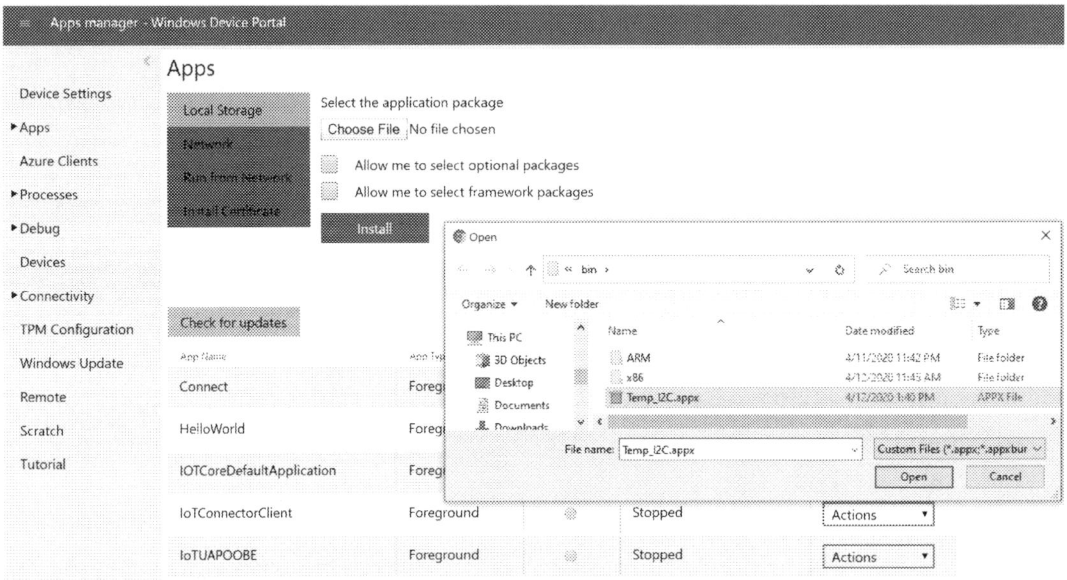

Figure 6-9. *Manually install .appx file using the Device portal*

Congratulations! You just deployed your first UWP application to a device running IoT Core and finished reading an analog-to-digital sensor.

Working with a DHT Sensor

I now propose a project using a DHT11 or DHT12 sensor, a basic, low-cost digital temperature and humidity sensor that can control the necessary conditions required for plants to grow hydroponically. Cultivators can also control agriculture remotely using IoT. DHT12 supports the I2C protocol; therefore, you can use the same code. DHT11 does not support I2C; therefore, you need to directly call the GPIO API.

Can you write the code for the circuit in Figure 6-10? Here is a hint:

```
var gpio = GpioController.GetDefault();
if (gpio == null)
{
    throw new ArgumentException("No GPIO controller found.");
}

var pin = gpio.OpenPin(17);
dht11 = new Dht11(pin);
```

```
var reading = await dht11.GetReadingAsync();
var Humidity = reading.IsValid ? (double?)reading.Humidity : null;
var Temperature = reading.IsValid ? (double?)reading.Temperature : null;
```

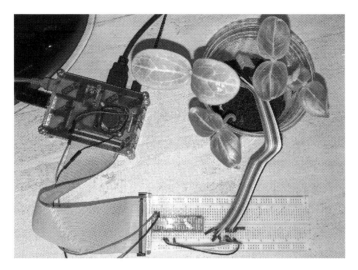

Figure 6-10. *Temperature and humidity reading using a DTH11 sensor*

Challenges of Using IoT in Agriculture

The benefits that farmers realize by adapting IoT are twofold. It has helped farmers to decrease their costs and increase yields at the same time by improving their decision making with accurate data. Each stage has its own challenges and thus opportunities. IoT in agriculture does have its own unique challenges, as defined here.

- *Security:* You saw in my initial chapters that security should come first. This sounds funny here, though. How will it affect a farmer if a hacker gets access to data about how much farmer's cows ate yesterday, moisture level of soil, or the growth rate of plants. I do agree that stealing these data might not be that advantageous to the hacker. What about hacking the device itself, though, and sending the wrong values. A low moisture level reading could start sprinklers and a higher reading of a cow's body temperature could trigger administration of antibiotics or medicine. Security is important everywhere.

- *Lack of infrastructure:* Even if the farmers adopt IoT technology they won't be able to take advantage of this technology due to poor communication infrastructure. Farms are located in remote areas and are often far from access to the Internet. Connection issues would cause any monitoring system to be useless.

- *High cost:* Initials costs of any IoT project are expensive. Sensors are the least expensive component, yet outfitting all of a farmer's fields with them would cost more than $1,000. To earn higher profits, it is important for farmers to invest in these technologies, but it would be difficult for them to make the initial investment to set up IoT technology on their farms.

- *Price influence:* Using hydroponics and aquaponics, farmers can produce multiple crop cycles. Using machine learning, producers can time the market and can inflate and influence market prices.

- *Transparency and control:* Sharing relevant data with a bank or insurance company could result in lower interest rates on loans or rewards. Therefore, the data must be accurate and near real-time.

Summary

By now you might be thinking if IoT can do everything, where is the research on high-yield seeds, and what about better fertilizer and high-performing pesticides? The overall goal of IoT is to actually reduce the need for all these. No seeds can provide high yield without genetic modification. No fertilizer can yield better results without using more chemicals, and we all agree avoiding the use of pesticides in our food is preferable. If IoT is able to increase yield without genetically modified seeds, better fertilizer, and higher use of pesticides, then this could be the solution we all need and have been seeking for decades.

We then discussed how drones allow farmers to monitor crops throughout their growth period. Additionally, farmers can spray fertilizers. Drones have become an invaluable tool for farmers to survey their lands and generate crop data.

I provided various application of IoT in agriculture. Later in the chapter we discussed challenges, as smart farming is capital-intensive. If you check ROI, though, IoT is helping farmers to improve yields and increase profits. In the lab section we first set up the Raspberry Pi 3+ with the Windows 10 IoT Core OS. Then we learned how to use an analog-to-digital sensor using PCF8591 and Thermistor to measure room temperature.

CHAPTER 7

IoT Applications in Energy

The industrial sector uses a variety of energy sources including natural gas, petroleum, electricity, renewable sources, and coal. Energy is used in industry for space heating, boilers, industrial processes, and feedstocks. Industry also uses energy to generate other forms of energy; for example, electricity operates industrial motors and machinery, lights, computers and office equipment, and equipment for facility heating, cooling, security devices, and ventilation.

As worldwide energy consumption is growing, some might argue that simply building more power plants would be more beneficial in areas where consumption is high. Instead of generating more energy, however, some major shifts are happening to make energy consumption more efficient. Moving to LED bulbs and increased adoption of smart light bulbs is a small but relevant example of energy efficiency. In this chapter we look at how IoT is being used or can be used to transform the energy sector from energy generation to transmission, distribution, and consumption.

Later in the chapter I will discuss two use cases of IoT in the energy sector: production-based consumption and the lesser known use of drone-mounted cameras. You will learn more detail about crack detection in physical structures in this chapter's lab. In that lab, we'll focus on the ML.NET Image Classification API and TensorFlow model. This lab does require some very basic knowledge of machine learning and C#.

Near the end of this chapter, we focus on the various benefits of IoT that power generation and utility companies are realizing. In Chapters 5 and 6, we discussed how easy it is to implement IoT in manufacturing and agriculture, respectively. However, the adoption of IoT and machine learning is not as straightforward in the energy sector. The energy sector has traditionally been a capital-intensive industry, be it oil, gas, hydropower, or even renewable sources such as solar or wind energy. This aspect of the energy domain makes it a slow adopter of technology. We will learn more about challenges in the last section.

© Nirnay Bansal 2020
N. Bansal, *Designing Internet of Things Solutions with Microsoft Azure*,
https://doi.org/10.1007/978-1-4842-6041-8_7

Energy

Energy has been evolving in terms of generation and has evolved through the Industrial Revolutions. We noted in Chapter 1 how we moved from steam-powered Industry 1.0 to all possible forms of energy today in Industry 4.0. IoT stands to be the most transformational aspect in the current generation of this industry. Therefore, worldwide energy consumption is expected to grow, and we need smarter energy solutions to fulfill our demands. Due to the large impact of IoT, it is hard to underestimate it anymore in the energy sector. The goal of today's power generation companies is to achieve sustainability and affordability while reducing the use of fossil fuel and carbon emissions. Companies want to become more efficient and reliable and want to create new value in areas ranging from dealing with unplanned outages to reducing waste.

Is the energy company a competitive industry? Yes, just like any other industry, energy companies are also prone to competition. There exists a barrier to entry because energy equipment and plants cost billions of dollars to commission and bring online, but installing rooftop solar panels is relatively inexpensive. Power-generating panels, called solar photovoltaics (PV), represent the fastest growing source of electric power in the United States. The cost of solar panels is decreasing every day and governments are offering more rebates and incentives to install them. If the cost of generating electricity from solar PV falls to the point of being competitive with energy companies, people will be motivated to install solar PV. Therefore, to keep costs down, energy companies are looking for IoT-based technology solutions to reduce cost and waste. As per one recent estimate, global energy prices are expected to decrease.

Energy has been evolving in terms of public demand, too. As population growth expands, so does the demand for electricity. Smart meters, green buildings, home automation, other products and concepts are delivering energy-saving results. Utilities are finding ways and with experimenting the use of IoT technology to limit energy demand. We will learn more about saving energy using smart thermostats, smart lighting, smart appliances, and so on, in Chapter 8.

There are basically three main pillars in the energy industry: generation, transmission, and consumption. IoT has proved its usability and advantage in all three areas. It is a debatable topic which area is biggest in infrastructure, but I believe transmission, the distribution network, is the biggest in infrastructure. Due to its sheer size, we need systems to optimize the efficiency of this energy infrastructure and reduce waste. IoT could certainly help. Today at any given hour of the day, an energy generation company knows about demand based on historical data. They increase or decrease production based on that information. Those are all approximate figures, though; technically companies keep power generation within a threshold range. For example, in nuclear power generation, the threshold of frequency is 47.5 to 52.5. When demand is low, they lower the power generation to keep the frequency within the given limit, or in some cases close one or two units, or in extreme situations shut down the whole power plant. Based on accurate forecasts, sensors can ensure precise generation of energy, thus optimizing production and control.

Companies generating renewable energy (solar, hydropower, geothermal, and wind farms) have been experiencing substantial global growth over the last couple of years. There is a lot that these companies can gain from keeping IoT at the forefront. Because of their newer infrastructure, they face the challenge of sustaining profits and productivity. They need reliability so that they can reduce the frequency and duration of outages. When demand is low, they lower power generation as well. When we are generating energy from renewable sources, reducing any energy generation creates a waste problem. The natural resource waste problem is particularly evident if we don't generate any power. For example, in 2016 China wasted enough energy to power the entire city of Beijing for a whole year.

IoT can reverse this business model through connecting consumers directly to the power distribution station, allowing for a two-way communication. Smart meters connected in a single network create smart energy grids and send critical operation information to the utility agencies in real time. UK-based utility company National Grid said that between 30 percent and 50 percent of fluctuations in the grid could be solved by consumers (i.e., households and businesses) adjusting their demand based on data from the grid. For example, a washing machine and dishwasher connected to the Internet could power on only when there's sufficient energy from the grid. Noncritical appliances would be switched off when the cost is high. It sounds like a more resource-optimized model if consumers change their behavior based on the amount of energy supply and point-in-time cost of the energy. I cover this new consumer-based model of energy in detail in the use case section of this chapter.

Note   A big UK hotel chain saves £700,000 a year by switching off air-conditioning compressors on the roof when demand is at its peak and rates are high. Customers don't notice the slight increase in room temperature.

One of the most popular uses of sensors in industrial applications is measuring wear, vibration, temperature, pressure, and the health of an asset. The data obtained from the sensors are used for estimating the time of failure and avoiding downtime for any unscheduled activities. IoT is very helpful in remote asset management and remote monitoring for safety and disaster prevention. Widespread adoption of this technology could prevent consumers from experiencing power outages in the future. The adoption of sensors in industrial applications is helpful for identifying the safety issues related to breakdown and leakages of harmful gas before causing any harm to equipment and workers, and hence is helpful for maintaining new safety levels.

Applications

As mentioned previously, the major driver for the use of IoT technologies in the energy industry is the need for efficient energy management. There are many more ways IoT energy devices can transform the industry, however. Some of the most popular IoT capabilities in energy use cases include optimizing the process of artificial lift, monitoring pipelines for metrics like optimized volume flow, and monitoring physical attributes of people to ensure and increase safety.

Note   Nissan was the first automobile company to invest in a vehicle-to-grid system. This IoT technology allows drivers to use energy, and stored extra energy can be returned to their household or to their local grid.

Use Case: Production-Based Consumption

This use case came from a problem that most countries are facing: stabilization of the power grid. Currently they have a good old system that is able to predict energy needs well in advance so that they can increase or decrease energy generation before a spike or a bust happens. This prediction comes from historical data or manual requests from big industries or events to the power sector; for example, shutting lights on Earth Day or lighting every part of the city on Christmas. This is called *consumption-based production.* Any big deviation in consumption can cause production or the grid to fail and cause a blackout. Blackouts can create problems for industries and citizens who are dependent on energy for their operations. Having a stable grid for energy generation reduces costs by providing a stable power economy versus if there is an unstable supply; the latter increases the cost of energy generation and has a deeper economic impact on the community.

Let's check the advancement of technology at the consumer end. In most big cities in India, real-time consumption of power can be monitored by consumers with the help of IoT-based electric devices known as smart power meters, shown in Figure 7-1. The regular usage and cost of power consumption are provided to user using an LED display panel. The power meter is helpful in providing the number of units that are consumed and transferring it to both the consumer and the electric board to reduce manpower needed. The user also can check the usage of power using a Web portal or smartphone app from anywhere and at any time. In case of a blackout, community-based power generation takes over (most of the time a diesel engine) and an LED flashes on the smart meter to notify the user that the source of energy has changed. As compared with regular cost of energy, the community-based power generation cost is several times higher. The flashing LED and beeping from the smart meter should prompt consumers to switch off nonessential appliances. Smart power meters are also prepaid, which benefits the supplier's finances.

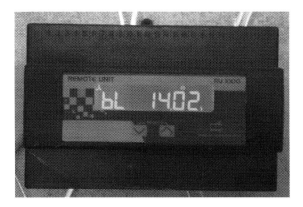

Figure 7-1. Smart power meter

Taken together, the problem on the producer side and the installation of a smart meter on the consumer side moves the industry to the next revolution in the energy sector, consumption-based production. Assuming the producer and smart appliances are connected to the Internet, IoT sensors connected with smart appliances can enable real-time monitoring of data from power grids and make data-driven decisions to switch appliances on and off without human involvement. Nonessential appliances like washing machines, dishwashers, and water heaters start to work in the night, when power consumption and cost are both low. This creates create flexible rates (i.e., higher rates during peak periods), giving consumers the choice of time of consumption. In such a model, the typical objective of individual consumers is the minimization of their own energy bill, while also respecting the total load on the grid. Consumers can also choose to use energy generated from renewable sources when available on the grid over energy generated by fossil fuels. Similarly, smart cities can switch off some streetlights when the load and cost are high.

Power companies cannot store energy. They reduce generation when consumption is low and bear the losses. With the introduction of the smart battery, though, individual consumers can take advantage of dynamic pricing and charge the battery when rates are low and offload energy back to the grid when the price goes up. This generates extra revenue for both parties. This time-of-use (TOU) pricing strategy results in better utilization of renewable energy by avoiding any waste when the sun is shining, the wind is blowing, and water is released from a dam.

A California voluntary pilot TOU between 2012 and 2015 saw very little reward for utility companies due to lack of consumer awareness and lack of smart appliances. Unfortunately, this initiative was stamped as a huge misconception about the benefits of TOU systems.

Use Case: IoT as a Catalyst in Reducing Energy Losses

Energy loss can be defined simply as the difference between energy generated and consumption. Energy losses are broadly classified into two categories: technical loss and nontechnical loss. Technical losses mainly come from energy devices like transformers, and from the materials used in the transmission and distribution system. Usually technical losses are known, measurable, and can be calculated well in advance. Nontechnical losses come from theft (including meter tampering or meter destruction), nonpayment, and error in measuring power when using manpower.

Losses are unavoidable, but can be reduced. Government and the private sector have faced heavy losses due to power theft. In 2012–2013, the United States had power theft of $6 billion. In developing countries, it is and even bigger problem; for example, in 2013 the government of Pakistan confirmed an average loss of $18 billion per for the last five years. To overcome this situation, energy providers are replacing legacy electromechanical induction meters, which operate by counting the revolutions of a disc at a speed proportional to the power, with electronic energy meters that are highly accurate and reliable energy measurement devices. In many cases, they are installing new electronic meters outside the customers' premises to avoid tampering. These steps are not preventing energy theft, however.

Manual detection of power theft is impossible; therefore, the industry is looking toward IoT-based power monitoring systems known as digital energy meters. Digital energy meters are different from electronic energy meters; they use processors to measure the electricity used. IoT is playing an important role in such digital meters. The main objective of smart energy is to provide an uninterrupted power supply, but the next most important objective is to reduce losses. Smart meters measure electricity usage and send these data to a centralized server at a more granular frequency (i.e., either daily or hourly). This technology helps in reducing electricity theft and also reducing manpower needed. Because these meters are connected to a centralized server, they are also used in power saving and identifying defective lights in near real time.

Figure 7-1 showed a prepaid meter, also known as pay-as-you-go meter. The payments are made upfront and customers avoid accumulating a debt for their electric usage. Other than consumer-level benefits, these are of greater benefit to utility companies. It improves cash flow, ends paper billing (hence saving on paper), reduces incorrect bills, and identifies energy theft when lower than regular or no usage is identified.

There are many more ways that IoT is helping the energy industry, specifically water utilities. A common goal in moving toward a greener earth is water conservation. For this reason, the popularity of smart water management is growing. It gives consumers the ability to monitor water consumption and provides useful information directly to the water utility company. By analyzing water loss data, companies are now able to detect water leaks from faulty pipes. Smart water sensors from home automation help reduce water consumption by maintaining the correct temperature and pressure. They can also reduce garden watering based on future weather conditions and data from rain sensors. All in all, IoT is significantly reducing water utility bills and reducing losses.

Use Case: Drone-Mounted Cameras

Usually renewable energy generation plants like solar, hydropower, geothermal, and wind farms are geographically dispersed and a setup could span acres. Physical monitoring of each farm is practically impossible. A quick solution is to implement enough sensors on equipment to remotely monitor and manage assets. Sensors can measure parameters such as vibration, temperature, and wear, so they can help companies optimize maintenance schedules. That's not enough, though, because sensors are not movable. They are attached to equipment and can sense physical parameters with certain limitation. There are around 6.8 million km of power transmission lines in the world, equal to 150 trips around the circumference of the earth. Conducting routine infrastructure inspections through sensors is practically impossible. Monitoring the health of power transmission towers in hard-to-reach areas requires eagle eyes. After all, machine learning needs data to analyze and predict or identify problems.

Many companies are testing drones to perform such tasks and enhance the safety and reliability of service. Drones opened up a whole array of new opportunities for companies involved in both the energy production and the transmission or distribution sectors. A drone can be equipped with several sensors of different types that are capable of collecting the extensive amount of data that is not accessible by humans. For example, a drone with a thermal camera might help identify overheating parts of an infrastructure. Drones can have one or more cameras that can live-stream video as well as take high-resolution images that can be later processed using AI and machine learning algorithms.

Consider the number of sensors that are used for collecting the extensive amount of data needed. They require enough network bandwidth to transmit the data to a ground station. As I mentioned earlier, transmission lines and towers can be situated in hard-to-reach areas where there are no network connections. Drones offer attractive opportunities here, as a drone can interconnect with these sensors when within a proximity range, copy and download the data, and then pass the collected information to the operator, which is further connected with a single IoT ecosystem. This use case for drones is very popular in the construction industry, too. Highly accurate images of construction sites make it easy for engineers to track changes and progress, and to compare them against plans. Drones are also used in chemical plants, nuclear factories, and mining companies.

National regulatory bodies have comprehensive regulatory frameworks and strict compliance guidelines for documentation of assets' technical condition to ensure the safety of critical infrastructure. Power and utility companies need to follow these guidelines. Previously such inspections required employees or contractors to work at heights and in dangerous environments, risking injury and causing lethal accidents. In some cases, with high voltage and magnetic fields, companies need to perform a partial shutdown of the facility. Today drones are helping in this case as well.

Drones are increasing their capabilities and can also work as robots; for example, they can trim vegetation growing around power lines and remove garbage on power lines. As trees grow, contact with nearby power lines is the main cause of power outages. Drones can identify such troublesome vegetation using photogrammetry methods or light detection and ranging (LiDAR) and trim those tree branches, too.

Drone manufacturers are working on technology to power drones with Edge computing, so that data captured from the sensors can be put into advanced applications like image recognition to find cracks in towers or tears in wires. There are a number of actions that can be performed by drones based on that physical, electrical, and magnetic data in real time. Hence, it can be said that the future technology of drones is totally based on the sensors in a number of ways.

Although there are numbers of advantages of drones, the Federal Aviation Administration in the United States has put restrictions on autonomous drones, which require them to be in the line of sight of pilots, and someone should be able to immediately take control of a drone. There are other restrictions in other countries; for example, drones need to be registered with the government in India.

Lab: Crack Detection in Structural Assets

We learned about predictive maintenance in Chapter 5. The same solution is applicable in the energy sector. When the RUL goes below a threshold, the machine learning algorithm flags the asset. Using this method of maintenance prediction, we use data from sensors to measure things like temperature, vibration, pressure, and so on.

Other things, however, like physical machines or engineering structures like concrete surfaces, beams, mobile towers, and in the context of this chapter in power grid towers, are often subjected to wear and stress that leads to cracks. As shown in Figure 7-2, solar panels are also prone to cracks due to extreme weather conditions and sometimes due to falling trees and debris. Early detection of such physical structural damage allows preventive measures to be taken to prevent further damage and possible disruption in energy distribution.

Figure 7-2. *A crack in a solar panel and a structural crack on a tower*

So, what kind of methods we can use to detect such cracks?

- *Visual examination:* Most of the time crack detection evaluation is done using visual examinations by employee or contractors. It is a very time-consuming process. Also, it is impossible to do a complete visual inspection in hard-to-reach areas, so these are often prone to error.

- *Testing methods:* To solve limitations with visual examination and human inspection procedures, big organizations use technology like ultrasonic testing, laser testing, and infrared or thermal testing. This requires special tools and workers with specialized skills to use those tools. Therefore, most of time these types of testing are done by contractors.

- *Machine learning (image detection):* Image classification is a computer vision problem. The major advantage of image detection over conventional manual methods is accuracy, most of which depends on training images, though. It is cost effective and very fast compared with other testing methods.

In the lab in Chapter 12, I will be using visual analytics using Cognitive Services, which does not require any experience in machine learning. Additionally, with just a few lines of code, you can classify the image, detect the object, and recognize the brand in a given image. If you are from a nonengineering background and would like to skip this lab, you can use the technique in Chapter 12 to identify a structural crack with very little change. However, the ComputerVision API has limitations with complex backgrounds, shadows, blurry images, and images with glare. Also, it doesn't allow much customization of the machine learning algorithm. A complex industry like energy demands more accuracy and therefore requires more control of the machine learning algorithm.

This lab bridges that gap. We now see how to build our own custom classifier model by natively training a TensorFlow model using the ML.NET API with our own images and detect the cracks. I first train a custom image classification model to perform an automated visual inspection of images to identify structures that are damaged by cracks. This might take a while, depending on your hardware and the number of images you selected for training. Once the training is complete, we will classify one image to check if the actual value matches the predicted value.

This lab assumes that you have images of physical structures taken by camera or using drones from hard-to-reach areas.

Note   The data sets for this tutorial are from "SDNET2018: A concrete crack image dataset for machine learning applications" by Marc Maguire, Sattar Dorafshan, and Robert J. Thomas (2018). See `https://digitalcommons.usu.edu/all_datasets/48`.

To create a sample .NET Core Console application that detects cracks, open Visual Studio. I am using Visual Studio 2019 Professional to create the .NET Core Console application. Name it CrackDetection or another name of your choice.

1. Create an assets folder in the project and copy all the images you downloaded to that folder.

2. Right-click the project in Visual Studio and add the following four nuget packages. At the time of writing, the newer nuget version 1.5.0 is in preview and prerelease state. I am still using stable version 1.4.0 for practicing this lab.

```
Microsoft.ML
Microsoft.ML.Vision
SciSharp.TensorFlow.Redist
Microsoft.ML.ImageAnalytics
```

3. Once that is done, add the following namespaces in `Program.cs`:

```
using Microsoft.ML;
using static Microsoft.ML.DataOperationsCatalog;
using Microsoft.ML.Vision;
using System.IO;
using System.Collections.Generic;
using System.Linq;
```

The `Microsoft.ML.ImageAnalytics` nuget is used to load a raw image into the preprocessing pipeline. The first thing we do is load all the training images from the given assets folder.

```
var projectDirectory = Path.GetFullPath(Path.Combine(AppContext.
BaseDirectory, "../../../"));
var workspaceRelativePath = Path.Combine(projectDirectory, "workspace");
var assetsRelativePath = Path.Combine(projectDirectory, "assets");

var images = LoadImagesFromDirectory(assetsRelativePath);

MLContext mlContext = new MLContext();
IDataView imageData = mlContext.Data.LoadFromEnumerable(images);

var preprocessingPipeline = mlContext.Transforms.Conversion.
MapValueToKey("LabelAsKey", "Label")
        .Append(mlContext.Transforms.LoadRawImageBytes("Image",
        assetsRelativePath, "ImagePath"));
```

`ImageClassificationTrainer` comes from the `Microsoft.ML.Vision` nuget. It is used to train a deep neural network (DNN) to classify images at the time of creating a training pipeline. There are four image classification models provided in `Microsoft.ML.Vision`: ResnetV2101, InceptionV3, MobilenetV2, and ResnetV250. I am using ResnetV2101.

ResNet V2 is a family of network architectures for image classification with a variable number of layers, published by Kaiming He, Xiangyu Zhang, Shaoqing Ren, and Jian Sun in "Deep Residual Learning for Image Recognition" (2015). The 101 denotes that the architecture Microsoft is using in the `Microsoft.ML.Vision` nuget contains 101 layers.

```
IDataView preProcessedData = preprocessingPipeline
        .Fit(imageData)
        .Transform(imageData);

TrainTestData trainSplit = mlContext.Data.TrainTestSplit(data:
preProcessedData, testFraction: 0.3);
TrainTestData validationTestSplit = mlContext.Data.
TrainTestSplit(trainSplit.TestSet);

IDataView trainSet = trainSplit.TrainSet;
IDataView validationSet = validationTestSplit.TrainSet;
IDataView testSet = validationTestSplit.TestSet;

var classifierOptions = new ImageClassificationTrainer.Options()
{
    FeatureColumnName = "Image",
    LabelColumnName = "LabelAsKey",
    ValidationSet = validationSet,
    Arch = ImageClassificationTrainer.Architecture.ResnetV2101,
    MetricsCallback = (metrics) => Console.WriteLine(metrics),
    TestOnTrainSet = false,
    ReuseTrainSetBottleneckCachedValues = true,
    ReuseValidationSetBottleneckCachedValues = true,
    WorkspacePath = workspaceRelativePath
};
```

The `SciSharp.TensorFlow.Redist` nuget is not directly used, but internally used by the training pipeline to fit the training set.

```
var trainingPipeline = mlContext.MulticlassClassification.Trainers
.ImageClassification(classifierOptions)
.Append(mlContext.Transforms.Conversion.MapKeyToValue("PredictedLabel"));

ITransformer trainedModel = trainingPipeline.Fit(trainSet);
```

Finally, we need to call a `classify` method to classify just one file or group of files, depending on your needs. Here I am giving you a method of single-image classification.

```
ClassifyImage(mlContext, testSet, trainedModel);

public static void ClassifyImage(MLContext mlContext, IDataView data,
ITransformer trainedModel)
{
    PredictionEngine<ModelInput, ModelOutput> predictionEngine = mlContext.
    Model.CreatePredictionEngine<ModelInput, ModelOutput>(trainedModel);

    ModelInput image = mlContext.Data.CreateEnumerable<ModelInput>(data,
    reuseRowObject: true).First();

    ModelOutput prediction = predictionEngine.Predict(image);
    OutputPrediction(prediction);
}
```

Additionally, we need some helper method and an input and output contract class we used in the preceding code.

```
public static IEnumerable<ImageData> LoadImagesFromDirectory(string folder)
{
    var files = Directory.GetFiles(folder, "*", SearchOption.AllDirectories);
    foreach (var file in files)
    {
        yield return new ImageData()
        {
            ImagePath = file,
            Label = Directory.GetParent(file).Name
        };
    }
}

private static void OutputPrediction(ModelOutput prediction)
{
    string imageName = Path.GetFileName(prediction.ImagePath);
    Console.WriteLine($"Image: {imageName} | Actual Value: {prediction.
    Label} | Predicted Value: {prediction.PredictedLabel}");
}
```

```
class ImageData
{
    public string ImagePath { get; set; }
    public string Label { get; set; }
}

class ModelInput
{
    public byte[] Image { get; set; }
    public Int32 LabelAsKey { get; set; }
    public string ImagePath { get; set; }
    public string Label { get; set; }
}

class ModelOutput
{
    public string ImagePath { get; set; }
    public string Label { get; set; }
    public string PredictedLabel { get; set; }
}
```

The architecture is shown in Figure 7-3.

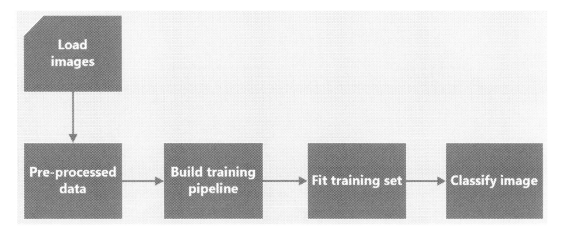

Figure 7-3. *ML.NET project architecture*

Compile and execute using F5. Your results should be similar to the output shown in Figure 7-4. You might see warnings or processing messages, but these messages have been removed from the following results for clarity.

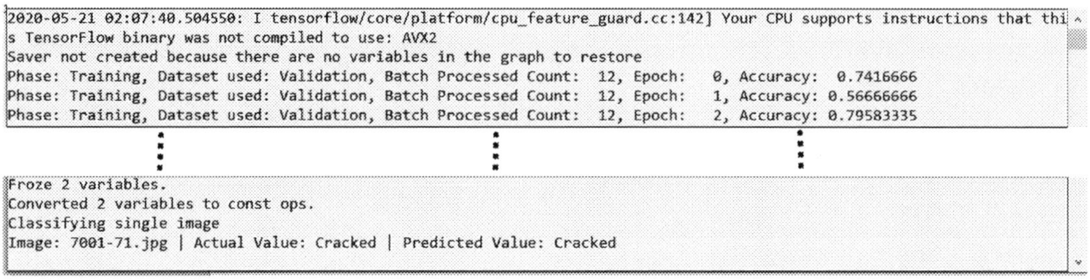

```
2020-05-21 02:07:40.504550: I tensorflow/core/platform/cpu_feature_guard.cc:142] Your CPU supports instructions that thi
s TensorFlow binary was not compiled to use: AVX2
Saver not created because there are no variables in the graph to restore
Phase: Training, Dataset used: Validation, Batch Processed Count:  12, Epoch:   0, Accuracy:  0.7416666
Phase: Training, Dataset used: Validation, Batch Processed Count:  12, Epoch:   1, Accuracy:  0.56666666
Phase: Training, Dataset used: Validation, Batch Processed Count:  12, Epoch:   2, Accuracy:  0.79583335
```

```
Froze 2 variables.
Converted 2 variables to const ops.
Classifying single image
Image: 7001-71.jpg | Actual Value: Cracked | Predicted Value: Cracked
```

Figure 7-4. *Execution result with the same actual and predicted values*

Congratulations! You've now successfully built a machine learning model for crack detection by reusing a pretrained TensorFlow model in ML.NET locally on your system, with no cloud and no special hardware requirements.

Once you train and test, pass your real images to test the result again using the following line.

```
prediction = predictionEngine.Predict(new ModelInput()
{
    Image = File.ReadAllBytes("<your image path>"),
    LabelAsKey = 1000,
    ImagePath = "<your image path",
    Label = "Image name"
});
```

The main intention of this lab is to learn use of the ML.NET Image Classification API and TensorFlow model and review the crack detection system based on image processing. With images I took with my camera, I found some false-positive results as well as some cracks that were not identified. Just like any other machine learning model, you need train the model with thousands of images for better accuracy.

After the first execution, did you notice a workspace folder created in your project directory? This folder contains generated files from our model; specifically, the .pb file is important. Using ML.NET, you can load this TensorFlow model .pb file (also called frozen graph def) using `context.Model.LoadTensorFlowModel` to make predictions with it from C# for scenarios like image classification. You can also export the TensorFlow model `.pb` file from Cognitive Services Custom Vision and load it to classify the images in a few lines. I cover the Custom Vision portal (`https://customvision.ai`) to import images, train models, and export final models in Chapter 12 without using any coding knowledge.

For the curious reader, you can use a tool called Netron to explore the `.pb` file (frozen TensorFlow model) and see the names of the input and output tensors.

Benefits of IoT Application in Energy

Use of IoT in the energy sector has a wide range of benefits for every part of the electric supply chain network, from power generation to the point when consumers pay their electricity bills. The benefits can be divided into two main categories, energy generation and energy consumption.

Benefits to energy generation are as follows:

- Reduced carbon emissions.

- Compliance with governmental audits.

- Predictive maintenance and remote asset monitoring.

- Automated processes to cut operational expenses and increase efficiency.

- Saving lives.

Predictive analytics help identify problems early to avoid unexpected downtimes or failures. Predictive maintenance of old plants is definitely a problem that IoT-based applications are solving for the energy sector, using inputs from sensors and devices to predict when maintenance is necessary. Predictive maintenance can also be done manually by periodically checking equipment with handheld vibration or audio sensors. For example, sensors can gather relevant real-time data on the condition of a mechanical lift.

As demand increased during peak hours, the power plant began creating more energy. When demand further grows above a threshold, the power plant or grid can trip. The impact of power loss can be fatal anywhere, but it's particularly devastating when hospital care and public transportation are affected.

Some of the benefits to energy consumption are as follows:

- Improved transparency of energy use.

- Reduction in energy demands.

- Empowering innovation.

IoT empowers users with actionable insight to better understand their energy consumption in real time and create personalized recommendations based on usage data. It could also drive forward lifestyle innovations, transforming the idea of a smart home into a reality.

It is possible to go completely green. First we need to cut the consumption of energy using smart things in households. Second, we need to generate our own energy from renewable sources and go completely off-grid. Every small or large initiative from industry and consumers reduces the carbon footprint and contributes to environmental conservation. This is the biggest benefit I see.

Challenges of IoT Application in Energy

Despite the number of undeniable benefits, IoT in the energy industry has some difficulties. Any level of integrating IoT devices in the complete energy system is not an easy task for any company and they face several challenges along the way. When considering the use of IoT technologies in the energy industry, you need to keep the following challenges in mind.

- *Security:* Once again security is the number one challenge because it is a common threat to all IoT solutions. Along with infrastructure security, data security and privacy also pose a challenge to IoT in energy. There is a lot of consumer data involved in this type of setup, which in the wrong hands can prove to be disastrous for consumers and completely destroy the reputation of a company. For security reasons, many companies rethink their decisions regarding IoT-based business models and delay their moves. With correct implementation, a company should be able to reap the benefits of IoT without the risk of being exposed to cyberthreats. One quick way is to take critical infrastructural assets off the public Internet and thus offline from cyberattacks.

- *Connectivity:* Without connectivity, distribution of energy is not possible. Now, you must be thinking, if connectivity is one of the important pillars of the energy sector, why is availability of connectivity a challenge in the energy sector? Much oil and gas exploration happens in deep oceans, out of reach of current mobile towers. The only option is to leverage satellite connectivity. I explain the role of 5G in detail in Chapter 13, and 5G will play an important role in increasing connectivity in such remote places.

- *Integration:* Most of our energy infrastructure is many decades old. Legacy equipment that does not have the capability to communicate using common industrial interfaces is definitely a big challenge for any energy company. Although the hardware might be new or improved, it is still based on outdated technology. Challenges arise when you need to connect your new IoT network with such existing such equipment. In some cases, companies need to first invest in improving the current infrastructure, and in some cases, it is a very complex process of integrating with the existing one.

- *Skill:* For many companies lacking the proper skill set, this integration becomes almost impossible, which is why the project is dropped before it even begins.

- *Regulation:* National bodies are defining legal regulations for flying drones to enable drone owners to deal with insurance of both drone and unmanned autonomous vehicle (UAV) pilots. Such a comprehensive regulatory framework prevents implementation of solutions using drones. Power and utility sector companies are working with governing bodies to get permission to perform beyond visual line of sight (BVLOS) flights, to open up new opportunities and allow drones to perform increasing numbers of operations.

These are the main reasons companies sometimes remain hesitant to implement a full IoT-based overhaul to improve their system, despite the many advantages.

The barriers to the adoption of these new IoT tools can be high, but the risk and cost of not pursuing them is greater. There is no one-size-fits-all implementation architecture for this sector. Every electric utility must evaluate its own path to overcome these challenges and keep innovation as the industry's heritage.

Summary

In this chapter, you learned that the main goal of power generation is to achieve availability, sustainability, affordability, and reduced carbon emissions. The adoption of IoT in power generation is helpful for identifying safety issues in plant equipment and grid infrastructure before they cause any outages. We saw some case studies from the energy sector: production-based consumption, IoT as a catalyst in reducing energy losses, and drone-mounted cameras. This case study brought to the forefront some of the opportunities energy producers and consumers have discovered.

In the lab, you learned how the entire machine learning solution can be created with a TensorFlow model using the ML.NET API to identify cracks in images of energy infrastructure elements.

However, security is considered one of the main challenges for IoT in the energy sector. Based on these challenges, the energy sector cannot run IoT projects on the public Internet.

CHAPTER 8

IoT Applications in Smart Homes

IoT is gaining popularity among millennials by providing smart devices that can be controlled remotely. Of all the IoT services, home automation and smart homes are the most representative. Smart homes include connected devices that make our lives easier, more convenient, and more comfortable. Home IoT services enhance the efficiency and comfort of users in their daily lives. Smart homes are no longer just a vision for future living. The concept has completely revolutionized modern living with unprecedented levels of indulgence, luxury, and relaxation, requiring less effort from residents. At present, there is a compelling demand for fast deployment of smart homes that has provided business opportunities for various organizations. Technologies including Insteon, X10, THREAD, ZigBee, Z-Wave, and Bluetooth LE are competing in this market.

In this chapter, I trace the history of the smart home and try to contextualize where the smart home movement sits in the larger technology category of IoT. The truth is that people have been talking about and building some variation of smart homes for decades, mostly custom automation. For example, almost a decade before the Nest thermostat came into existence in 2011 from Nest Labs, I was already using a programmable thermostat from Honeywell. I must huddle with blanket any day I arrive home early, though, because I programmed my heater to start at 6 p.m.

Smart home systems have achieved great popularity in recent years as they increase the comfort and quality of life. I know you are familiar with digital assistants like Google Home, Amazon Echo, Apple HomePod, or Microsoft Cortana, and you might even have one in your home. In this chapter, though, I introduce you to advanced automation with some unique use cases. Later in the chapter we will do a lab as well.

© Nirnay Bansal 2020
N. Bansal, *Designing Internet of Things Solutions with Microsoft Azure*,
https://doi.org/10.1007/978-1-4842-6041-8_8

Finally, I close with the benefits of smart home systems, technological limitations that create hurdles, and challenges of privacy and security associated with the connected nature of modern smart homes.

Smart Homes

Imagine that you're driving home on a hot summer day. Rather than turn the air conditioner on when you get home and wait for your house to cool down, you simply use your smartphone when you leave your office to tell your smart thermostat to lower the temperature. You then tell your coffee machine to start preparing decaf and finally set your lights based on your mood. Smart homes have transformed the way we live. The technology fascinates me, and smart home space fascinates me most, first because it promises to transform the way I live, and second, because even after a decade it is still a luxury (i.e., not all builders offer it).

X10 was the first communication protocol designed for such home automation. It was designed to work on 120 kHz radio frequency (RF) through existing electric wiring. These signals command the operation when they reach programmable outlets or switches. A transmitter could, for example, send a signal to turn on switch at a specific time. I got access to an Insteon (competitor of X10) protocol-based wireless device for the first time in 2008 when I won the device in the INETA Tampa meetup group's raffle. I learned how to open and close a wall/ceiling register using a Web-based portal. (Can you do that today?) I was amazed with the technology in those days. Around 2009, numerous companies started investing in home automation products. For example, Nest Labs started in 2010, and launched its first product, the smart thermostat, in 2011, which today you see as Google Nest.

The beauty of Smart Homes lies in the fact that one can remotely control entire home devices using smart phones or other web-based applications. The common goal of Home IoT devices is reducing cost and conserving energy, helping low carbon emission thus contributing into greener earth.

According to a forecast by Zion Mrket Research, the global smart home market is expected to reach $53.45 billion by 2022. The home automation sector consists of smart kitchens, security and access control devices, smart irrigation, smart lighting, smart appliances, and so on. All devices are controlled by a master home automation controller, often called a smart home hub. Most of the hubs facilitate easy integration of new devices and appliances sharing the same protocol. Therefore, homeowners can easily upgrade to the latest lifestyle technology by adding a particular suite of devices in place of older ones. This will help the residents to improve appliance effectiveness and enrich their overall lifestyle.

Government is playing important role, too, among the main drivers, finding IoT to be a solution to a major problem of global warming and fulfilling growing demand for electricity as reasons to adopt this technology.

Hardware and software are the two bases for any device, and communication is another important building block in IoT-based home automation devices. Appropriate communication protocols help in avoiding the performance bottlenecks that restrict device integration capabilities with other IoT gateways. Unfortunately, this embedded protocol support continues to affect the growth and acceptance of smart home market. Instead of standardizing protocols, companies are divided, and tightly couple their devices with random or proprietary protocols. For example, Amazon has embraced Zigbee in its Echo Plus devices, and Google Nest is leveraging its own Thread protocol to communicate with sensors.

Figure 8-1 shows the smart home architecture with its main components and the connection and data flow among them.

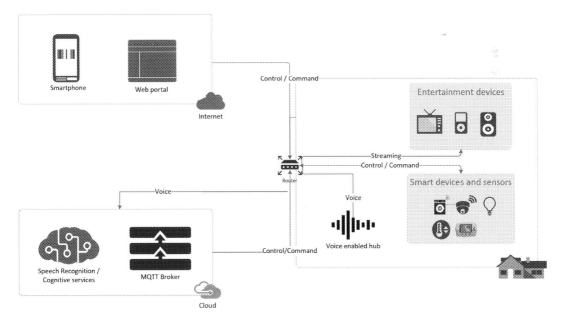

Figure 8-1. *Home automation architecture*

Just like any typical IoT platform, home automation also includes device security and authentication, message brokers and message queuing, device administration, protocols, data collection, analysis capabilities, integration with other web services, scalability, and APIs for real-time information flow. I am not focusing those technicalities in Figure 8-1. My focus is on the core components.

- *Smart devices and electrical instruments:* Sensors in home automation include but are not limited to temperature, lux, water level, air composition, surveillance cameras, voice and sound, pressure, humidity, infrared, vibrations, and ultrasonic. These devices are categorized into two types. The first type only takes commands or can be triggered based on a set time. For example, pet care can be automated with connected feeders. The second type is bidirectional communication devices, which take commands and send notifications or alerts when they read values outside set limits. Few of them are Edge devices, which include Edge computing to predict values based on a machine learning algorithm.

- *Entertainment devices:* These include televisions, portable audio devices and smartphones, for streaming digital content.

- *Hub:* This could be a voice-enabled device with cloud services to translate a user's voice into meaningful commands (for security reasons, in some hubs the speech recognition and cognitive services are inside the hub itself using Edge computing) or non-voice-enabled hub to program smart devices.

- *Communication infrastructure:* This is the most important component. It seems simple, but if you look closely, this architecture has three communication systems: an external network, gateway, and an internal network. External networks are cable television networks, telephone networks, and the Internet. The Internet is mostly used as a multimedia network for transmitting audio and video streaming services. An intranet is used to interconnect the great diversity of household appliances, electrical instruments, and sensors. Finally, the home gateway is a network device that connects the external network and home intranet to provide the smartphone and web portals that control the function of interconnecting devices in the home.

In this architecture I used the philosophy of a single device manager (hub) for handling different communication protocols. Supporting multiple protocols is a greater challenge with most of the voice-enableds hub on the market. Fortunately, several commercial solutions such as Revolv, SmartThings, Insteon, Vera, and Wink, are bringing interoperability to several supported devices and protocols. Each one of these offers its own smartphone app to use as a remote control for the systems. It works even if a user is outside the house, which makes the solution a fully functional, ideal Plug-and-Play home gateway.

Application

The application of smart home devices is continuously evolving with new up-and-coming technologies in computer networking, embedded systems, human–computer interfaces, and wireless sensor networks. Millennials are bringing new expectations and interpretations about what a smart home system is expected to do. Brands are focusing on better mobile experiences for their consumers and voice is the next generation use case. The following use cases are some of the most relevant today.

Use Case: Smart Home Personal Assistants

At present, there are several personal assistant products available on the market. I am neither rating nor reviewing any of these devices, nor I am recommending one over another. In this section, I am exploring the opportunity to implement personal assistants, a first step in automating your home.

Google and Amazon are among the companies that produce top voice-activated personal assistant products that provide platforms and solutions for home automation. Smart home devices such as Amazon Echo, Apple HomePod, and Google Home provide a more interactive, easy to set up, and user-friendly experience. These AI-powered smart devices are streamlining our lives and allowing us to perform everyday household tasks with ease, all with a voice command or touch of a button. Referring back to the architecture in Figure 8-1, when you speak to these voice-enabled devices, a recording of what you asked is sent to the company's cloud, where natural language processing (NLP) services process the request more efficiently, to finally respond to you or to the other device as a command. Every device is designed with distinctive architectural elements and can have built-in skills, support third-party skills, plug-and-manage other smart devices, and prepare shopping lists for you. Commonly, all smart home personal assistants are Internet-based systems that can get regular and new updates. For example, you can develop your own skill or command remote web service host developer by third-party developers. Due to such extensibility, they are popular.

In the competitive market of screen-based assistants, LUCY features a large-format screen. It can be installed on a refrigerator door or simply on a wall like a digital photo frame. It is an AI-enabled device with a microphone and camera through which it can see, hear, and connect to other devices like the other personal assistants.

We talked about Raspberry Pi in previous chapters. It can use Google's speech recognition interface. This device receives voice or gesture commands or collects data from sensors and then interprets those commands or data to administer household devices like fans, TV, heaters, lighting, doors, and more. For example, it collects data from sensors and turns off lights in a room, if there is no one sitting in that room.

Voice technology will become a primary interface to the digital world as we become more comfortable and reliant on it. A lack of knowledge makes it particularly hard for companies to adopt a voice strategy. There is a lot of opportunity for much deeper and much more conversational experiences with customers. These smart home personal assistants would get skills from different service providers to offer customer care. Children will get tuition, and financial services could be available in the future. Every manager should take this as a new opportunity to connect with the customers.

Use Case: Green House System

Home automation not only can make your life safer and more convenient; it can also help you to save energy and money. An important factor in monthly expenses is utility consumption, which can be reflected in terms of gas, water, and electricity. The average home spends almost $2,000 on utility charges related to energy every year. This average household could cut a third of its current energy bill by switching to energy-efficient appliances, thermostat controls, and smart lighting. Almost half of these total utility charges go toward HVAC systems. There exist many types of programmable thermostats that offer the flexibility to control the climate in your home efficiently to save energy and lower energy bills. Some of them are smarter, learning from your habits and setting the temperature based on AI. Another third of the total utility charges goes toward electricity.

There exist many types of products that can better use energy, like programmable timers to turn on or off the patio or porch lights at dusk and dawn. These daylight sensors are efficient and can reduce your usage. Motion-sensing bulbs or occupancy sensors turn off lights when a room is left unoccupied. Dimmer switches allow you to set the brightness levels of lighting to match the occasion. The remaining household utility costs go to water charges. For that you have various products to maintain pumps and heat in your pool and irrigate your lawn based on local weather conditions.

Going beyond this usage, I would like to highlight one important device I love. How many times have you left your laptop cord connected while system is either shut down or in sleep mode? The same is applicable with an iron, phone charger, monitors, massage chairs, and so on. This standby mode accounts for 10 percent of residential electricity usage. Smart power strips or smart power bars can cut energy to your devices while they are in standby mode, which is an overlooked yet significant energy-saving tool.

How many times have you let the shower go for couple of seconds (or minutes) before warm water actually starts flowing? Kids often play under the shower. In addition, the quantity of water is based on the angle and holes in the shower head. A smart shower with time limiters can boost your water savings significantly. A thermostatic temperature control attached to the valve lets you select temperatures and it only allows water to start flowing once the temperature reaches that selected temperature. A voice-controlled shower sounds entirely unnecessary or even slightly ridiculous. Once you start using it, though, its convenience might just grow on you. As a parent, you can program the water to turn off after a certain length of time if you need to hurry along any household teenagers. All of this can be achieved with the awesome power of voice commands.

Lab: Working with Personal Assistants

It is not a science fiction fantasy to have a mirror that shows you information about the weather, your daily schedule, a shopping list, and birthday reminders before starting your day. In this lab, I am building a smart mirror that will show you all this helpful information while you are getting ready in the morning.

In the lab in Chapter 6 we installed Windows 10 IoT Core on Raspberry Pi. In this lab, I introduce you to another OS, Raspbian. It is a custom OS based on a variant of Linux called Debian.

Installing Raspbian Operating System on Raspberry Pi

The following are the standard hardware components for any Raspberry Pi project:

- Raspberry Pi 2, 3, or 4

- MicroSD card

- Monitor

- Mouse and keyboard

- HDMI cable

Just like we installed Windows 10 IoT Core on Raspberry Pi in Chapter 6 using your local system, we will again use the local system to install the Raspbian OS on a MicroSD card.

1. Connect a MicroSD card to your local computer and format it with FAT32 format. You can use the quick format option.

2. Open `https://www.raspberrypi.org/downloads/noobs/` and download NOOBS (Offline and network install) on your local computer. NOOBS (New Out of Box System) provides a choice of Raspberry Pi OSs and installs them for you.

3. Unzip the file you downloaded.

4. Copy all the files from the NOOBS folder to your MicroSD card.

Your card is ready! Carefully insert the MicroSD card to Raspberry Pi. It will only fit in one way, so if it is difficult to put it in, flip the MicroSD card over. Connect the HDMI cable connected to the monitor to Pi. Connect the keyboard and mouse. Finally, connect the power cable to Raspberry Pi and switch it on. When Raspbian loads for the first time, you will see the Welcome screen shown in Figure 8-2.

Figure 8-2. *Raspbian welcome screen (first time only)*

Click Next, then select your time zone and preferred language and create a login password. You're now ready to get online. Choose your Wi-Fi network and type any required password. The older model only supports 2.4 GHz, whereas the newer models support both 2.4 GHz and 5 GHz. Connect with your wireless network displayed in the list.

Once connected, click Next to allow Raspbian to check for any OS updates. When it's done, it might ask you to reboot so the updates can be applied.

Congratulations! You have successfully installed a new Raspbian OS and you're ready to start using Raspberry Pi.

Installing Smart Mirror Platform

There are many smart mirror platforms available. MagicMirror was developed to run on Raspberry Pi. It is a platform that can be easily installed on Raspberry Pi. It is a very powerful and user-friendly platform that allows users to customize it to make it their own. It comes under an MIT license. It is a true modular plug-in system. Various modules come preinstalled with it, like a clock, weather, calendar, news feed, and so on. On top there are various modules available from third parties, like health, sports, and entertainment applications.

Note   I am using MagicMirror because it requires no programming knowledge and installs with just one simple command.

To install Magic Mirror, open the terminal window on your device as shown in Figure 8-3 and type the following command.

```
bash -c "$(curl -sL https://raw.githubusercontent.com/sdetweil/MagicMirror_
scripts/master/raspberry.sh)"
```

Relax! The screen might look frozen for some time, but the actual installation is running in the background. Installation will take between 10 and 20, minutes depending on the version of Pi.

At one point, the installer will ask you to install pm2 as shown in Figure 8-3. Type y and press Enter. pm2 is a production process manager that allows MagicMirror to reload without downtime and to facilitate common system admin tasks. In this case we will use it to keep a MagicMirror shell script running and also to autostart MagicMirror each time you start Pi.

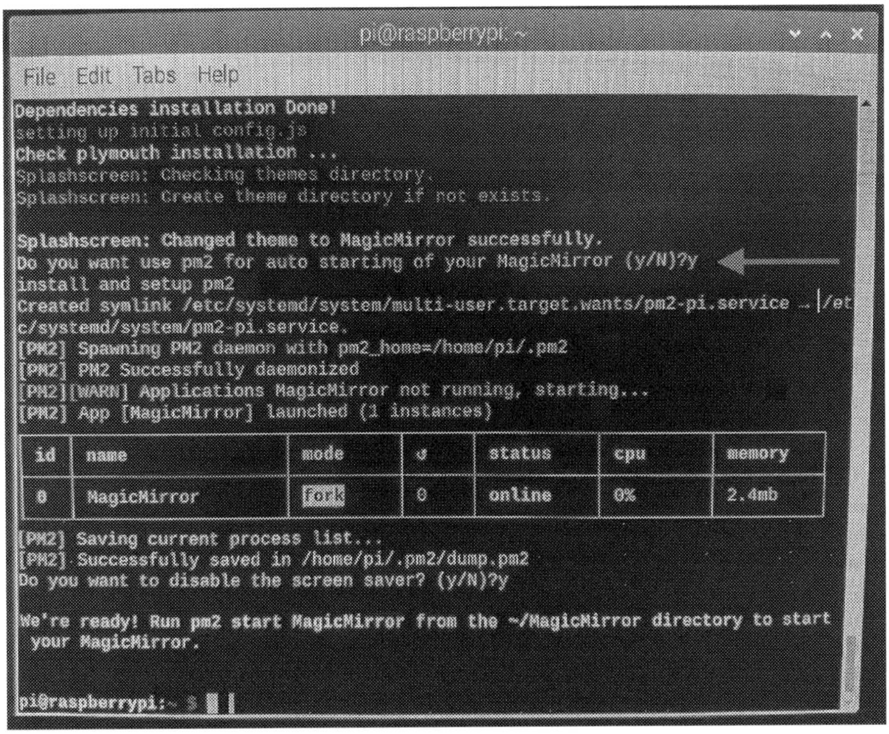

Figure 8-3. *Raspbian home screen, terminal window with MagicMirror install command*

Congratulations! Your smart mirror is ready. If you are using a vertical mirror, you need to perform one more step to rotate the screen. In the same terminal window, type the following command:

```
sudo nano /boot/config.txt
```

Add the following line at any number you like:

```
display_rotate=1
```

Press Ctrl + X and then press Y to save and close.
Restart your Pi or type the following command to reboot:

```
sudo reboot
```

You're all set to start enjoying your very own Raspberry Pi-based smart mirror. Now it's time to turn the MagicMirror into your own smart mirror. To add or delete a module or change the location of a module you need to make a very simple change in the config.js file. Open the config.js file, located under Home -> pi -> MagicMirror -> config.

145

Inside the config.js file, there are separate modules to customize the interface, such as language, calendar, weather forecast, newsfeed, and more. One example is the module displaying a clock shown in Figure 8-4. The clock on the top left is configured as module="clock" and the calendar below it is configured as module="calendar". Similarly, you can add more preinstalled modules and install modules from third parties.

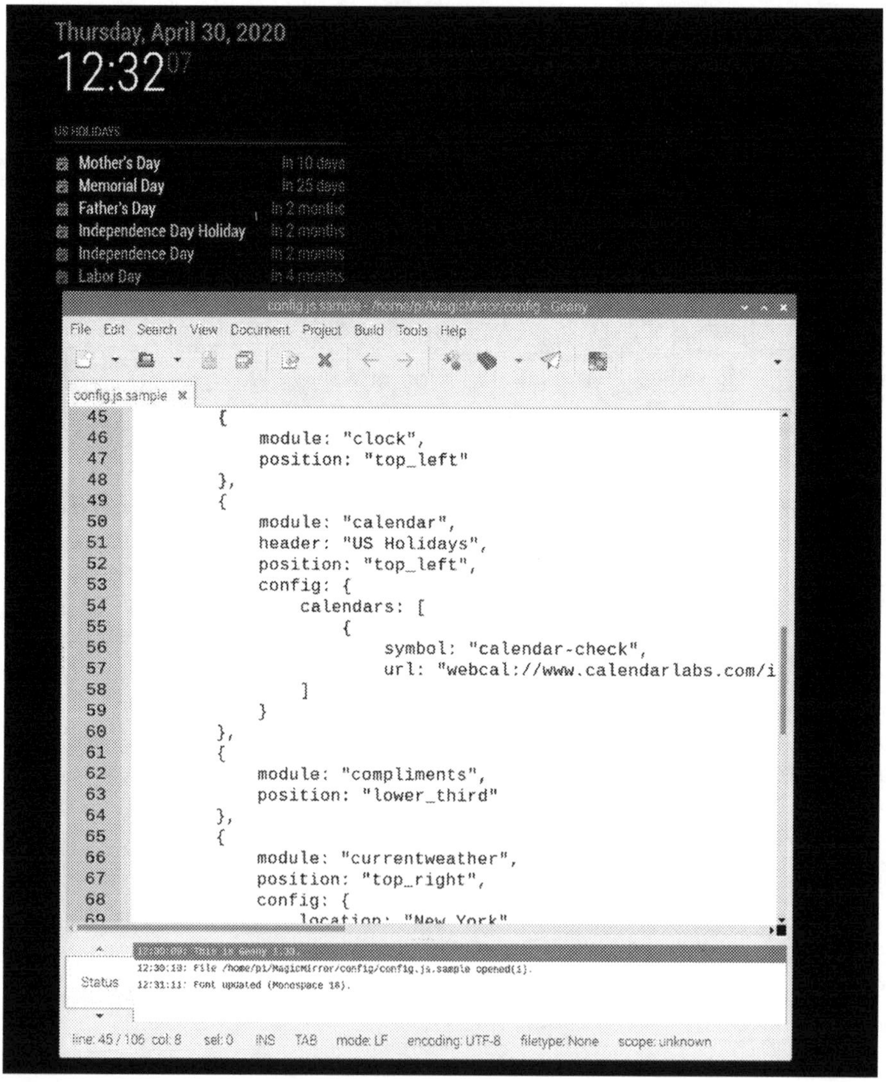

Figure 8-4. *MagicMirror clock module*

The following are some of my favorite third-party modules.

- *Traffic:* Shows current commute time to office.

- *Email-mirror:* Shows the ten most recent emails.

- *Weatherforecast:* Shows weather forecast for the week.

- *awesome-alexa:* Activate an Amazon Alexa module when you say "Alexa" without any Alexa device.

Additionally, for this smart mirror to finish and look good, you need a wood frame and a two-way mirror. Building a wood frame is outside the scope of this lab, as is sticking a two-way mirror on top of the monitor screen. I would like to see your creativity and choice in creating the wooden frame.

You can move further and make it a touch-based smart mirror using an IR touch overlay or touch foil. The main difference is the IR touch sizes are standard and match monitor sizes with a 16:9 ratio, whereas with the touch foil you can use any size screen and mirror, so this does open up more possibilities for ordering a premade frame and standard mirror size.

Exercise

Next, add the voice control module awesome-alexa to your mirror, so that you can update your calendar, play Spotify playlists, and start your coffee machine while you are taking a shower. It's really awesome to have voice-enabled mirror, a futuristic device.

The full set of instructions is listed on the module's official website at `https://awesome-alexa.js.org/`. It is not necessary to copy the steps here.

Smart Mirror Using Microsoft Technologies

One of my favorite parts about developing the smart mirror was the fact that I could do so from the comfort of Visual Studio and leverage the unlimited possibilities of Microsoft Azure. Most of my business applications are developed on the cloud and I would like to see the status of my projects, health, and alerts generated while I was sleeping, without opening my laptop. Here I am developing a simple UWP app in C# that can be installed on my MicroSD card with Windows 10 IoT Core OS I installed in Chapter 6.

Other than current local weather and forecasts, it displays a clock, you can use Microsoft Cognitive Services to perform facial recognition, and use it to show your upcoming calendar events, emails, and reports. Also, with the Emotion API it can play music based on your mood. Finally, it can also include a camera, microphone, and sound bar, enabling voice-based interactions.

Adding all these requirements, the hypothetical user interface layout is shown in Figure 8-5. Let's have a look at the various components that our application is built on.

- Clock

- Weather

- Commute time

- Cryptocurrency rate

- Outlook email

- Text messages (SMS)

- Music

- Voice-enabled

- Business charts

Figure 8-5. *UWP smart mirror application prototype*

I am not going to code all of these in this chapter. I will start with a UWP clock application and leave the rest to you.

1. Open Visual Studio 2017/2019.

2. Create a new project with File | New Project.

3. Select the template Blank App (Windows Universal).

4. Add the following code in `MainPage.xaml`:

```
<Grid Background="Black">
    <TextBlock x:Name="txtClock" HorizontalAlignment="Left"
    Margin="58,74,0,0" Text="TextBlock" TextWrapping="Wrap"
    VerticalAlignment="Top" Height="99" Width="271" Foreground="White"
    FontFamily="Verdana" FontSize="55"/>

</Grid>
```

5. Add the following code in `MainPage.xaml.cs`:

    ```
    txtClock.Text = DateTime.Now.ToString("hh:mm");
    ```

Make sure the app builds correctly. For Raspberry Pi 2 or 3, select ARM. Select Remote Machine as shown in Figure 8-6.

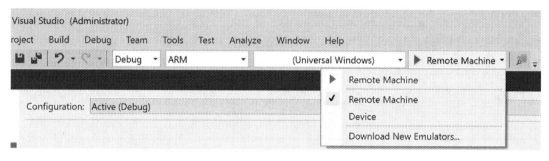

Figure 8-6. *Build and Debug settings*

As shown in Figure 8-7, Visual Studio will present the Remote Connections dialog box. Enter the IP address or name of your IoT Core device (in this example, we're using mypie3) and select Universal (Unencrypted Protocol) for Authentication Mode. Click Select.

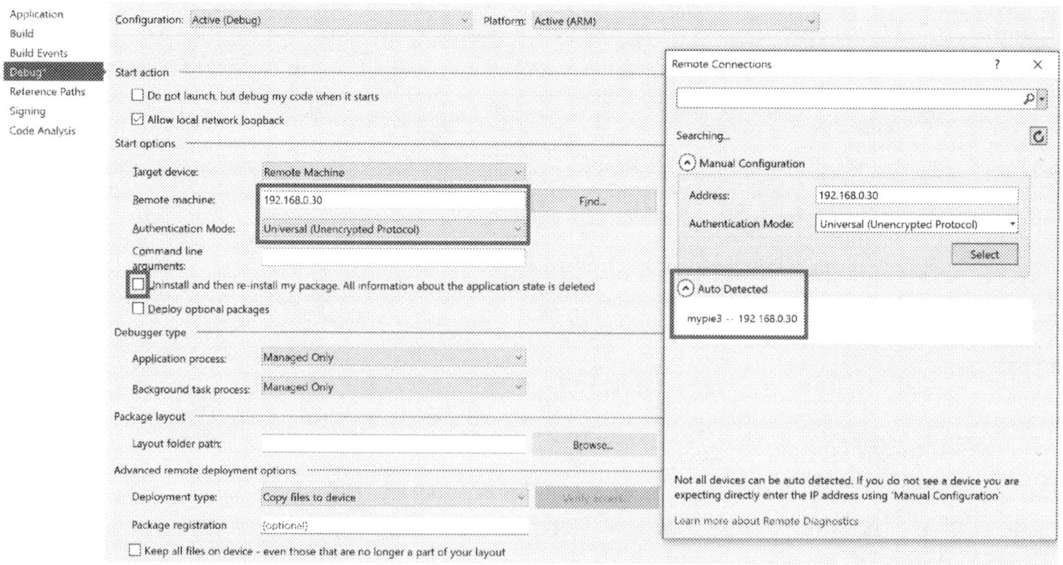

Figure 8-7. *Project properties to deploy application on Raspberry Pi*

Deploy the app to your Windows IoT Core device.

To add a sports calendar, add the following code in `MainPage.xaml`.

```
<ListView.ItemTemplate>
    <DataTemplate x:DataType="local:Events">
        <Grid>
            <Grid.RowDefinitions>
                <RowDefinition Height="*"/>
                <RowDefinition Height="*"/>
            </Grid.RowDefinitions>
            <Grid.ColumnDefinitions>
                <ColumnDefinition Width="Auto"/>
                <ColumnDefinition Width="*"/>
            </Grid.ColumnDefinitions>
            <Image Grid.Column="0" Grid.RowSpan="2" Source="Assets/
            grey-placeholder.png" Width="32"
        Height="32" HorizontalAlignment="Center"
        VerticalAlignment="Center"></Image>
            <TextBlock Grid.Column="1" Text="{x:Bind Summary}"
            Margin="12,6,0,0"
        Style="{ThemeResource BaseTextBlockStyle}"/>
            <TextBlock  Grid.Column="1" Grid.Row="1" Text="{x:Bind
            Datetime}" Margin="12,0,0,6"
        Style="{ThemeResource BodyTextBlockStyle}"/>
        </Grid>
    </DataTemplate>
</ListView.ItemTemplate>
</ListView>
```

Add the following code in `MainPage.xaml.cs`.

```
public class Events
{
    public string Datetime { get; set; }
    public string Summary { get; set; }
}
```

```
    public ObservableCollection<Events> EventList { get; } = new Observable
Collection<Events>();

    protected override void OnNavigatedTo(NavigationEventArgs e)
    {
        base.OnNavigatedTo(e);

        HttpWebRequest myRequest = (HttpWebRequest)WebRequest.
        Create("http://sports.yahoo.com/nfl/teams/cin/ical.ics");
        myRequest.Method = "GET";
        WebResponse myResponse = myRequest.GetResponseAsync().Result;
        using (StreamReader sr = new StreamReader(myResponse.
        GetResponseStream(), System.Text.Encoding.UTF8))
        {
            Ical.Net.Calendar calendar = Ical.Net.Calendar.Load(sr.
            ReadToEnd());
            foreach (var events in calendar.Events)
            {
                EventList.Add(new Events() { Datetime = events.DtStart.
                ToString("dd-MM hh:mm", null), Summary = events.Summary });
            }
        }
    }
}
```

Once again, compile and deploy on your Pi. You will see the screen shown in Figure 8-8.

Figure 8-8. *Smart mirror UWP app*

Similarly, Microsoft Cognitive Services offers a ton of programming. We are covering Cognitive Services in detail in Chapter 12.

This is just a small sample, introducing you to a UWP app developed using Visual Studio on Windows 10. Try it out for yourself.

Benefits of IoT Application in Smart Homes

New devices that supposedly make your home smarter emerge in the market every day. I identify the following categories of benefits according to the device's use.

- *Home security:* This is one of the main reasons people opt for home automation systems. IoT home automation provides more control over home security and users are less worried about security of their homes. Users are notified of all the entries into their home through smartphone notifications. Homeowners can also adjust lighting and lock doors through their phones if any unauthorized person tries to enter the house. Advanced devices are using AI like facial recognition algorithms in identifying people at the door.

- *Energy saving:* Although the system installation might be a high initial investment, it can be a cost saving in the long run because of the savings it can provide. Energy savings can be increased by controlling electrical devices and irrigation systems. For example, intelligent irrigation systems react to weather conditions and save money by applying exactly the correct amount of water to a lawn.

- *Live-saving alarms:* IoT-enabled smart homes have alarms that alert users in case of fire or theft. For example, heat sensors can set off alarms and summon firefighters in the event of a short circuit. These notifications can prove to be life-saving for the owners and they can prevent all sorts of disasters before they occur. Insurance companies reward customers with low premiums if they have such alarm and security systems.

- *Convenience and comfort:* IoT automation in homes makes it convenient for users to access all devices remotely through the Internet. Users can turn off appliances, monitor security from inside the house or around the world. Users can easily perform all household operations through their mobile phones while laying comfortably on a sofa. With the rise of adaptive learning and AI, devices capable of learning your habits are getting closer to reality. Automation can be useful for people with disabilities and for the elderly. Even blood pressure sensors and blood sugar levels can be incorporated into these systems, providing peace of mind to relatives.

The IoT smart home is still in its infancy, but these benefits will shift consumers' habits and make smart homes part of our daily lives.

Challenges of IoT Application in Smart Homes

IoT application in home automation improves the convenience and efficiency of everyday household tasks, as all home electronic appliances are controlled centrally through smartphones and tablets. However, there are certain common challenges like privacy and some difficulties like lack of standardized devices. The following sections cover some of the key challenges:

Lacking Smart Knowledge

There is a lack of understanding of smart home solutions and what they can offer. This lack of understanding not only exists among consumers, but suppliers, too. For example, I visited Home Depot recently, and an automated blinds supplier believed that the only good way to operate the blinds was with a dedicated remote control that comes with the blinds. Having a number of remotes in your hand is a challenge they don't accept. Similarly, lot of hardware supports its own hub. This tight coupling pushes away better devices available on the market.

Interior designers and home builders also need to improve their knowledge and offer home automation as a standard practice. This is the next big market for existing homes.

If you have never lived in a properly automated home, you probably lack the adequate context to understand what you really want. Most do-it-yourself enthusiasts start with a voice-enabled hub like Amazon Alexa or Google Home, then go for smart lights, smart switches, and a smart television with popular streaming applications. You can plan and install security cameras that you can monitor using your smartphone. Unfortunately, professionals think about home automation differently.

Security

I have mentioned security in almost all of the chapters. This chapter is no different. In home automation, this is an even a bigger bucket. Some examples follow.

- *Surveillance camera hacking:* This can expose home residents and prove to be a threat to their physical privacy. Some devices have security vulnerabilities that can lead to theft of personal information.

- *Snooping:* Monitoring of users' daily conversations using cameras and microphones comes with these devices. Smart speakers can leak personal information to third parties. Surveillance cameras can be used to monitor all the activities inside and outside of a house, and they can also be used to record and distribute sensitive videos of the residents. Recently, Google admitted having hidden microphones in Nest home security devices.

- *Accident:* Smart plugs can result in an insecure communication protocol and cause a threat to a user's life if a medical device is implemented using that plug. Remote control hacking can lead to unintended lighting, temperature control, door locking, and so on.

- *Home security:* Smart locks can be used to trap users inside their own homes and can be opened remotely via hackers.

Manufacturers are aware of these concerns and already pursuing solutions for them. For example, Z-Wave Alliance has already launched a new certification program that requires manufacturers to implement the strongest security mechanisms.

Cost

Because automation technology is so cool, it's easy to think that it makes your home look more impressive, and thus is considered a luxury. In reality, the technology can help reduce your monthly energy bill and promote sustainability. I live in the Greater Seattle area, a hub of big technology companies, a home to thousands of people who worked on making these smart devices. Still, I don't see builders offering new houses with preinstalled home automation. Therefore, costs are increased if you try to implement a smart home after you purchase it.

At present, due to the high cost of new smart appliances, to allow control of traditional appliances, intelligent outlets are used to control the household appliances or to collect limited information about them.

Lack of Standardization

I covered this earlier, but I would like to bring it up again. The lack of standardization leads to these devices being purchased indiscriminately. Some devices allow connection of devices from other vendors. However, assembling IoT devices disjointedly could create significant vulnerabilities. Insurance mights deny your claim because you use smart appliances, HVAC, or other systems that are not approved. Depending on the nature of the insurance agreement, this could jeopardize a successful insurance claim due to issues of liability.

Government and relevant authorities have yet to institute common secure standards for IoT devices to ensure safer use.

Summary

I look forward to the day when you go for shopping window blinds and the only obvious option you see is smart motorized blinds. This is a great opportunity for tech startup entrepreneurs. One day, I would like to just say "Goodbye" and expect my blinds will close, lights will be switched off, thermostat will adjust, security will be enabled, and so on, without touching multiple remotes, a smartphone, or web applications.

I did an in-depth analysis of two IoT user cases—that is, smart home personal assistants and a green house system—identifying benefits and describing challenges relevant to IoT application in smart homes.

In the lab, I described how easy is to make a smart mirror using Raspberry Pi on Raspbian and on Windows 10 IoT Core OS. We configured a prebuilt MagicMirror application with just one command, and also developed our own UWP application. Execute this lab for the mirror in your guest washroom and impress your relatives and friends with your new learning.

Despite the numerous benefits, IoT devices are accessible to attackers and cause some significant security threats and privacy concerns for residents if not implemented correctly. All in all, IoT applications in home automation and smart homes will exponentially evolve in coming years and completely revolutionize our way of living.

CHAPTER 9

IoT Applications in the Supply Chain

Whether you're in manufacturing, retail, agriculture, finance, or any other industry, at any given point in time you are planning and managing the flow of raw materials, finished goods, or both through your supply chain. IoT devices like smart thermostats, appliances, and fitness bands are starting to have a very noticeable impact on the everyday lives of consumers, but now it's time to understand how IoT is making significant changes in supply chain management and changing the world of business. In this chapter, I will provide IoT applications to improve different areas where we will be seeing the most advancements and change, with the ever advancing IIoT in supply chain management solutions.

This chapter provides an overview of exciting and relevant services and solutions that are essential to running a successful IoT project in the supply chain industry. IoT is set to revolutionize the supply chain both in terms of its operational efficiencies by using forecasting, and oversight applications and revenue opportunities by adding decision-making transparency.

This chapter covers the following topics:

- Introduction to the supply chain

- Application of IoT to gain an edge on your competitors and even build your own brand using use cases of getting financing and competitive transparency

- Working with RFID

- Challenges of using IoT in the supply chain

© Nirnay Bansal 2020
N. Bansal, *Designing Internet of Things Solutions with Microsoft Azure*,
https://doi.org/10.1007/978-1-4842-6041-8_9

The Supply Chain

The supply chain is a network of nodes. These nodes start from suppliers of the raw materials, to manufacturers of the goods, and finally end at the customer, the consumer of that product. Examining these nodes, they are comprised of organizations, people, activities, information, and resources involved in this journey. Next, to make it more complex, it is not one-way traffic. If you notice, raw material suppliers are actually a mining company or a manufacturer of that raw material. Finally, at each stage we have a packaging, transportation, and distribution network and storage, to move one piece to the next node. Therefore, modern supply chains are often very complex, spanning multiple countries and involving many steps. If you are thinking about replacing a traditional human workforce with smoothly running, self-regulating robots and process automation, then you are still in the fourth Industrial Revolution.

Thinking about capturing, integrating, and analyzing high-quality, real-time logistics and supply chain data for predictive analytics and AI takes you into the fifth Industrial Revolution. Actually, logistics is an activity within the supply chain, but I don't mind using the terms *logistics* and *supply chain* interchangeably, as IoT is essential at each stage to achieve competitive advantages, customer satisfaction, and transparency. For IoT to be most effective, all members of this global supply chain of logistics must be connected. Most of the managers are aware of the advantages of IoT use and managers from leading companies are already exploring its possibilities.

Historically consumers rarely thought about where their products came from, how they got transported, or how a store handled them. Today's customer is not just aware, but feels responsible to see that the products are sourced ethically and vendors are acting responsibly. Therefore, the need for IoT in this industry is greater than ever before.

Let me explain this with a story. The Japanese have always loved fresh fish, but to feed the growing population and meet increased demand, fishing boats need to travel farther with each passing day. The problem is that the return trip started taking more time and fish were not fresh like they were before. To solve this problem, fishing boats installed freezers. This allowed the boats to travel much farther and still keep the fish fresh. Consumers easily differentiated between fresh fish and frozen fish, however, and frozen fish sold at a lower price. The fishing industry faced an impending crisis.

Fishing companies turned to IoT for solutions. First, they increased the size of the ships. Second, they replaced freezers with huge fish tanks on the fishing boats. Finally, due to the additional weight of the water, they reinforced boats to carry more weight. Fishers now catch the fish and stuff them in the tank. IoT companies added sensors and devices to track and keep water temperature the same as the water temperature at the source. Also, automatic feed dispensers are used to keep fish healthy. The retailers know the amount of fish coming and the arrival time, so they can start selling them in advance. Because orders come in before the actual fish arrive, the retailer arranges the logistics to ship them to the customer. This reduces port-to-door time for each fish. I think aquaculture will be the most important food industry of this century. The data gathering and remote sensing has increased efficiency, improved quality, made business more profitable, and increased customer satisfaction.

Applications

Some of the common application of IoT in supply chain are asset management and tracking, fleet tracking, and scheduled maintenance. They are so common that I am not going to repeat them here. I am taking a different approach, discussing some of the most important use cases of IIoT in the supply chain. Here are the most prominent applications of the IoT in supply chain to gain an edge on your competitors and even build your own brand.

Use Case 1: Getting Financing

For small and medium-sized businesses, it is sometimes hard to get financing through traditional sources because of lack of evidence of creditability and assets. Due to the involvement of multiple nodes in the distribution channel of a supply chain, the business entities are fragmented and dependent on other vendors to share the same kind of information about assets, inventory, and transactions. The manual data management providers don't prove any repayment ability of the small or medium-sized business.

With IIoT, a company can make an asset digital as well as creditable. When both side of businesses (i.e., sellers of raw goods and purchasers of a product) start data sharing, along with the data sharing from the company itself, it gets the data automatically verified. Data capture needs to be done for each entity and at each stage, including assets, current inventory, orders in the pipeline, transactions, invoices, logistics, and cash flow.

You can start with an introduction of IoT throughout the supply chain to automate tasks related to inventory, shipment, and quality control; collect and report physical aspects, such as amount of spoilage or damaged packaging; and introduce systems and processes to track delivery, processing refunds for damaged goods, losses from theft or shrinkage, and late shipment by logistics. These data make an order certain and thus show verified receivables in the financial sheet.

Using these data, financial companies create a virtual credit rating for your business, based on a buyer's proven transaction history. The same data could be used to predict demand and thus how much financing the business will need to fulfill that demand.

We will see in the lab for this chapter how small and medium-sized businesses can easily collect these data with low-cost RFID technologies.

Use Case 2: Competitive Transparency

Organizations have started sharing data with customers, not just about their actual products, but about the organization's internal culture; for example, data about the gender gap in each department, diversity in the workforce, and employees' working conditions. Customers would also like to know the social responsibility of the company and where they are investing a part of their profit. The primary impetus behind sharing these data is to boast of transparency as a business value. In the modern world, customers feel responsible and their choice is often based on those nonvisible factors.

As shown in Figure 9-1, a customer can get a clear picture of how a product is manufactured, processed, and gets to the marketplace. When you want to buy chicken from your favorite grocery store, for example, you might be able to track data about the facility where the chicken was born and raised, the food the chicken ate, and how it finally got packaged, in what temperature it was stored, and shipping time. Increased visibility of the supply chain and the business process helps to build trust and reliability for a brand. In addition to telling a customer that food is organic, providing such data quickly validates its claim of intrinsic quality. One study in 2015 found that 66 percent of shoppers were willing to pay more for a product if the company was committed to environmental change and maintained a transparent supply chain.

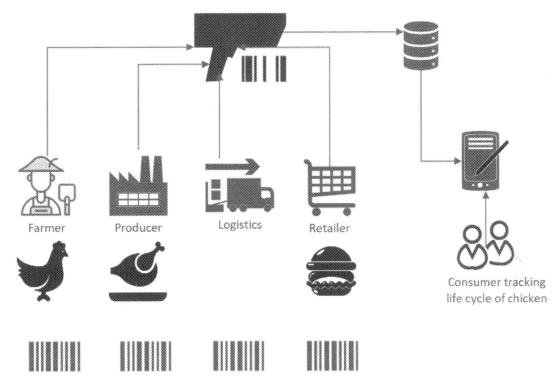

Figure 9-1. *Competitive transparency in the supply chain using a barcode*

Implementing IoT in the supply chain just for obtaining more customers might not seem to justify the initial and operation costs. The same data transparency, though, can help managers prevent disruptions that could put the entire business in jeopardy. You will determine quickly and accurately if something goes wrong with one of your suppliers or product quality. For example, in pharmaceutical product storage, a temperature variation of fewer than 2° could ruin an entire batch of product.

We will see in the lab that follows how you can easily collect data about the chicken life cycle using low-cost RFID technologies.

Lab: Working with RFID

For purposes of this chapter, I assume that your supply chain is comprised of the producer, logistics, wholesaler, and the retailer, as shown in Figure 9-2. Different players in the supply chain could use RFID data for different applications such as shelf replenishment, inventory management, time-to-arrive tracking, automatic product ordering, and product recall.

Technically speaking, because the technology behind RFID scanning and data storage would be same at each stage, I am choosing a producer to architect this lab.

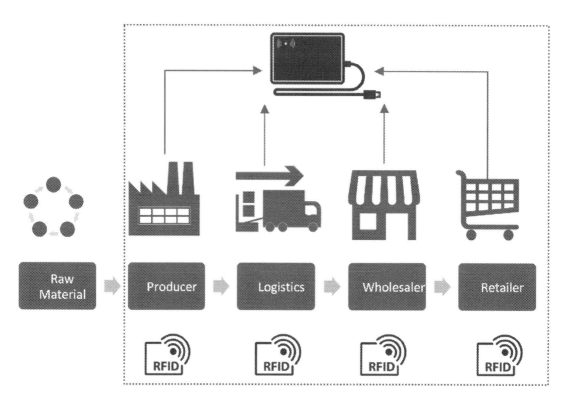

Figure 9-2. *The transition of a product with an RFID tag from the manufacturer to the consumer*

As shown in Figure 9-3, I focus on the data models of producers for storing the data generated by product packaging and RFID transactions. I assume that when the product is manufactured, an RFID tag is placed on the product, which generates the product ID and creates the first RFID transaction at the manufacturing facility.

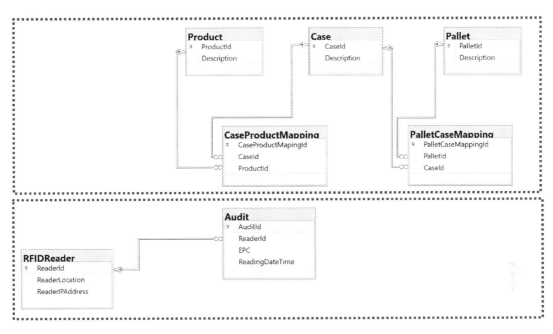

Figure 9-3. *The data models of the producer*

The data model shown in Figure 9-3 is divided into two parts, the inventory management part and the audit part. Most companies already have an inventory data model like this. The unique design here is that the ID of the product, case, and pallet is equal to the unique RFID tag (EPC). The ID of the product, case, and pallet is the link between the existing data model and the RFID data model for audit as shown in lower dotted box in Figure 9-3. To simplify this lab, I defined a Deception column in each table. Technically a product table has several attributes pertaining to the product, manufacturer, ingredients, and so on. Similarly, case and pallet tables include several attributes pertaining to dimension and maximum weight. The two mappings tables define a one-to-many relationship between case and product and between pallet and case.

I define an RFID audit to be an event that corresponds to the reading of an RFID tag by an RFID reader. Each RFID transaction generates data including the reader ID, RFID tag (EPC), and other relevant information. For example, placing a product into a case, placing the case into a pallet, and loading a pallet into a delivery truck generate different RFID audits.

Table 9-1 shows various type of transactions for a product with an RFID tag as it moves from one location to another in the supply chain. The RFID tag will be read at several different locations between producer and customer.

Table 9-1. *Transactions for Supply Chain Events*

Facility Type	List of Transactions
Producer	Product manufacturing
	Product arranged in case
	Case loaded in pallet
Logistics	Pallet loaded in delivery truck
Wholesaler	Pallet placement in warehouse
	Pallet loaded in delivery truck
Retailer	Pallet unloaded in retail store
	Unpacking of pallet
	Unpacking of case
	Product placement on shelf
	Point of sale (POS) machine

At the logistics level, loading the pallet (to be delivered to the wholesaler's warehouse) would generate an RFID audit of all the products being loaded as well as an RFID audit of the case and pallet itself.

At the wholesaler's warehouse, placing the pallet onto a warehouse shelf and loading the pallet onto a delivery truck (to be delivered to the retail store) generate RFID audits. I assume that there also exists an RFID tag on the delivery trucks. Scanning a delivery truck will generate various RFID audits of product, case, pallet, and truck itself. Any loading of the wrong product, case, or pallet should be flagged by the RFID data processing system.

In a retail store, events such as pallet unloading, shelf replenishment, movement of an item from one shelf to another, and sale of an item generate RFID audits. It depends on the retailer whether they ask for an individual tag on each product or only on the case. For example, a grocery store like Walmart needs an RFID on each product, as compared with Costco, a wholesale store, which might only need an RFID on each case.

After a reader reads a tag, the tag, together with the ID of the RFID reader, are sent to Azure Function (Step 1 of Figure 9-2). The Azure Function app then queries the inventory database to translate the tag (Step 2) into product ID, case ID, pallet ID, truck ID, and so on.

Solution

The solution I developed here will work as follows: The RFID tag reader will stream data to the cloud through Azure IoT Hub. These data will be analyzed in real time by an Azure Function app. The job will have one output directly to the Azure Logic app. If Azure Function found that sensor data are not aligned with the inventory management system database, it will trigger the Logic app, which eventually triggers a notification. Hence, the information about abnormal values will be directly delivered to the user in real time. Figure 9-4 shows the complete architecture of this solution.

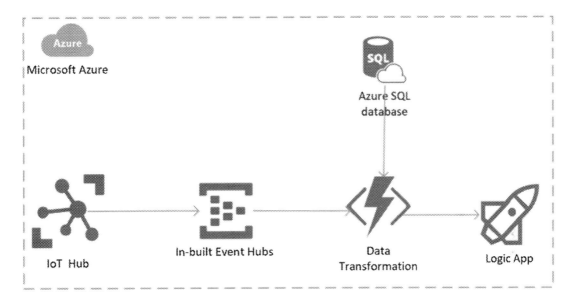

Figure 9-4. *Solution architecture*

We start by creating IoT Hub, which I defined in Chapter 3. When the IoT Hub is ready and receiving data from a device, in our case an RFID reader, you can now create the following components.

- Logic app, which will be triggered by the Function app, and send a notification.

- Azure Function app, which will analyze data in real time.

- Azure SQL, which stores inventory master data and reader audit data.

Logic App

You can create a Logic app using Azure Portal. Click Create A Resource, select Logic App, and click Create. The Create Logic app screen, shown in Figre 9-5, appears. Use the Basics tab to define your Logic app.

Select a resource group, set the Logic app name, select Region, click Review + Create, and finally click Create.

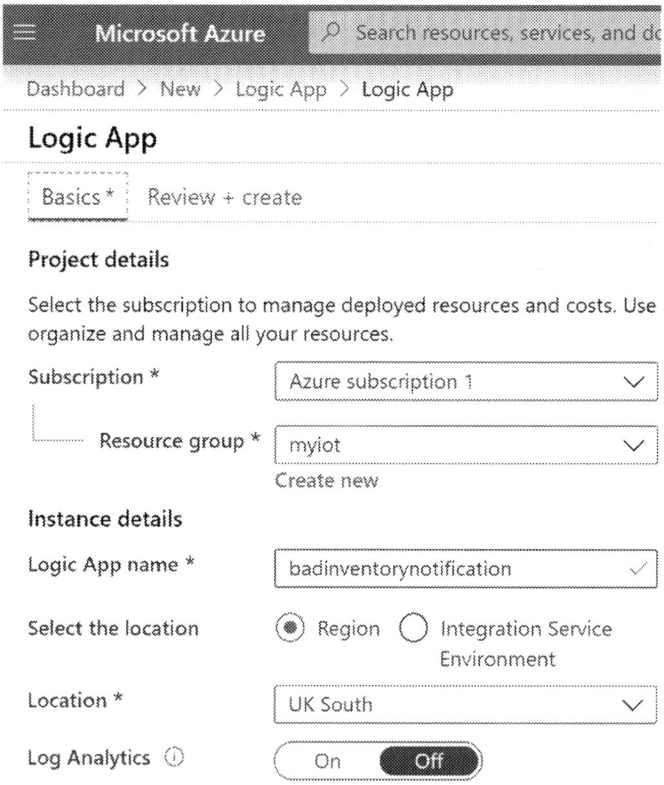

Figure 9-5. Logic app configuration

As shown in Figure 9-6, on the Logic App Designer screen, add "When a HTTP request is received" and enter the following JSON schema.

```
{
    "properties": {
        "rfidepc": {
            "type": "string"
```

```
      }
    },
    "type": "object"
}
```

Add a "Send an email" step and configure your Microsoft Office 365 email. Enter a valid email ID in the To field, then add a subject and body. Click Save.

Copy the HTTP post the URL generated. We will need this in the Function app in the next step.

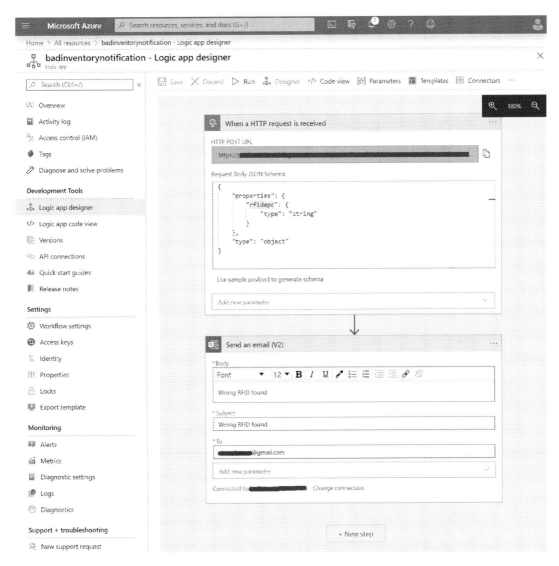

Figure 9-6. *Logic app steps*

Azure Function App

You can create a Function app using Azure Portal. Click Create A Resource, select Function App, and click Create. The Create Function app screen appears, as shown in Figure 9-7. Use the Basics tab to define your Function app.

Select a resource group, set the Function app name, select .NET Core as the runtime stack, and select a region.

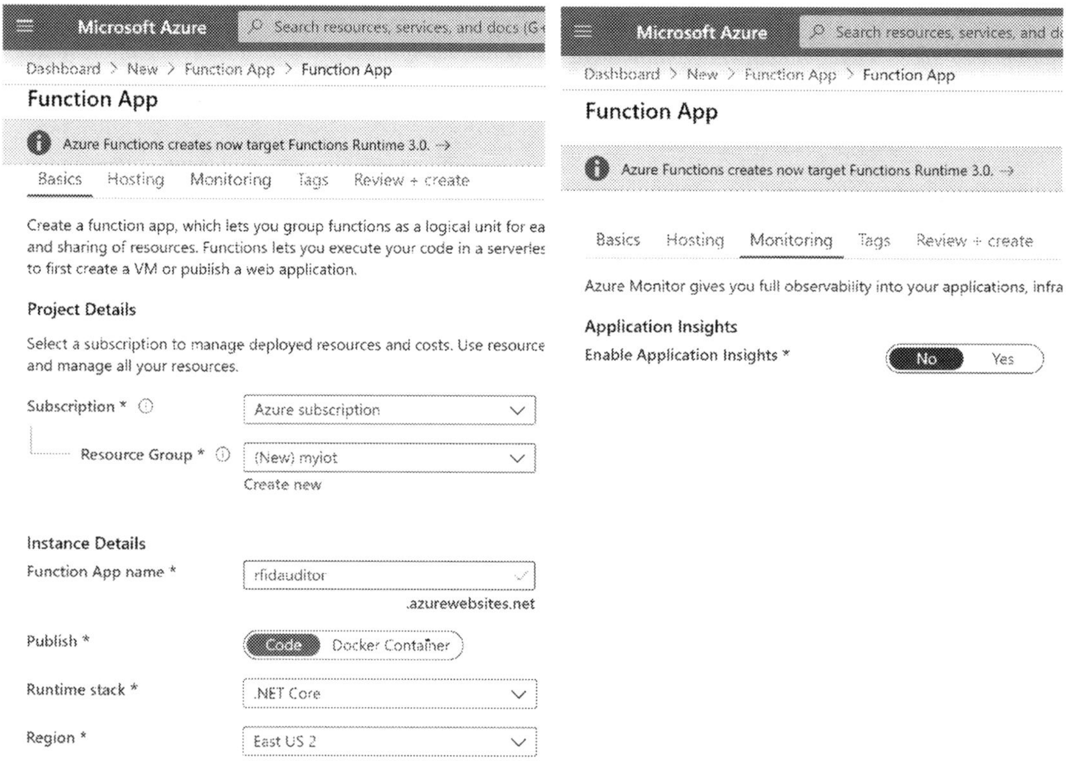

Figure 9-7. *Function app configuration*

Note   For resources like the Function app, always remember to select No on the Monitoring tab. Otherwise Azure will create an Application Insights instance for you. For this book and to save your Free Azure subscription credits, you don't need Application Insights. You will most likely consider enabling this feature for data-critical applications in production.

Wait for the resource to be created. Click Go To Resource. Click the + sign next to the Functions menu item. Select the In-Portal tile, click Continue, select the More Templates tile, click Finish, and view template. In the Choose A Template Below dialog box, enter iot in the search box and select the IoT Hub (Event Hub) tile. As shown in Figure 9-8, you will see the New Function blade.

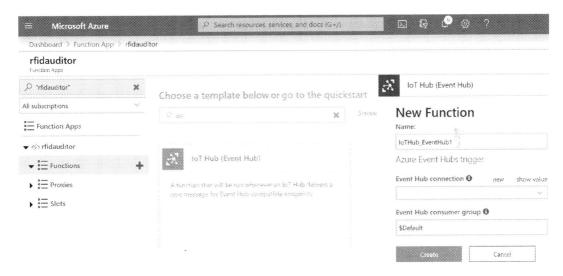

Figure 9-8. *IoT Hub (Event hub) Function app template configuration*

On the New Function blade, under Event Hub Connection, select New Hyperlink. As shown in Figure 9-9, select IoT Hub and Azure will automatically show your IoT Hub in this subscription. Click Select.

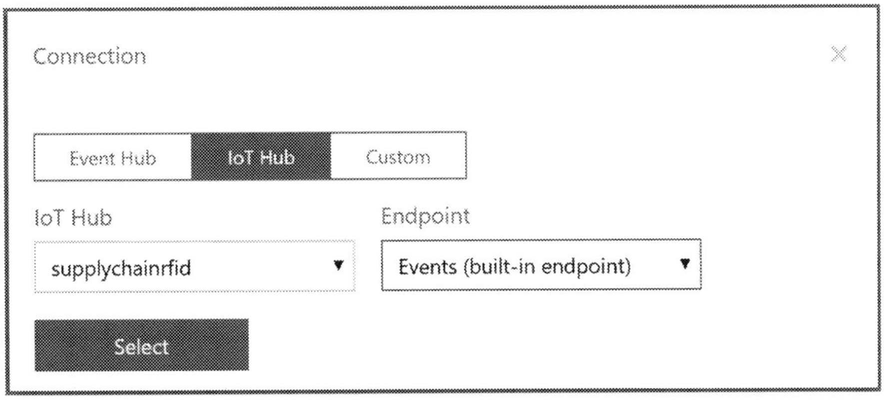

Figure 9-9. *IoT Hub (Event Hub) connection*

Go to the Function app and click your function. On the run.csx screen, paste the following code.

```
using System;
using System.Threading.Tasks;
using System.Net.Http;
using System.Text;

private static string logicAppUri = @"<logic app http post url here>";


private static HttpClient httpClient = new HttpClient();


public static async Task Run(string myIoTHubMessage, ILogger log)
{
        //your logic here
        //connect to SQL Server
        //Select if coming RFID EPC tag is a valid RFID EPC. If not Trigger
          Logic app

        log.LogInformation($"IoT Hub trigger with message:
        {myIoTHubMessage}");
        var response = await httpClient.PostAsync(logicAppUri, new
        StringContent(myIoTHubMessage, Encoding.UTF8, "application/json"));
}
```

Azure SQL

You can create this using Azure Portal. Click Create A Resource, select SQL, and click Create. As shown in Figure 9-10, on the SQL Deployment Option screen, select Single Database and click Create.

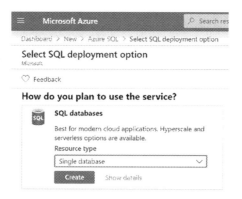

Figure 9-10. *SQL database service option*

The Create SQL Database screen appears. Use the Basics tab to define your SQL Server and SQL Database information.

As shown in Figure 9-11, under Server, click Create New. The New Server dialog box opens. Enter values for the Server Name, Server Admin Login, and Password. Click Create. Back on the Basics tab, select a resource group, set a database name, and set Compute + Storage to Basic. Click Create and Review, and finally click Create.

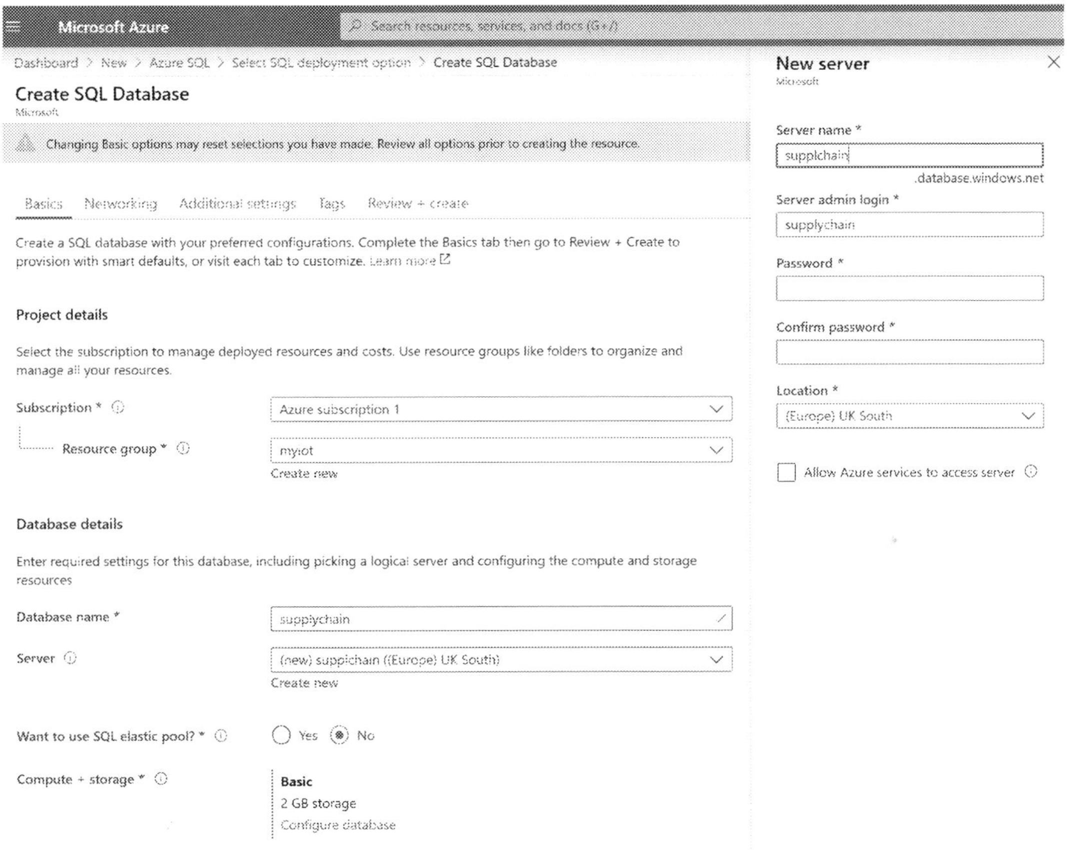

Figure 9-11. *SQL Server and database configuration*

Go to the database you just created and click Query Editor (Preview). As shown in Figure 9-12 , paste the following query into the Query 1 window and click Run.

```
CREATE TABLE [dbo].[Product](
      [ProductId] [int] NOT NULL,
      [Description] [varchar](50) NOT NULL,
      CONSTRAINT [PK_Product] PRIMARY KEY CLUSTERED ([ProductId] ASC)
)
```

171

```
CREATE TABLE [dbo].[Case](
        [CaseId] [int] NOT NULL,
        [Description] [varchar](50) NOT NULL,
        CONSTRAINT [PK_Case] PRIMARY KEY CLUSTERED ([CaseId] ASC)
)

CREATE TABLE [dbo].[CaseProductMapping](
        [CaseProductMappingId] [int] NOT NULL,
        [CaseId] [int] NOT NULL,
        [ProductId] [int] NOT NULL,
        CONSTRAINT [PK_Mapping] PRIMARY KEY CLUSTERED (
        [CaseProductMappingId] ASC),
        CONSTRAINT [FK_Mapping_Case] FOREIGN KEY([CaseId]) REFERENCES
        [dbo].[Case] ([CaseId]),
        CONSTRAINT [FK_Mapping_Product] FOREIGN KEY([ProductId]) REFERENCES
        [dbo].[Product] ([ProductId])
)

CREATE TABLE [dbo].[RFIDReader](
        [ReaderId] [int] NOT NULL,
        [ReaderLocation] [varchar](50) NOT NULL,
        [ReaderIPAddress] [varchar](11) NOT NULL,
        CONSTRAINT [PK_RFIDReader] PRIMARY KEY CLUSTERED ([ReaderId] ASC)
)

CREATE TABLE [dbo].[Audit](
        [AuditId] [int] NOT NULL,
        [ReaderId] [int] NOT NULL,
        [EPC] [int] NOT NULL,
        [ReadingDateTime] [datetime] NOT NULL,
        CONSTRAINT [PK_Audit] PRIMARY KEY CLUSTERED ([AuditId] ASC),
        CONSTRAINT [FK_Audit_RFIDReader] FOREIGN KEY([ReaderId]) REFERENCES
        [dbo].[RFIDReader] ([ReaderId]),
)
```

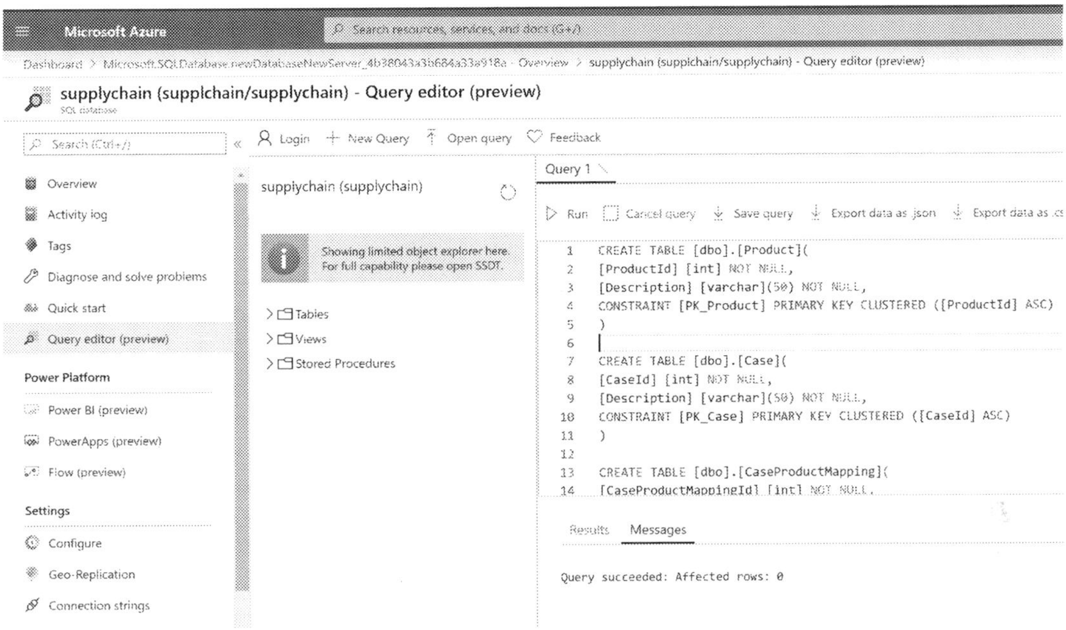

Figure 9-12. *Creating a database schema*

IoT Device Configuration

Our server code is ready, and now it is time to configure our IoT RFID reader to send data to IoT Hub. Assume you have an RFID tag on each product, each case, and also on the pallet. This tag corresponds with the ID column of the Product, Case, and Pallet tables.

When a pallet moves, the scanner scans all the tags and sends the data to the IoT Hub, where Azure Function verifies the tags.

Due to the size of this code, I don't provide it here. You can download the code from this book's git repository. The readme.txt file will contain detailed steps to execute the code on your Raspberry Pi 3.

To test the rest of the components, let's use a simulated IoT device using Visual Studio Code. Open Visual Studio Code and connect to Azure: Sign in from the command palette. Then select the subscription using the command palette Azure: Select Subscriptions. You will see your IoT Hub in the Explorer pane. Click ... and select Send D2C Message To IoT Hub as shown in Figure 9-13.

Figure 9-13. *Visual Studio Core connected with Azure subscription*

Finally, enter the line in the message box and click Send as shown in Figure 9-14.

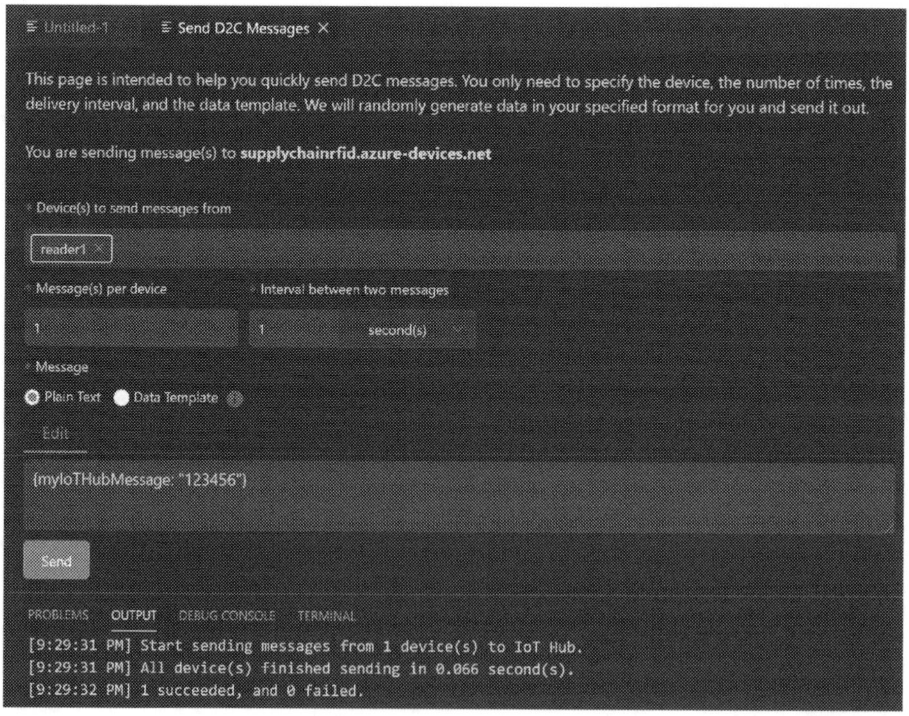

Figure 9-14. *Sending a message to Azure IoT Hub*

Congratulations! You received an email. Let's understand the full solution end-to-end using our serverless architecture defined in Figure 9-4. We have seen how we can simulate an IoT device using Visual Studio Code and send messages to the IoT Hub. Our device ID was a simulated device, as Visual Studio Code picked automatically. Then, we route the messages into the default Event Hub. The message triggered the Function app automatically. The Function app applied our logic from the database and called the Logic app using an `Http Post` call. Finally, the Logic app sent an email notification instantly. Now you can perform any actions with these data; I will leave that to you.

Challenges of Using IoT in Supply Chain

Despite the growing popularity of IoT in the logistics and supply chain sector, there are challenges most managers face. In an age when companies are investing in IoT, the biggest challenge today is global adoption. In a supply chain, products move from one location to another and are exchanged between multiple vendors before reaching the customer. For IoT to be more effective, all members of this global supply chain must be connected. There is so much more we need to do to make the supply chain industry even more efficient, namely the adoption of Edge computing. We will discuss in the upcoming chapters how Edge computing is continuing to take form. The following are the biggest challenges for managers in creating a supply chain vision in their company.

- *Connectivity issues:* IoT heavily relies on connectivity, which is usually in the form of an Internet connection. Because fleets are moving from one location to another, there's not always a reliable network available. Connectivity issues could be solved by satellite-based Internet connections. Technology companies are aware of the demand and are actively investing in satellite-based Internet connectivity.

- *Security threats:* When we talk about connecting our fleet, temperature-controlled storage, and increased data storage, security obviously comes to the fore. Any vulnerabilities in these systems could result in tanking the company's reputation and increasing costs. Edge computing is the solution to make decisions using machine learning as close to hardware as possible and cryptographic hardware monitoring to detect outside security threats.

- *Skill gap:* It is hard to find technology-trained warehouse workers and vehicle drivers. A supply chain manager should understand that with the existing tech talent shortage, hiring skilled professionals is a time-consuming process. Adopting the IIoT means people in the system using data from trusted sensors and devices need to make the right decisions; for example, when machines need scheduled maintenance. Managers are solving this challenge by offering training courses and compensation to continue education for their existing employees.

Summary

IIoT has already penetrated deep into the business processes and supply chain management of companies. It is continuously pushing managers to use this technology to improve efficiency, performance, and business output. We saw some not-so-plain-vanilla use cases of IIoT in the supply chain using examples of getting financing and competitive transparency. To be honest, these are my two favorite use cases because they give you a different perspective, rather than thinking about fleet management, inventory management, and last-mile delivery.

Later we saw a working serverless architecture that we used to simulate an IoT device using Visual Studio Code and send messages to the IoT Hub. Finally, we routed the messages into the Function app and finally the Logic app to send an email notification. This has a lot of use case(s).

Let's take another example of a delivery van. The system picked the correct box or envelope to ship, and scanned the correct RFID, but now the delivery person is walking toward the wrong house (address). Do you want to create a system for this use case? You are already sending RFID data to server; can you send delivery person location data and correlate that with the package?

RFIDs can be used in agriculture to track the movement of animals, in the jewelry industry to mitigate the challenge of jewelry security, in defense for weapon and soldier movement tracking, in laundry automation to track maintenance and age of uniforms, and in libraries to enhance the efficiency of circulation operations (libraries often use barcodes with proper positioning and line of sight).

The part that we didn't cover is the use of SQL Server database to flag incorrect or missing products, which can be programmed in Azure Function using ADO.NET.

CHAPTER 10

IoT Applications in Financial Services

In the world of interrelated things, the financial services industry is communicating with customers, offering them advices and verifying information via cell phones. Financial services companies also collect data with regard to the spending habits of customers. Therefore, there are multiple way for banks to connect with their customers by offering advice and rewards in other areas of life, not necessarily just financial. This chapter is focused on the application and benefits of IoT in this sector. We start with understanding goals of the financial industry and how IoT fits in. Then we discuss possible applications of IoT in the financial services business.

In this chapter, I will provide applications of IoT to improve different areas where we will be seeing the most advancements and change, with the ever advancing IIoT in financial services. Later, managers will learn how to run an IoT-enabled security system in financial services businesses using AI.

Developers will gain hands-on experience building a real-time weapon recognition security system easily and quickly using Microsoft Azure, without much knowledge of machine learning or AI. Finally, we will discuss benefits and challenges of using IoT in this industry.

The Place of IoT in Finance

Although IoT is adopted by various organizations falling under various industry verticals to share data and make significant decisions based on them, the primary objective of this chapter is to elaborate how IoT-enabled applications prominently aid the financial services industry in identifying which data could be useful and understanding the possibility of using these data at various levels. What could IoT could do in transferring your money from Bank A to Bank B? How could IoT help in trading in stocks? Remember

© Nirnay Bansal 2020
N. Bansal, *Designing Internet of Things Solutions with Microsoft Azure*,
https://doi.org/10.1007/978-1-4842-6041-8_10

that the intrinsic value of the IoT lies in the data, and financial services also generate data, which can be gathered, exchanged, and analyzed. Therefore, it is necessary for financial services institutions to also adopt this technology, as it provides a variety of applications for different sectors of the finance industry, as shown in Figure 10-1; examples include monitoring the transactions entering a bank or entering a country. Such payments transferred from origin to destination can be monitored easily to defend against threats. After the retail industry, banking is one of the most customer-centric business models. Therefore, the vision and modus operandi of banks moving are away from their traditional designs toward the modern era of digitization and going completely paperless, providing smartphone applications to do most (if not all) types of transactions. We know this by the name of mobile banking.

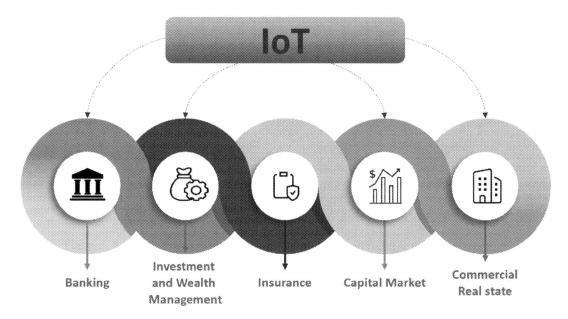

Figure 10-1. *IoT potential in five specific financial industry sectors*

Even though this technology helps finance sectors to monitor the primary goal of the institution (i.e., to monitor the money trail and insure it is a safe, accurate, and verifiable transaction), there exist other meaningful possibilities in this sector. Some are obvious, like enabling insurance companies to collect data about insured goods in real time; allowing consumers to make instant contactless payments; providing the framework for retail banks to collect information on each customer who enters one of their locations; simplifying debt collection, capacity calculation, and demand forecasting; and providing enhanced fraud detection systems to continue their business operations efficaciously.

Among these, fraud detection is the most common term you probably have heard in the past few years. As each credit card transaction goes through a fraud detection system, you might get an email from your bank, a short message, or a phone call from the bank to verify a transaction. When this happens, you know the fraud detection system is at work in your financial institution. This should give you peace of mind and confidence in your institution, thus increasing customer satisfaction.

IoT devices used in the financial services industry are customer-facing as well as non-customer-facing devices. Most of the discussion in previous chapters has been on analyzing data for effective and timely decision making. We also talked about RFID tracking in logistics in Chapter 9. Financial services are mostly customer facing, though. IoT can facilitate a personalized customer service experience by recognizing customers as they come through the door, displaying a personal greeting and personalized product advertising while waiting in line for a teller, providing mobile applications to submit checks, and offering wearable smart devices to use like traditional credit cards in making wireless payments and cash withdrawals from ATMs.

Note   Short code-based and voice-based authentication is old school. Do you know about wristbands that use an individual's heartbeat for biometric authentication?

Other applications of IoT in financial services such as tailored marketing, blockchain-based smart contracts, and chat bots to improve customer experience are outside the scope of this chapter.

Application

Some of the most common applications of IoT in financial services are fraud detection, financial health tracking, and customer geolocation tracking. They are so common that I am not going to expand on them here. I am taking a different approach of discussing some of the most important use cases of IIoT in finance. Here are the most prominent applications of IoT in this industry to gain an edge on your competitors and even build your own brand.

Use Case 1: Blockchain Smart Contracts

Blockchain has revolutionized many industries, including education, health care, supply chain, banking, and so on. Some core components of blockchain are that they can be written and read by certain participants, and entries are permanent, transparent, and searchable. Data are replicated and stored across the system over a peer-to-peer network. Finally, it facilitates peer-to-peer transfer of value without a central intermediary. On the top of blockchain itself, there exist smart contracts that significantly help finance services to manage agreements among users. These agreements are digitally signed, and cryptography is used to secure the data. I believe banking might be the industry where smart contracts appear to be the most significant alternative to the traditional model of transactions.

IoT and blockchain are a perfect pair. Data security, one of the main issues with IoT, can be solved by blockchain; that is, securing the data from IoT sensors. Therefore, a blockchain-based IoT system can make financial connected objects—"Bank of Things"—more reliable and secure. In recent times, it has been observed that blockchain has enough potential to secure records of every authenticated transaction made by customers. Moreover, the Commonwealth of Australia has already completed the first global trade transactions made between two banks using IoT technology and smart contracts. I must admit that blockchain and IoT projects have complex architecture, so I am not going much further here.

Use Case 2: Online Transactions and Authentication

An early prototype of an IoT device in retail banks was the ATM. Since their widespread adoption, ATMs have been one of the top IoT devices that make banks far more efficient, eliminating long wait times to see a teller at a brick-and-mortar bank.

The traditional way of banking was largely dependent on manual recording of entries, onsite visits for transactions, and inefficient authentication in terms of time and financial cost. The emergence of digitization and IoT has changed this. The most commonly used IoT devices (i.e., cell phones [smartphones], smart watches, and tablets) have the ability to connect to the Internet and use banking services.

Tablets are being used increasingly, both by bank employees and customers for 24/7 banking, eliminating the need for a physical visit to a branch. Smart watches and smartphones come equipped with near field communication (NFC) chips that can be used for wireless payments at various outlets all over the world. As almost all new smartphones come with at least one biometric authentication option like a fingerprint reader, facial recognition, iris scanner, and such, they can be and are being used as authentication tools for online and wireless payments, adding an extra layer of security to our banking transactions and eliminating the need to carry credit and debit cards everywhere.

The customer data available through IoT will help banks identify their customers and their needs. Customer information will also help banks provide value-added services, financial assistance, and customized products. For example, based on historic crop yield data, frequency, and market rate, banks can provide flexible terms for farming loans. In another example, by installing sensors in a borrower's warehouse, a bank can track raw materials, production, and inventory. This helps the bank make a quick decision and stop borrowers from engaging in fraudulent practices. Insurance companies have already started providing incentives to users who install On-board diagnostics (OBD) devices in their vehicles to send their driving habits to the company. This is a win–win situation for insurance company and consumer.

Note   As part of corporate responsibility, U.S Bank started an IoT initiative that motivates its clients to stay fit. For completing achievements, users receive bonuses and financial rewards.

Use Case 3: IoT as a Vehicle for Greater Security

Financial services organizations have to be security conscious, and therefore they are invested and continue investing heavily in networks of security cameras and other visual sensors to ensure the viability of their facilities. Companies in this sector are also well ahead in terms of visual analytics adoption, as they have developed and implemented capabilities employing cameras and visual sensors connected to AI and analytics systems. Mobile phones are the leading endpoint choice for financial companies to collect customer data and to provide paperless services. Financial firms have lot of room to employ IoT as vehicle for greater security.

In the wake of recent incidents in educational institution, large public gatherings, and office premises, I chose this chapter's lab work on identifying firearms using IP cameras and the Azure cloud. I trained the model with about 20 images, and that model is running on an IoT Edge device to detect objects in real time. Please proceed to the lab for more information on this use case.

> **Note**   You need no prior knowledge of machine learning to use this system or to practice on your machine.

This simple system delivers highly scalable, resilient, and near-instant emergency warning notifications. As soon as the system detects a firearm, the alerting system notifies law enforcement, neighborhood residents, and individuals working close to that building in real time.

Lab: IoT as a Vehicle for Greater Security

This lab is based on integration of hardware and software to deliver intelligence at the edge along with integration of Azure Machine Learning and Azure IoT Hub. Figure 10-2 shows a simple architecture for object detection. For this lab, this architecture is referenced to build our security system to detect firearms. You are already familiar with most of the components. The new offering in this architecture is Custom Vision. You do not need any knowledge of machine learning to create an object detection model using Custom Vision.

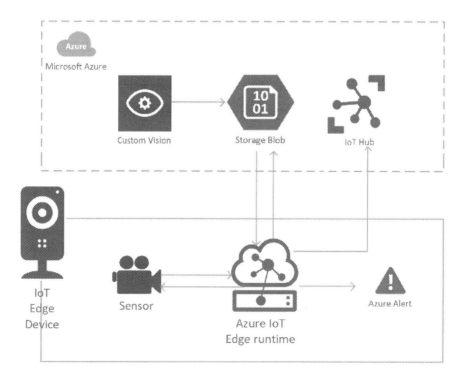

Figure 10-2. *Object detection architecture*

Looking at the two boxes here, the top box with the dashed line contains services we are using in the cloud like Custom Vision, Storage, and IoT Hub. The bottom box with a solid line contains components on the Edge device, like the camera sensor itself, along with the IoT Edge runtime.

The two main components in this architecture are Custom Vision and the Edge runtime. Custom Vision is a cognitive service provided by Microsoft to let you build, train, and deploy two types of project: image classification and object detection. Image classification tags whole images, whereas object detection finds the location of content within an image. We will be using object detection in this lab to identify and mark firearms in the live video feed.

Custom Vision

Custom Vision is an AI service that has the ability to perform functions that emulate human cognition (i.e., knowledge, memory, evaluation, and reasoning). Humans memorize patterns, sense physical and nonphysical objects near them, visualize objects, and understand voice commands. Humans are able to learn this from their experience (i.e., knowledge). Similarly, we provide a few examples of images, define labels for the objects in those images, and let Custom Vision learn it.

Prerequisites

We will need at least 15 images of the object we need to identify, but I recommend 20 images. For this lab I choose an AR-15 rifle. Use your favorite search engine to find images of an AR-15. Try to download images with several backgrounds and rifles at various angles to train your detector model. If you hesitate to search for rifles, use your favorite object, like a cowboy hat, musical instrument, or frying pan.

Custom Vision Resources

Custom Vision provides SDKs in .NET, Python, Java, Node.js, and Go. As promised, though, you need no prior coding skills or machine learning skills for this lab, as we are choosing the web portal itself.

1. Navigate to `https://customvision.ai`.

2. Log in using your existing Azure Portal credentials.

3. Select New Project. The Create New Project dialog box will open, as shown in Figure 10-3.

4. Enter a name and a description for the project.

5. Select a resource.

6. Under Project Types, select Object Detection.

7. Under Domains, select General (Compact).

8. Under Export Capabilities, select Vision AI Dev Kit.

9. Finally, click Create Project.

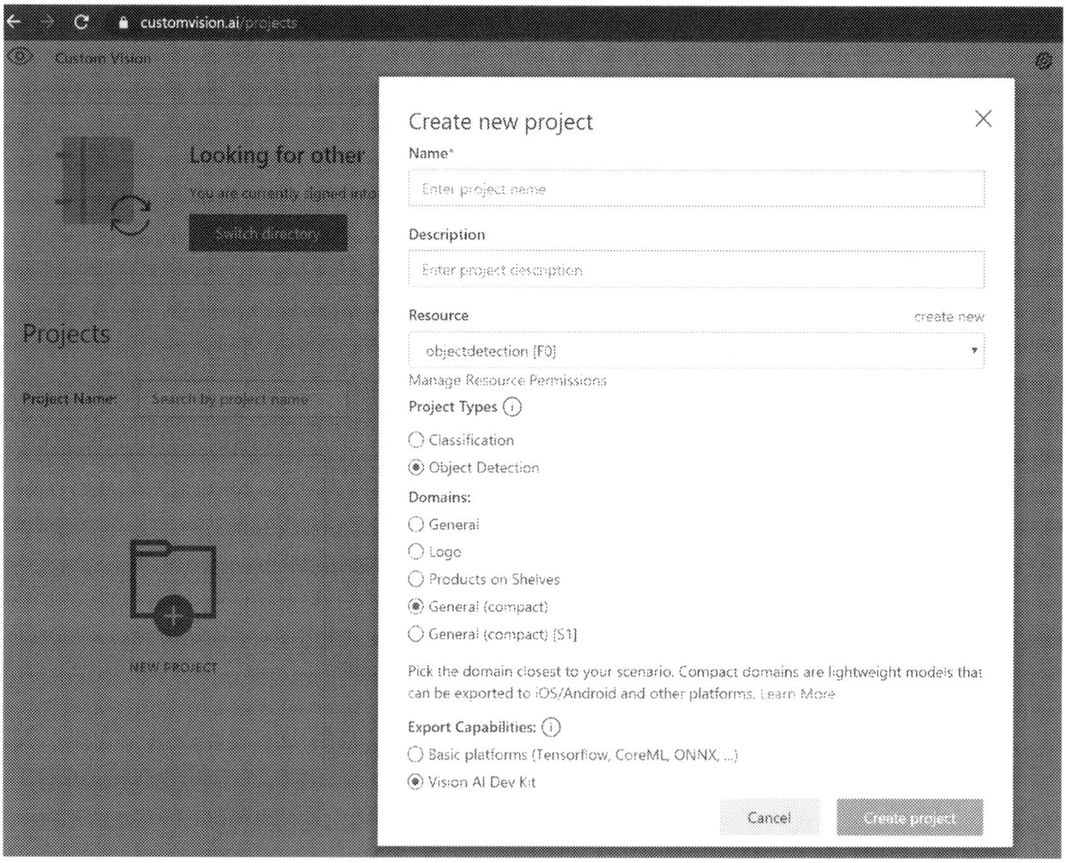

Figure 10-3. *Create New Project dialog box*

The Training Images tab, shown in Figure 10-4, lets you upload and manually tag images. Click Add Images and then click Browse Local Files to locate your files. You can select all desired files at once. The files will take some time to upload based on image size, and all images will display as Untagged.

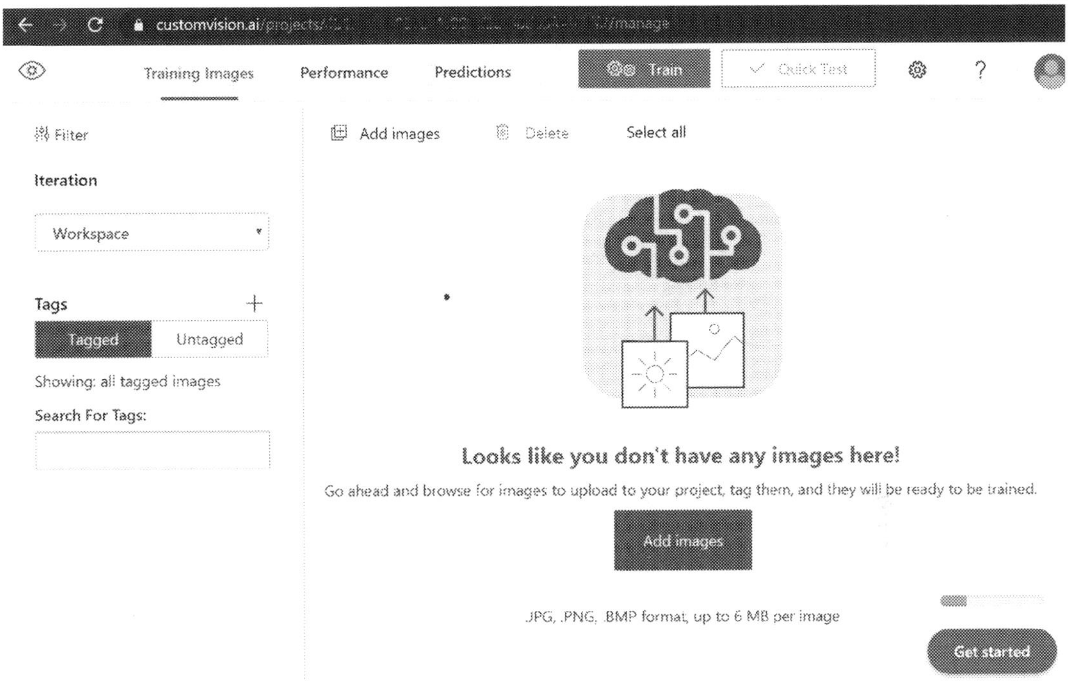

Figure 10-4. *Training Images tab to add images*

To manually tag the objects that you want the detector to learn to recognize, click the first image. Click and drag a rectangle around the desired object in your image, then enter a new tag name with the + button, or select an existing tag from the drop-down list, as shown in Figure 10-5.

In a multilabel project, you can add more than one tag to your images, but in a multiclass project you can add only one. To upload another set of images, return to the top of this section and repeat the same steps.

The system might suggest a tag based on a previous training model, so keep uploading and tagging.

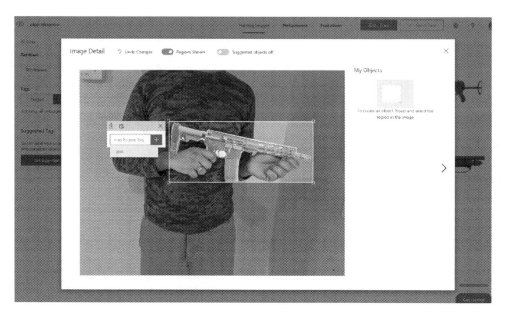

Figure 10-5. *Selecting an object in an image and tagging it*

As we uploaded enough images, it's time to train our model. Click Train. Under Training Type, select Quick Training and wait for it to finish. Depending on the number of images, it might take a couple of minutes to train your model. Once it is finished, click the Performance tab to view your model performance, as shown in Figure 10-6.

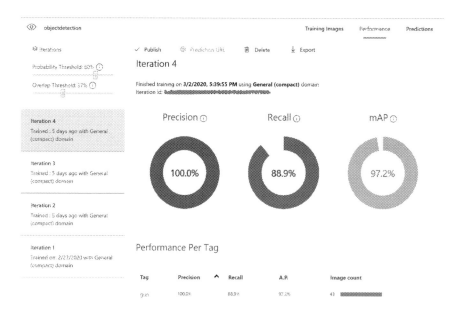

Figure 10-6. *Performance of your model*

Precision indicates the fraction of identified classifications that were correct. Recall indicates the fraction of actual classifications that were correctly identified. In this example, I reached precision of 100 percent in Iteration 4. I added about 30 images to reach this stage. If your precision is low, add more images with different camera angles, backgrounds, and visual styles. Alternatively, you can change Quick Train to Advanced Train, but this takes more time and cost. Each time you train, the system will create a new iteration with a number. Then it will show you the new performance metrics. Don't be surprised if your precision goes low. You can view all of your iterations in the left pane of the Performance tab. If you don't want to use a specific iteration, you can delete it.

Click Export and select Vision AI Dev Kit. Right-click Download and select Copy Link Address. Store this URL, as you will need it in the next stage.

If you don't have an IoT Edge device, you can stop here and test the model from Azure Portal itself. Click Quick Test and upload any other image you didn't upload and tag before. The model will try to detect your object and will provide you a Probability number. The higher the probability, the more likely the returned results will be a high-precision detection.

IoT Edge

Now you have the file location for the Vision AI Dev Kit version of your object detection. In this section, you configure and deploy it on IoT Edge as a module. Azure IoT Edge can make your IoT solution more efficient by moving workloads out of the cloud and to the edge.

Prerequisites

Before beginning this section, you should have gone through the previous chapters and already set up your IoT Hub. If you have any existing devices, routines, or settings, you can keep them.

Creating an IoT Edge

To get started, log in to Azure Portal.

1. Click Dashboard.
2. Click your IoT Hub resource.
3. Under Automatic Device Management, click IoT Edge.
4. Click Add An IoT Edge Device.
5. Enter the Device ID, as shown in Figure 10-7.
6. Do not change anything else and click Save.

Figure 10-7. *Adding an IoT Edge device*

Find your newly created device on the IoT Edge page and select it. You will see a configuration page for the IoT Edge device, as shown in Figure 10-8. Click the Show Field Content (eye) button next to Secondary Connection String and store it, as you will need it in the next stage.

You will see edgeAgent and edgeHub. These are two modules that make up the IoT Edge runtime. Both are the module twins for the IoT Edge. $edgeAgent reports three properties, status of the last seen, currently running on the device or not, and a copy of the desired properties currently running on the device. $edgeAgent coordinates the communications between the IoT Edge agent running on a device and IoT Hub. On the other hand, $edgeHub coordinates the communications between the IoT Edge Hub running on a device and IoT Hub. It reports version, status code, and last connected and disconnected time.

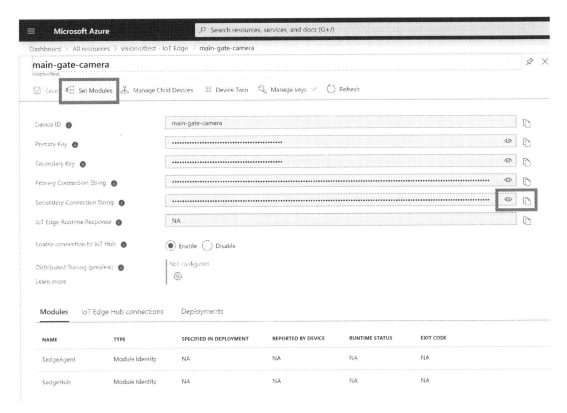

Figure 10-8. *IoT Edge device with edgeAgent and edgeHub modules*

Next, we need to add the Vision AI model that we created in the Custom Vision portal. It needs a lot of settings, though. To avoid all those manual settings, we can add the default Vision AI model provided by Microsoft. To do so, click Set Modules. You will see the Set Modules On Device page shown in Figure 10-9. Under IoT Edge Modules, click Add and select Marketplace Module.

On the IoT Edge Marketplace Module blade, type vision in the search box and select Vision Get Started Module. You will notice an AIVisionDevKitGetStartedModule module added to the IoT Edge Modules section. Click Review + Create and then click Create.

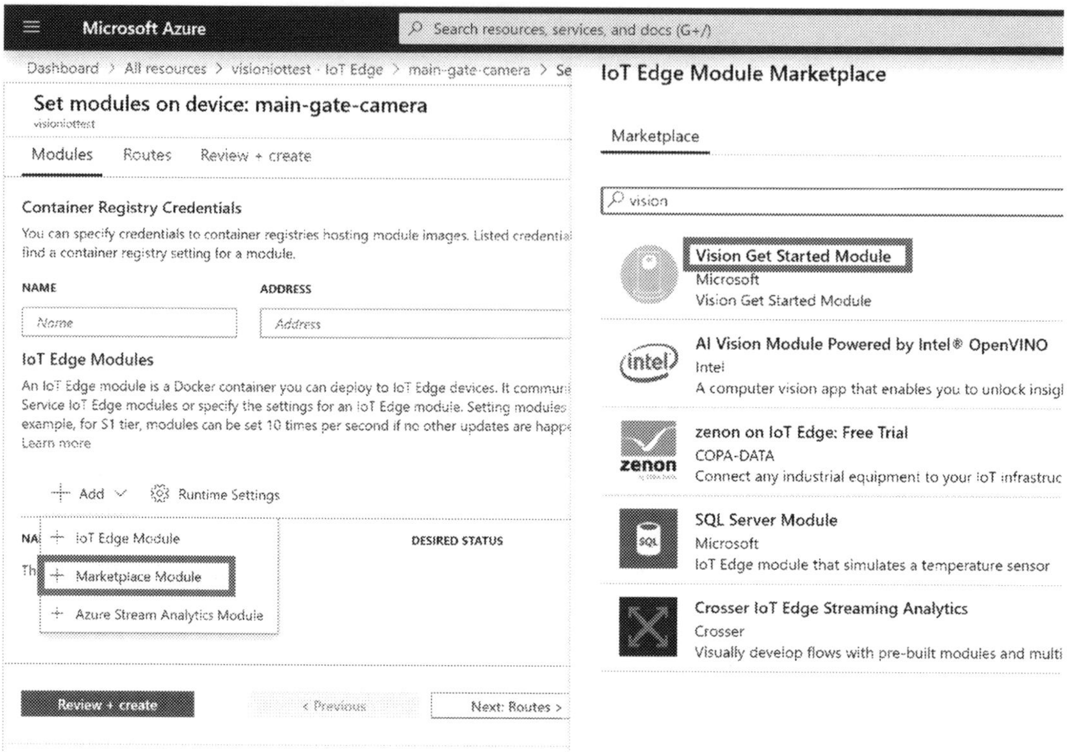

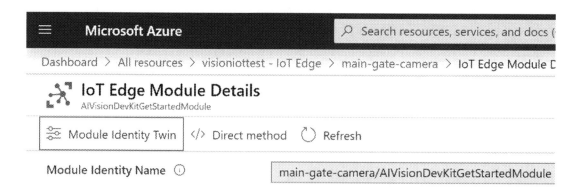

Figure 10-9. *Searching for and adding the AIVisionDevKitGetStartedModule module*

In the IoT Edge Modules section, click the AIVisionDevKitGetStartedModule module. Click Module Identity Twin, as shown in Figure 10-10.

Figure 10-10. *AIVisionDevKitGetStartedModule module*

You will see a large Module Identity Twin screen with a lot of properties. We are only interested in the property ModelZipUrl. First paste the URL you copied from the Custom Vision portal Download button into value of the property ModelZipUrl as shown in Figure 10-11. Click Save.

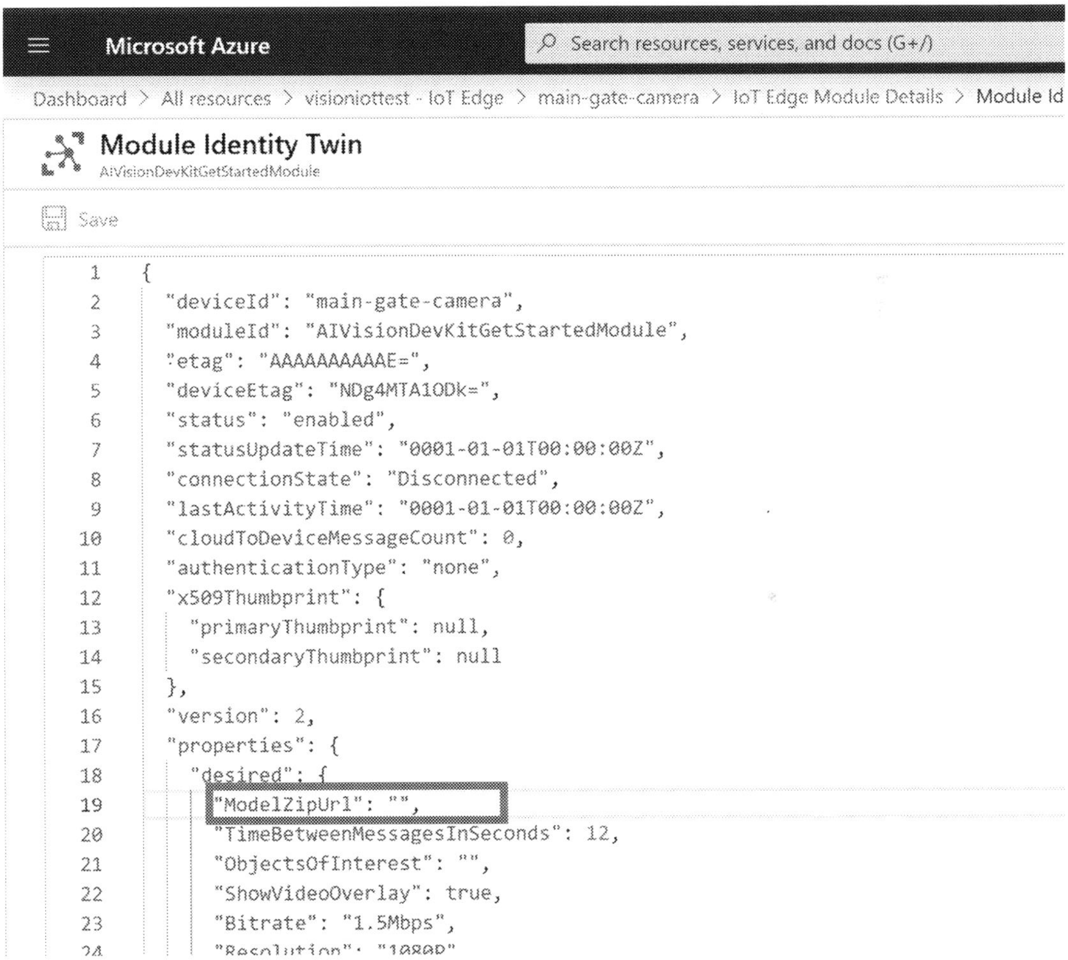

Figure 10-11. *Updating AIVisionDevKitGetStartedModule module with Custom Vision object detection model*

Monitoring Cameras (Security Camera)

You have created a Custom Vision module and an IoT Edge device on your IoT Hub. This is the third and last step. For this lab I selected a monitoring camera from Qualcomm that can run on-device visual and audio analytics using the Qualcomm Vision Intelligence Platform (`https://azure.github.io/Vision-AI-DevKit-Pages/`). This camera supports Azure IoT Edge for efficient deployment and connected device management capabilities. The `camera` can download any custom code, Azure Stream Analytics, and Azure Cognitive Services from the Azure cloud to run locally on the edge.

Set up the camera with the instructions that came with it. As shown in Figure 10-12, enter the IoT Edge device URL you copied from the Secondary Connection String setting of your device earlier. Wait for the camera to download your module from Custom Vision storage.

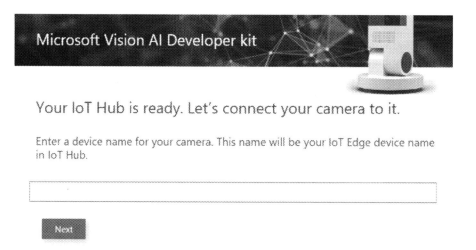

Figure 10-12. *Setting up a camera with the IoT Edge device connection string*

Congratulations! Your security camera is ready. Let's test it, as shown in Figures 10-13 and 10-14.

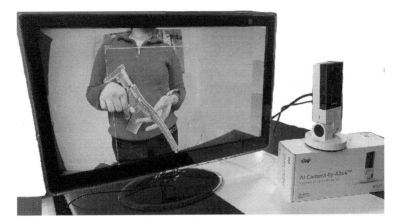

Figure 10-13. *Testing the object detection module at a different angle*

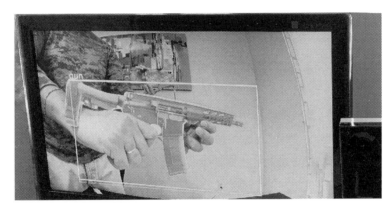

Figure 10-14. *Testing the object detection module*

Advanced users can use Raspberry Pi with a camera attached to it or another IP camera like NVIDIA AI Camera, Altek AI Box, or any Certified Azure IOT Edge camera.

Benefits of IoT Application in Financial Services

There are numerous benefits of adopting IoT. Here are the three that I believe provide the largest value-add to the financial industry and provide you an edge over your competitors.

- *Ease of access:* One of the most important benefits of using IoT applications
  in financial services is rewarding and providing easy-to-access services
  for both credit and debit cardholders. With the help of an IoT application,
  banking sectors can analyze the total usage of particular areas, and
  take actions to increase or decrease the number of ATMs, for example,
  depending on the total usage volume. Banks can use these data to provide
  on-demand services to customers to improve their overall experience.

- *Customer data availability:* One of the major benefits of adopting
  this sophisticated technology is related to the availability of customer
  data, which can be accessed from remote locations 24/7. It allows
  organizations to gather in-depth information about the insights.
  Moreover, mechanisms such as fault detection and fault recovery
  help to identify the faults in the network and automatically take the
  necessary steps to recover data to ensure high data availability.

- *Easy fraud prediction:* In terms of security, IoT-enabled applications
  help identify the transactions made by users with credit and debit
  cards. The prime reason for identifying fake transactions is to create
  a secure environment and to secure the data resources of customers
  from black hat hackers. For instance, if a user is paying for some
  product using a debit or credit card, the payment made by user
  should be verified with the server to determine user authenticity. If
  the credentials do not match, fake transactions can be blocked.

Challenges of IoT in Financial Services

We are Chapter 10, and by now you know the power of IoT devices is boundless and
thus is vulnerable. When discussing finance, this fragility is compounded because these
systems possess vast amounts of highly sensitive and valuable consumer information
that can reap significant rewards for hackers. The following are the top challenges for IoT
in financial services.

- *Security threats:* This is the most important challenge, but because
  we have covered it previously, I am not detailing it there. That doesn't
  mean it is less challenging or can be ignored in this industry.

- *Protecting data and consumer privacy:* Security and privacy risks associated with IoT is no less compared with other industries. Smart sensors used for transaction monitoring are capable of collecting all information including location data. Finance systems keep sensitive information like Social Security numbers, payment data, biometric data, and investment details. Therefore, banks are a prime target of hackers. Some common terms you might have heard are third-party data breaching and user-influenced data. By far, one of the biggest challenges the financial sector will encounter is the ability to securely share sensitive data. Data infringement and data hacking can cause massive damage to customers, and banks could lose trust, along with their customer relationships.

- To overcome these various challenges, organizations require proper data infrastructure. Avoiding this risk removes the IoT adoption hurdle and will keep data generated from devices at the center of decision making. As discussed in Chapter 9, tracking units produced, machine downtime and uptime, and customer account details can, in turn, be used to create new products and services tailored for the customer.

- *Outdated devices:* We also talked about this previously. Devices from unknown manufacturers or small manufacturers that don't update firmware regularly are at risk. If smart devices are not updated regularly, they it can become a target for newly exposed vulnerabilities. Skipping regular updates to the hardware devices or deploying devices without proper testing can present a major challenge for financial sectors in maintaining the flow of device interconnection. If key issues around devices can be overcome, the IoT presents a huge opportunity for the banking sector. To overcome these various challenges, managers should procure devices from known manufacturers and update the devices regularly.

Summary

IoT is quickly establishing itself within the banking and financial services industry at a lightning pace. It might not always be appropriate to simply replace the existing system with a modern one. If the existing system works, managers often don't want to take any risk, especially in the case of banks and insurers. However, we saw applications that could be developed without affecting existing systems and discussed opportunities in developing various applications.

Later we saw a working serverless architecture in which we used an IP camera and machine learning model to detect firearms. I showed you how to explicitly use selected AI algorithms available through Microsoft Cognitive Services and how to build a custom AI module using Azure Custom Vision. In the lab, you trained a Custom Vision model and deployed it as a module onto an IoT Edge device. Finally, we discussed the benefits and challenges managers should consider before choosing technology and applications.

CHAPTER 11

IoT Applications in Health Care

Believe it or not, health care has changed a lot in recent years due to acceptance and implementation of revolutionary technologies. The greatest obvious technological leap forward in the last several decades has been the development of electronic health records (EHR) systems. Although we might think that is the biggest change because we directly benefit from EHR, actually the biggest change in recent years is how the health care industry does research, recommends medicines, and accurately diagnoses patients using technology. The increased prevalence of life-threatening diseases challenged the health care industry to integrate advanced technologies such as data analytics, machine learning, IoT, and AI.

At this point I am not debating which is the biggest change, but among all of these, in this chapter I emphasize how IoT has attained maximum consideration in the health care industry. IoT can be described as a centralized network of interconnected physical devices that can be controlled remotely using the Internet. I discuss how IoT is beneficial for everyone in this industry: patients, physicians, hospitals, and insurance companies. Later in the chapter I look at some major implementations through use cases to describe the diverse applications of IoT in medicine.

In this chapter I emphasize challenges more than benefits, because even though health care is such a vast ecosystem, full of opportunities and human priorities, the global health care regulatory bodies worldwide are gatekeepers for any new process or technology. Sometimes this slows down acceptance and implementation of new processes and technologies.

Finally, we will look at the three major stages of storage, analytics, and visualization of Apple Watch data using Time Series Insights (TSI). For the same, we will provision a new TSI environment and connect it to our IoT Hub. Finally, we design various reports, all of this without any knowledge of coding and query language.

© Nirnay Bansal 2020
N. Bansal, *Designing Internet of Things Solutions with Microsoft Azure*,
https://doi.org/10.1007/978-1-4842-6041-8_11

Health Care

If chronic diseases do not kill you, you could easily live through your 100th birthday, but EHR was not the reason. There is some other force that keeps pushing the boundaries of the health care industry to adapt new ways of monitoring your health. Wearable monitoring devices made remote monitoring possible and empower physicians to deliver exceptional care. There are so many wearable devices available that this technology is commonly referred to as the Internet of Medical Things. Figure 11-1 introduces IoT in health care with its four different consumers.

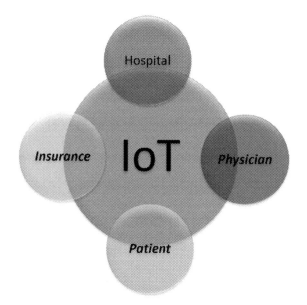

Figure 11-1. *Stakeholders of IoT in the health care industry*

IoT for Hospitals

IoT can turn a regular hospital into a smart hospital, by streamlining processes and enabling health care professionals to conduct tasks in a timely manner. Apart from monitoring patients' health, there are many other areas where IoT devices are very useful in hospitals. Examples include tracking the real-time location of medical equipment like wheelchairs, defibrillators, nebulizer machines, and the nearest oxygen tank; maintaining near-perfect temperature of rooms and smart fridges for vaccines to keep them safe; and providing a real-time inventory of life-saving drugs. Another example is smart beds that can sense the presence of a patient and automatically adjust to the correct angle and pressure to provide proper support without the need for a nurse to intervene. All data can be tracked and collected in real time. IoT has thus provides a myriad of possibilities to enhance efficiency and convenience and even provide cost-saving alternatives to hospitals.

At the time of writing, COVID-19 was spreading on almost all continents. The spread of infection is a major concern for patients in hospitals. During this difficult time, I noted how IoT-enabled hygiene monitoring devices were helpful in preventing patients from getting infected in hospitals. The disease monitoring tools merged IoT data with GIS data, social media streams, and other sources to detect emerging public health threats from COVID-19. By collecting such data from remote locations, clinical researchers are better equipped to make an evidence-based analysis of the outbreak, suggesting preventive measures and avoiding ineffective processes other countries or hospitals used.

IoT for Physicians

I have two doctors in my family, and in my experience, physicians don't like too many gadgets. A primary care physician isn't going to sit and stare at a live feed of your blood pressure or check it on a smartphone on a regular schedule. However, IoT does enable physicians to make evidence-based, informed decisions and it provides absolute transparency when needed. Taking again the example of COVID-19, during this pandemic with hospitals full of patients, IoT-based health care helped physicians with remote monitoring of physiological parameters of other patients in need, like pregnant women, elderly patients, and infants. Physicians can create different metrics to see any changes in the patients' health conditions remotely. This provides an effective interaction between the physicians and patients, leading to patient satisfaction, as they can now interact more easily and efficiently with their doctors. Medical staff can monitor and analyze patients' condition efficiently connected to their smartphones, removing the physical barrier to diagnosis and prescribing drugs. Timely and correct diagnosis is important, and that's exactly what IoT device provides: It helps in effective decision making by analyzing data generated through IoT devices and ensures quality health care.

IoT for Patients

Smart medication dispensers could automatically upload information to the cloud and alert doctors when patients don't take their medicine. At first it feels like an overengineered product, but you would be surprised that among elderly patients this is a very helpful service, because if patients don't take their medication in appropriate doses or at the right times, symptoms could worsen, increasing the threat to life. We are familiar with wearables like fitness bands (including smart watches), portable monitoring devices like blood pressure monitors, and thermometers, as other wirelessly connected devices that keep track of your vital signs like blood pressure, heart rate, distance walked, running speed, calories burned, and so on. Sharing these data with physicians allows them to spend less time on logistics and more time treating conditions and consulting with patients. These wearable devices have changed people's lives, especially for elderly patients, by enabling constant tracking of health conditions. Devices integrated with IoT flag results in relation to a target range and can alert you to take necessary action before the onset of any disease when they pick up on critical changes in such numbers. In this chapter's lab, we will learn how to make all these data useful by analyzing them using an IoT data analysis platform such as Microsoft Azure to draw meaningful insight and notice actionable trends.

We all are aware of such wearables, but to add value, here I would like to discuss some more intense recently developed IoT devices that are life-saving for many. Continuous glucose monitoring (CGM) devices with smart insulin help continuously monitor of blood glucose levels at regular intervals and calculate the correct insulin dose at the right time. Alternatively, you can also monitor blood glucose level with Google's smart contact lenses (although commercialization of such a device is still far from reality.) Smart inhalers monitor the physical environment that causes asthma symptoms, and also records the number of times and the amount the patient inhales. Other notable devices are Bluetooth-capable hearing aids, ingestible pill-sized sensors, and mood-enhancing devices. Robotic surgery is now a reality. Artificial organs are already a viable alternative to waiting for organ donation.

IoT for Health Insurance

IoT is an industry-agnostic technology that includes insurance companies related to health care. The IoT has changed the way the health insurance industry currently interacts with hospitals and patients. Some well-known systems that have been working for decades are clearinghouses, EHR, online prescriptions, and online payments. Beyond this, health insurance has become one of the key industries disrupted by connected devices. I don't know of any not-for-profit insurance companies. Just like any other business, insurance companies are also looking to make a profit, but that requires precise data to fine-tune policies to the needs of each specific customer and minimize the risk of losing funds. Like the auto industry using OBD devices to track your driving habits and offer insurance based on those data, health insurance companies incorporate devices such as biosensors, wearables, and mobile apps to track customer behavior, workout schedules, and stress levels to identify the kind of care needed for each policyholder and set the premiums accordingly. For example, residents of "Cancer Alley," a location in Louisiana where a plant emits 99 percent of U.S. chloroprene pollution, are more likely to get cancer due to chloroprene air emissions. What do you think the health insurance premium would be for 29,000 residents of that town as compared with your town? This risk calculation helps determine the cost of the health care premium the individual will pay.

Toxic air or water is not the only cause of chronic diseases; they can arise from simple factors like poor nutrition, lack of exercise, and high levels of stress. IoT solutions combine insightful analytics and allow policyholders to avoid being generalized; they can be quoted more precisely. On the other side, collecting these data helps insurance companies launch new products, use flexible pricing models, and market specific coverage. Conventionally, customers are often directly engaged with agents or brokers. Converting this indirect customer contact to direct contact can offer considerable benefits in customer relationships as well as in handling of insurance claims.

There is one common benefit to all health care stakeholders: the Cost of health care. Using machines to deliver patient care means that health care becomes increasingly affordable for all parties involved. The data collection, reporting, and analyses become more accurate, ultimately saving time and reducing the need for in-person visits. The data collection and early warning from devices saves the cost of unnecessary lab tests. The IoT can also improve care while patients are in the hospital, cutting down on expenses for all parties.

Applications

From wearable devices to advanced analytics, there are several applications of IoT in health care. It's hard to find an industry with more potential for IoT than health care. Wearable devices such as fitness bands, smart watches, and so on monitor real-time data, IoT-enabled labels integrated in a patient's ID card reduce admission time in hospitals, and medical equipment can enable better management of medical resources. IoT benefits everyone associated with the health care industry: patients, physicians, and health care and health insurance companies.

Let's have a look at some of the major IoT implementations in the health sector.

Use Case 1: Mobile Health

Mobile health, or mHealth, is an emerging field that has proved to be a true lifesaver for modern patients. mHealth is a term used for the practice of medicine and consumer health supported by mobile devices. Remote and wireless medical care solutions based on wireless communication networks are rapidly expanding. The mHealth system will benefit patients in many ways, such as quick diagnosis, remote monitoring, and home rehabilitation. mHealth is the combination of mobile apps and devices that can be used to deliver, access, or record medical information, or provide clinical services. mHealth makes use of health tracking devices such as smart watches and fitness bands connected to a central server. It can serve as a potential health care hub to collect valuable medical information and then generate medical reports. mHealth solves the problem of people who don't get time to visit providers for regular checkups, by giving them everyday health notifications on their smartphones. There are several mHealth applications available on the market, differing in functionality and purpose.

Fitness Apps and Devices

These provide users a nudge in the right direction and help them to make certain modifications in their lifestyle and self-report these data to their health care provider. These apps can track exercise time, distance covered, calories burned, and vital signs like heart rate and blood pressure during this period. There are other devices, primarily smart watches, that track additional parameters like sleep time quality of sleep. There are already hundreds of off-the-shelf sensors, wearables, and mobile devices that can gather such data. The self-report reduces the cost and burden of travel, improves patient recruitment and retention, and captures more reliable and accurate outcomes.

Some advanced devices have the ability to continuously measure the period of time between heartbeats—a metric called heart rate variability (HRV). The variation in this metric indicates stress. The introduction of low-energy Bluetooth (4.0) is helping these devices do more with less energy. I am excited to see the changes in the more granular load of data from these devices once 5G is widely available.

Pregnancy Monitoring

Pregnancy monitoring devices are used to track pregnancy health and monitor fetal development. They can also be used to schedule doctor visits, observe the growing baby, and notify women to take prenatal vitamins. A simple ultrasound device connected with a smartphone allows health care workers to perform ultrasounds on pregnant women to see if their pregnancies are progressing normally. Because these ultrasounds can be performed almost anywhere, and the images can be shared via Wi-Fi, cellular, or USB connections, these are often used in cross-country health care services.

Use Case 2: Wearable Sensor

Other than smart watches and fitness bands, various other advanced devices demonstrate what medicine is becoming capable of. Some notable IoT wearable devices in health care are listed here.

- Ultraviolet radiation devices measure UV sun rays and warn of overexposure in certain hours.

- ECG monitors can measure electrocardiograms (ECGs) and detect atrial fibrillation.

- Blood pressure monitors can measure blood pressure and daily activity, like steps taken, distance traveled, and calories burned.

- Biosensors are self-adhesive patches that can collect data on movement, heart rate, respiratory rate, and temperature.

- Electrozyme temporary tattoos have the ability to measure lactate, a chemical compound generated by muscles. They can monitor muscular exertion, fatigue, hydration levels, and electrolyte balance.

- Posture correction devices helps correct a user's position by alerting (by sound or vibration) when he or she is walking or sitting with poor posture.

- CGM devices continuously monitor blood glucose levels at regular intervals. Additional insulin sensors can calculate the correct insulin dose at the right time.

- Smart nicotine patches can gradually dispense smaller doses of the addictive ingredient to help smokers try to end their addiction.

- Google smart contact lenses are made for people who suffer from diabetes and those who simply wear glasses.

- Smart bras have the ability to track conditions and rhythms in the breast tissue to alert to the possibility of cancer.

The most common among all wearable sensors are smart watches and fitness bands. In the lab we will be using heart rate data from an Apple watch, as displayed in Figure 11-2.

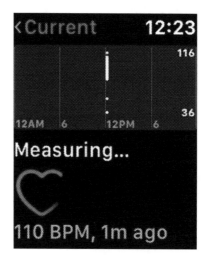

Figure 11-2. *Exporting data from the Health app*

Lab: Analyze Heart Rate Data from Your Apple Watch

Wearable devices such as fitness bands, smart watches, and so on, are integrated with real-time tracking systems and can be used to monitor and observe people's health conditions. Patients can use wearable devices to keep track of their physical activities and monitor their overall health. The data generated by wearables can also be used by physicians for effective diagnosis and treatment. These medical devices gather information about oxygen, blood pressure, blood sugar level, ECG, and so on. These real-time patient data can prove to be critical in the case of a medical emergency such as an asthma attack, diabetes, low blood pressure, heart failure, and more.

Therefore, the data generated from IoT devices are important, but the aspect of analyzing data is where the actual benefit is. In this lab we will analyze these data using Azure TSI. TSI can be integrated with the data coming from these devices in real time or can perform an on-demand dump and conduct analysis on top of it. Such continuous patient monitoring and real-time data analysis helps in diagnosing diseases at an early stage or even before the disease develops, based on symptoms.

As we know, IoT has a four-step architecture that is connected so that data captured or processed at one stage yields value to the next stage.

- *Stage 1:* Data generation from deployed interconnected devices includes sensors, actuators, monitors, detectors, camera systems, and so on.

- *Stage 2:* Aggregate the data. If data received from sensors are in analog form, they are converted to digital form for further data processing before aggregation.

- *Stage 3:* Preprocess, standardize, and move data to cloud storage.

- *Stage 4:* The final step is to analyze the data to bring actionable insights for effective decision making or trigger action.

Apple Watch does the first two steps for you, so this lab starts with Stage 3; that is, I will show you how to download the data, ingest it in Event Hub, and analyze the data generated from your Apple Watch Heart Rate monitor sensor using Azure TSI. I briefly covered Azure TSI in Chapter 4.

Azure TSI is a fully managed offering primarily developed for data generated from IoT devices that guarantees the sequential order of data arrival. TSI stores, aggregates, and visualizes telemetry and trends in graphical format without writing any code. It follows the look-back architecture used in root-cause analysis, detects anomalies, and flags low and high values. That's exactly what we would like to do with our heart rate, blood pressure, glucose level, and oxygen level data.

Note   Azure TSI doesn't require any coding knowledge and does not require writing any scripts.

Exporting Apple Watch Health Data

Exporting the data is easy. Open the Health app on the iPhone, select the Name icon at the top right corner on the Summary tab, and then click Export All Health Data, as shown in Figure 11-3. You will see the export being prepared, and once it finishes, your sharing options will appear.

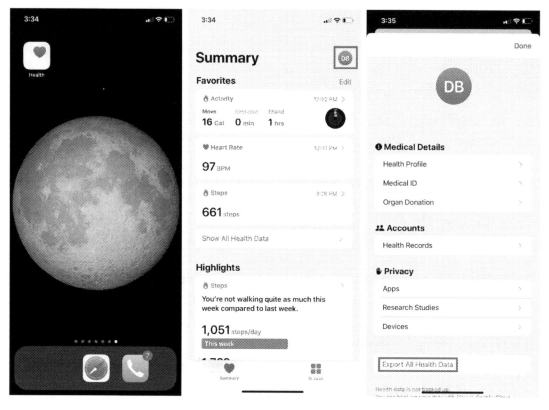

Figure 11-3. *Exporting data from the Health app*

This will send the file export.zip to a location you choose. Once you have downloaded the export.zip file, you can extract the files. In this case there was export. xml and export_cda.xml. I looked at export.xml and found the heart rate data shown in Figure 11-4. I looked at export_cda.xml and didn't know what that was, so I ignored it.

```
6597    <Record type="HKQuantityTypeIdentifierHeartRate" sourceName="Apple Watch" sourceVersion="6.1" device=
        "&lt;&lt;HKDevice: 0x281f53f20&gt;, name:Apple Watch, manufacturer:Apple Inc., model:Watch,
        hardware:Watch3,3, software:6.1&gt;" unit="count/min" creationDate="2020-04-23 12:16:41 -0700"
        startDate="2020-04-23 12:16:40 -0700" endDate="2020-04-23 12:16:40 -0700" value="92">
6598
6599    </Record>
6600    <Record type="HKQuantityTypeIdentifierHeartRate" sourceName="Apple Watch" sourceVersion="6.1" device=
        "&lt;&lt;HKDevice: 0x281f5c000&gt;, name:Apple Watch, manufacturer:Apple Inc., model:Watch,
        hardware:Watch3,3, software:6.1&gt;" unit="count/min" creationDate="2020-04-23 12:16:46 -0700"
        startDate="2020-04-23 12:16:43 -0700" endDate="2020-04-23 12:16:43 -0700" value="92">
6601
6602    </Record>
6603    <Record type="HKQuantityTypeIdentifierHeartRate" sourceName="Apple Watch" sourceVersion="6.1" device=
        "&lt;&lt;HKDevice: 0x281f5c0a0&gt;, name:Apple Watch, manufacturer:Apple Inc., model:Watch,
        hardware:Watch3,3, software:6.1&gt;" unit="count/min" creationDate="2020-04-23 12:16:51 -0700"
        startDate="2020-04-23 12:16:50 -0700" endDate="2020-04-23 12:16:50 -0700" value="98">
6604
6605    </Record>
6606    <Record type="HKQuantityTypeIdentifierHeartRate" sourceName="Apple Watch" sourceVersion="6.1" device=
        "&lt;&lt;HKDevice: 0x281f5c140&gt;, name:Apple Watch, manufacturer:Apple Inc., model:Watch,
        hardware:Watch3,3, software:6.1&gt;" unit="count/min" creationDate="2020-04-23 12:16:56 -0700"
        startDate="2020-04-23 12:16:53 -0700" endDate="2020-04-23 12:16:53 -0700" value="97">
6607
6608    </Record>
```

Figure 11-4. *Heart rate data from* `export.zip` *file downloaded from the Health app*

IoT Hub with TSI

Let's see how we can detect high and low heart rate.

1. Sign into the Azure Portal using your Azure subscription account.

Note   I assume you already have an IoT Hub. If not, follow the steps to create a new IoT Hub given in Chapter 3, as that is not a part of this lab.

---

2. Select + Create a resource in the upper left.

3. Select Time Series Insights as shown in Figure 11-5.

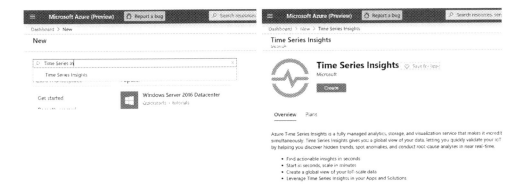

Figure 11-5. *Azure Time Series Insight on Azure Portal*

4. On the Create Time Series Insights Environment page, on the Basics tab, set the parameters as shown in Figure 11-6.

5. We're going to start by creating a new resource group, but you can select the existing resource group.

6. For the Tier, S1 is selected in this example, but that bills monthly and is not dependent on actual usage. I usually recommend choosing the PAYG (Preview) tier. The downside is that you must create your own storage and partition keys. For this lab, these extra settings could be confusing and therefore I prefer the S1 tier.

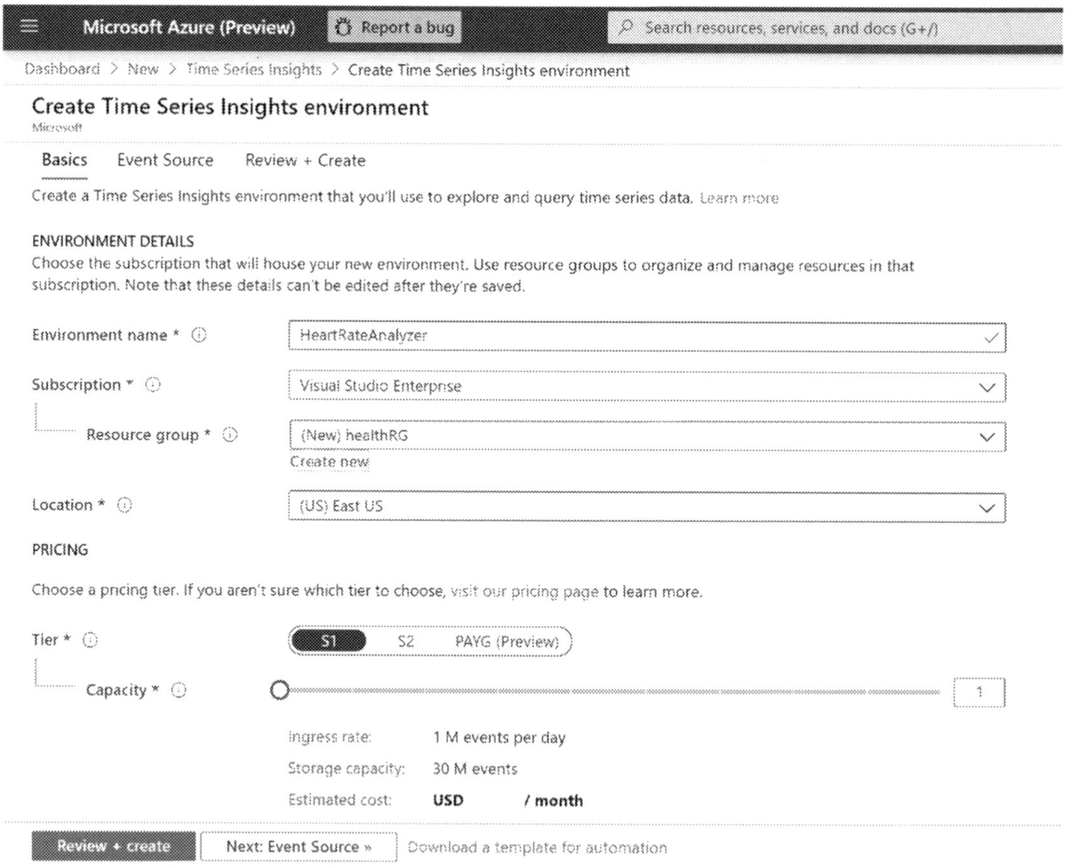

Figure 11-6. *Creating a new new Azure Time Series Insights environment on the Basics tab*

7. Click Next: Event Source or click the Event Source tab. Set the parameters as shown in Figure 11-7 to select the existing IoT Hub.

8. Click Review + Create.

9. Click Create and wait for the resource to be created. It might take few minutes to provision.

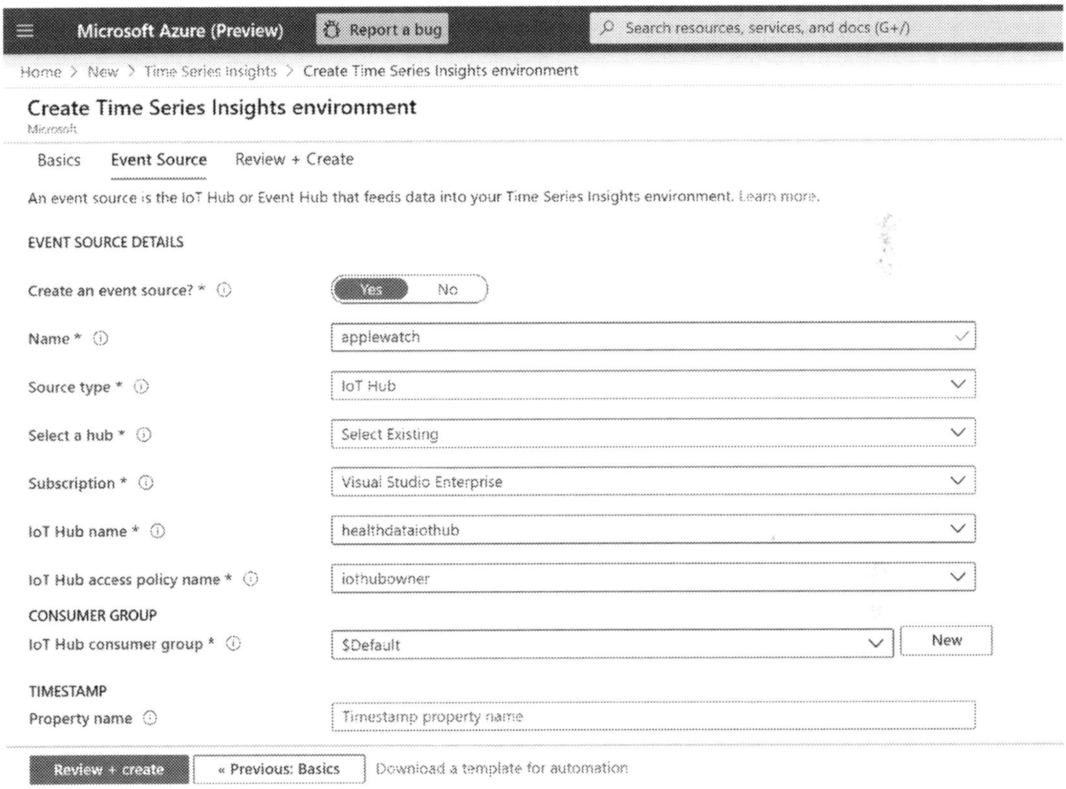

Figure 11-7. *Event Source tab to create a new Azure Time Series Insight environment*

Stream Data

There is no easy way to send the data you exported from Apple Watch to IoT Hub or Event Hub. As this chapter is focused on TSI, I will leave it to the user to provide real heart rate data. For now, I am using Visual Studio Code to quickly send hundreds of heart rate messages to IoT Hub, as shown in Figure 11-8.

I used the following data template to generate these data. You can also use the same format you downloaded with export.xml, but you need to convert it into JSON format.

```
{
  "heartbeatSensor": [
    {
      "value": "{{float 60 70 round=0.01}}"
    }
  ]
}
```

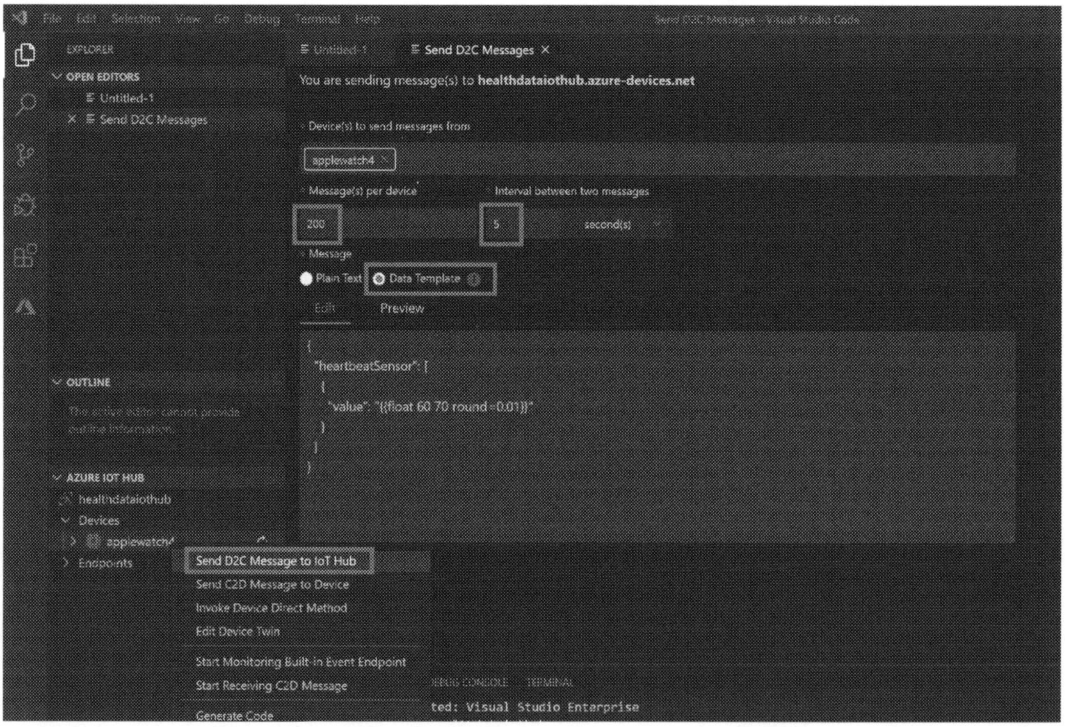

Figure 11-8. *Simulating heart rate using Visual Studio Code*

Exploring Reports

From the overview page of your TSI, click Go To Environment to launch the reporting dashboard. This takes you to the Time Series Insights page shown in Figure 11-9.

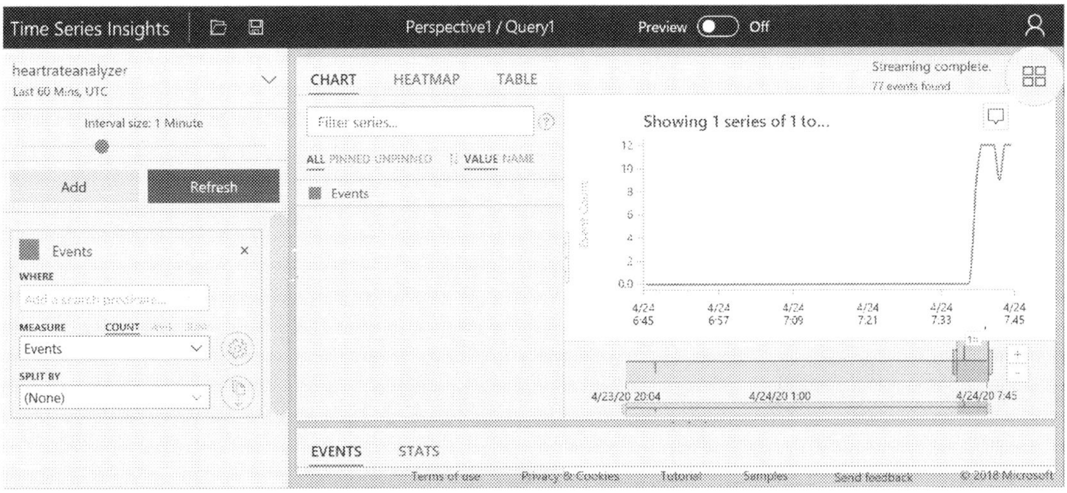

Figure 11-9. *Time Series Insights perspective explorer (dashboard)*

Our dashboard is divided into three sections. On the left there are query options and on the right is the visualization of our current query. At the bottom, we can see the raw events or statistics from our result set.

By default, the perspective shows you the count of events; that is, the total number of messages IoT Hub received, which are read by TSI. The number of events isn't always helpful. In our example we are interested in a graph of my actual heart rate. Change the query on the left from Events to heartbeatSensor.Value, as shown in Figure 11-10 to graph real values. It shows there was a big spike and suddenly a big drop in my heart rate. Right-click the graph and select Explore Events, as shown in Figure 11-11, to see actual values used to create this graph. In our case this is value of heart rate.

Congratulations! You just have visualized your health data using Azure TSI.

Other notable reports are the HeatMap chart and Table-based report of the same data. Based on different sensor data from your Apple Watch like ECG, blood pressure, and heart rate, you can create up to four different reports by clicking the tile button in the top right corner.

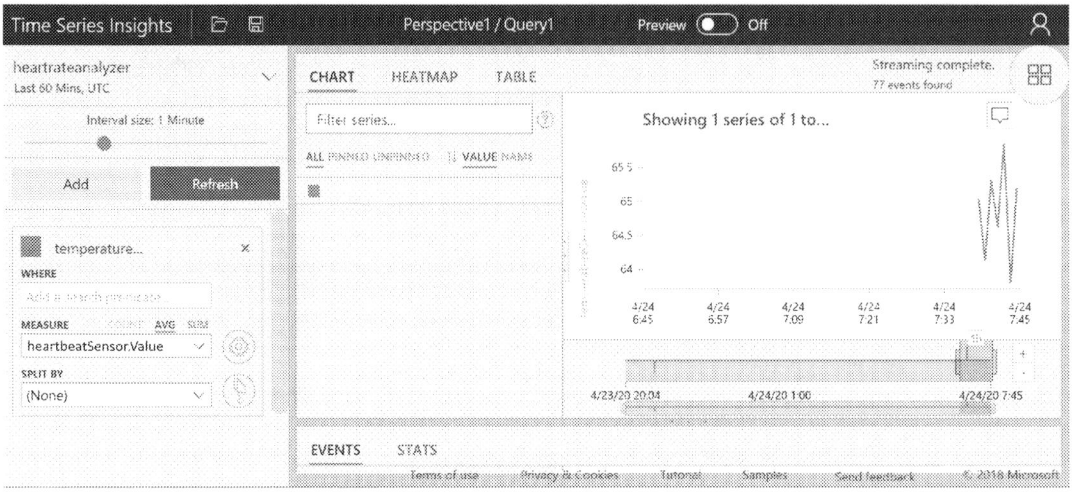

Figure 11-10. *Perspective on heart rate values*

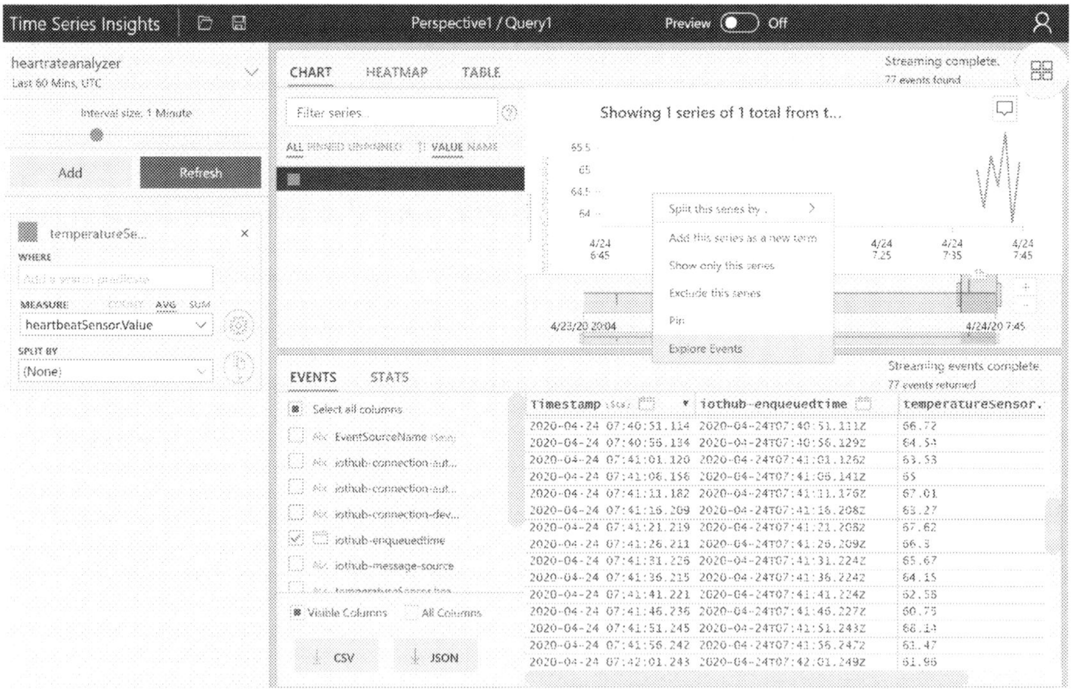

Figure 11-11. *Event received on heart rate*

This process would be mostly the same with real data because TSI is built for this type of analysis on an IoT scale with time-series data sets.

TSI Preview has some notable changes. For example, you can create a model to enhance your browsing and visualization experience. You can add types, hierarchies, and instances to complete your model. Because this is in preview mode, I will leave it to you to further explore new features when Generally Available (GA).

TSI is costly because we selected the S1 tier. You can either delete the entire resource group by selecting Delete or remove TSI only.

Benefits of IoT Application in Health Care

IoT technology affects the whole range of operational, medical and managerial services in the healthcare sector. Following are the key benefits of IoT Application in healthcare:

- *Affordability:* Using devices to offer patient care makes health care increasingly affordable for all parties involved. Use of IoT solutions and connected medical devices in the Health care sector provides real-time patient monitoring to the medical staff. Efficiently automated health care systems require less maintenance and can be employed long term. Furthermore, these systems reduce unnecessary visits to the hospital and provide accelerated diagnostics and treatment.

- *Better patient experience:* IoT-enabled health care systems involve better engagement of patients in their treatment. Patients can regularly monitor their own health status through wearable devices. These devices also enhance the diagnosis process by providing doctors digital reports. This ensures medical staff has to spend less time looking for drugs, tracking supplies, and monitoring hygiene processes in the hospitals. It also ensures patients adhere to their treatment procedures and facilitates tracking of patient compliance with medical prescriptions.

- *Reduced wastage and errors:* Using IoT for medical data collection and hospital workflow automation can curtail waste related to medical tests. It can also reduce system errors that can occur in ordinary hospital systems.

- *Improved treatment outcomes:* IoT-based health care solutions are integrated with the concept of big data and cloud computing. They allow doctors to access real-time health status of patients, so they can make better decisions that will enhance treatment outcomes.

The future of IoT in health care is very bright. Regular use of common things on a global scale to reduce physical visits to hospitals is only a small picture of the success of the IoT in medicine. Business Insider estimates that the installed base of IoT devices in health care will be more than 161 million units by the end of 2020. I am pretty confident that if you ask most medical professionals about their opinion on the subject, they will say that full IoT integration and adaptation is the only logical way foward for the advanced medicine of the future. The results are higher efficiency and reduced waste. That is just the beginning of a future where medical systems work to their fullest potential.

Challenges of IoT Application in Health Care

IoT applications in health care facilitate the lives of both patients and health service providers. Although IoT implementation in the health care sector seems to be revolutionary and highly effective, there are still a number of challenges posed by IoT applications in this sector. In certain situations, these challenges nearly outweigh the benefits. The following are some of the major challenges of adopting IoT in health care.

- *Data security and privacy challenge:* Data security and privacy are among the most significant challenges posed by IoT implementation in any industry, but this challenge is greatest in the health care industry. Security is the most pressing concern about the IoT in health care. IoT-enabled devices collect real-time patient health data, which are categorized as confidential information. Therefore, these data provide a myriad of opportunities to cybercriminals and are susceptible to privacy threats. The U.S. government enacted guidelines in the Health Insurance Portability and Accountability Act (HIPAA) on how to store, process, and use medical data. Most of these devices do not follow proper data protocols and standards, however, because of ambiguity in ownership. The legal parameters for using data collected from connected devices are being defined by government bodies and must be verified as well as audited for

214

risk assessment regularly. Such security does increase the overall cost. Many consumers are ready to pay for premium services with advanced security. A more detailed list of other cybersecurity issues is provided in Chapter 14.

- *Integration of multiple devices and protocols:* The implementation of IoT in the health care sector is hindered by integration of multiple devices. Medical device manufacturers have no standard communication protocols and standards for medical equipment. As a result, each medical device manufacturer establishes its own environment for IoT devices that cannot interact with devices of competing manufacturers. This nonuniformity of synchronous data protocols slows down the process of data aggregation and curtails the scope of IoT in the health sector. The medical IoT still has to be approved by global health care regulatory bodies. This will take time and might keep many innovations at bay because of formalities. Another challenge is handling regular updates. The software must be regularly updated with the latest version to run devices securely. Such constant updates will require great effort and might spawn many technical issues.

- *Data accuracy and overload:* For IT departments of health care facilities, the sheer amount of data that comes through connected devices can be overwhelming, requiring a steep learning curve. IoT-enabled devices gather data in bulk that needs to be processed in small chunks for better accuracy of results. However, due to nonuniformity of communication protocols and standards, it becomes quite difficult to collect the data required to gain insights and analysis. As a result, data segregation without overloading becomes nearly impossible, which affects decision-making procedures in the health care sector over the long run.

Note   As previously mentioned, systems can be hacked. Lots of attention will need to be focused on data security, which requires significant spending.

Despite these challenges, the future of health care will undoubtedly involve the IoT. International health governing bodies are already issuing guidelines that must be strictly followed by medical establishments integrating the IoT in their workflow. One such guideline issued by the U.S. Department of Health and Human Services on cybersecurity best practices for medical device manufacturers is available at `https://www.healthit.gov/sites/default/files/page/2020-02/Medical-device-manufacturers-IOT-Code.pdf`. Such guidelines could restrict possible innovations to some extent, but that will improve over time.

Summary

IoT is set to transform the health care sector even more in the coming years. IoT has played a specific role in improving quality of life and creating a new technological environment in health care, helping medical organizations to manage the bottlenecks of care and bridging the gap between health service providers and patients.

I analyzed IoT in health care using two different use cases, mobile health and wearable devices. The integration of IoT in these health care sectors has brought numerous benefits. mHealth serves as potential health care hub for monitoring patients' health using smartphones.

We discussed several benefits of IoT in health care, such as cost savings, better drug management, better patient experience, and reduced waste. However, any advancement in technology poses some challenges. Health care is no different: With game-changing IoT integration in the health care sector there arise myriad of technical difficulties and adoption issues like data security, integration of multiple devices, and accuracy.

At the end we used TSI to pull data from IoT Hub using a mechanism that involves the existence of a consumer group and created a report using Apple Watch heart rate data exported using the iPhone Health app.

CHAPTER 12

IoT Applications in Retail

IoT makes conventional devices and machines smart by allowing them to transmit data over the Internet, enabling the system and other IoT-enabled things to connect with each other and serve a meaningful purpose. Similarly, IoT makes traditional businesses smart, too. Holistically, we are moving toward technology solutions that can improve the quality of our lives and retail shopping does comes under that umbrella. A growing expectation of retail customers requires stores to deliver the best in-store experience to draw them in. Customers don't want to passively spend their money. In this chapter I discuss how retailers can offer information, personalization, socialization, and experiences to their customers using a more digital experience.

Retail sales here should not be confused with e-commerce, as this chapter focuses on in-store experiences covering all retail categories like hardlines (appliance and furniture) retailers, soft goods (clothing and footwear) retailers, consumables (personal products) retailers, and edibles retailers like grocery stores. All types of retailers like to increase footfall and thus improve sales.

In traditional retail, a transaction deals with limited amounts of products, whereas wholesale deals with large-scale sales of products. In this chapter we are focusing on different types of retail deals and how we can harness the power of AI to make it more attractive. Maximizing footfall, customer experience, and revenue are the reasons that this chapter focuses on the core principles of IoT in retail.

Finally, this chapter explores a number of practical solutions for creating different types of models, like computer vision, that make a store smarter, and how basic AI makes it easier for retailers to provide what today's customers want. I will be providing detail steps to perform face detection, brand detection, and a virtual glass demo. You will see how easy these solutions are; they require no machine learning or AI knowledge.

217

© Nirnay Bansal 2020
N. Bansal, *Designing Internet of Things Solutions with Microsoft Azure*,
https://doi.org/10.1007/978-1-4842-6041-8_12

Retail

Retailers are looking for innovative ideas that can bridge the digital world, where customers spend so much of their day, with the physical world, where physical products reside. In retail, the fashion industry is my favorite topic. A growing need to deliver the best in-store experience in the fashion (clothing and garment) sector is driving the adoption of the IoT.

Smart stores provide the ability to analyze the entire pre- and postshopping journey of a customer and constantly customize the in-store shopping experience. Retail IIoT is recognized as one of the major game-changing factors in making a store smart. Although retail companies do not consider IoT applications to solve all of the problems they face, there still exist many solutions that can help these organizations strengthen their ROI and build a stable base on which they can grow even better and implement more complicated IoT applications later on.

The typical journey of IoT in retail stores starts with loss prevention. This is a priority all retailers share. Loss prevention is one of the most difficult tasks to manage. It includes shoplifting, missed transactions, and spoiled food. Sellers worldwide lose billions of dollars each year in these areas. Reducing theft, catching unscanned items in a cart or bag, and reducing food waste while capitalizing on opportunities that would otherwise go unnoticed will not only bring those billions of dollars back to retailers, but will greatly affect employee time management and future purchasing decisions. RFID is the ultimate low-cost solution retailers use to strengthen their loss prevention defenses. A smarter way is the use of battery-powered Bluetooth low-energy enabled sensors, which can prevent theft and keep track of the whereabouts of merchandise. Are you thinking of finding same style but in size 8 on the floor? This solution could help.

Next is detection and logging arrival and departure of your staff using keypads, biometrics, or a card swipe. Retailers need this for many obvious reasons, like payroll processing, labor regulation compliance, and enforcement of attendance and time-off policies. IoT can go further, though, measuring exactly how many consumers are in a store, tracking the products they were interested in, and displaying these data using a heat map. Heat mapping is used to track customers' habits, such as popular store areas, products, and times for shopping. Finally, this hot spot alerts employees to serve that demand immediately and convert a lead into a sale.

One of the main concerns for retailers is how they can become more competitive and improve sales. Retailers keep records of customers using credit card information, promotions drawing forms filled out at the store, and business card drops. Some retailers still believe in and therefore send printed advertisements in the mail, but IoT can go further with these capabilities.

- Retargeting customers on social media based on their previous in-store product interest, using the amount of time they stayed in a specific department, in a specific aisle, and with a specific brand.

- Sending personalized printed marketing mail tailored using product customers searched online or visited in store with no purchase.

- Upselling and cross-selling items based on past purchases. A customer might need an HDMI cable, a gaming chair, and a set of wireless headphones if he or she purchased a gaming device.

The next traditional approach is promotions. Promotions are an important part of a retailer's sales and marketing mix, and for good reason: They can drive sales and help move inventory. Types of retail sales promotions include percentage discounts, $x off, buy one get one (BOGO), and multibuys (e.g., buy 2 and get a 30 percent discount, or buy 3 and get a 50 percent discount). IoT can go further, though. We need to identify consumer psychological choices that encourage shoppers to check out more products. Different customers have different choices of promotions that tempt them to accept it and want to take advantage it. Sometime offers are only extended to a certain shopper segment based on their past business.

Retailers need to keep some food items cold in refrigerators and need to continuously keep vegetables moist to keep them fresh. Using sensors and devices placed at targeted locations, they can get information on moisture and temperature levels. Implementing such a simple IoT project can save a retailer substantial energy and water costs, as well as keep vegetables fresher by not over- or underwatering them. More than ever before, consumers want high-quality items.

So, what is next after these innovations just described? Retail companies now enhance the way consumers move around their stores. The IoT allows for the addition of sophisticated digital technologies to this process, thus significantly enhancing it. Rather than having a person tracking traffic patterns and then attempting to find a link with trends, IoT will actually provide retail companies with more reliable and precise data about how their customers are acting using sensors, beacons, and smart cameras.

Do you like the free Wi-Fi in stores? Retailers can detect the presence of customers via Wi-Fi. Offering free Wi-Fi can help stores engage with consumers and deliver mobile coupons on signup. Beacons detect consumers' proximity and allow a wide range of interactions, delivering both proximity-based content and product information, in addition to consumer visitation insights. Using beacons, IoT offers traditional retailers with a brand new opportunity to give their potential customers promotional materials that are shaped toward the current demand. Have you ever noticed low-cost watches and earrings laying on a simple table? Beacons are irreplaceable for tracking customer in-store navigation and collecting data about customer behavior. Those watches and earrings are placed based on data the store collected.

One of the most efficient ways to reduce the amount of workforce involved in store management is to use robots for repetitive activities. Robots have the potential to significantly change the retail sector. Target, for instance, tested robots in one of its San Francisco locations to help stock shelves. Restaurants in China have started replacing waiters with robots. Needless to say, the IoT does not remove the need for a retail human workforce; instead workers will be able to concentrate on activities that are not tedious and boring, but need top-notch human support. More and more retailers are trying to incorporate the IoT to boost their performance. There are already a lot of companies that have embraced assistance from IoT service providers and the number of these companies is expected to increase in the future, particularly if you consider the fact that such solutions can improve customer satisfaction and revenue.

Digital signage helps retail companies provide a personalized and interactive shopping experience. We will discuss this further in a use case in the next section.

At the time of writing, the COVID-19 pandemic was ongoing. Retail store supply chains are becoming more complicated and longer, requiring better management than ever before. Retailers need to monitor their inventory from the moment it leaves production until it is eventually shipped. It is also no longer enough for a retail company to merely monitor inventory, because many retailers now need to know the state of their products inside the supply chain at any given moment. Online orders are growing and footfall in stores is decreasing. As a store manager, what you might have done to keep up the sales and stable revenue was invest in logistics and supply chain. Supply chain is major aspect of retail. A supply chain is a mechanism between businesses and suppliers to deliver goods to end users. Retailers need to consider their supply chain to ensure they obtain the correct goods within a reasonable time frame at an affordable price. When something goes wrong somewhere in the supply chain, it could result in a rise in the cost of the product and delivery time. The application of IoT and challenges related to logistics and supply chain management were discussed in Chapter 9. At this point, though, I again would like note that this element of the retail industry is also an important horizontal aspect.

Applications

IoT is changing retail forever. It is personalizing the in-store experience with offers built on data collection from previous purchases and browsing history. It is providing unprecedented insight into buyer behavior, so retailers can offer a better customer experience across every channel. IoT-based solutions provide actionable insights that allow retailers to implement new business models and increase their ROI. Next I present a few use cases of how IoT could seize on new opportunities for revenues.

Use Case 1: Smart Shelves

Once again, take a shelf, add some sensors, and make it a smart shelf; in the retail sector this is a creative business model. The concept of a smart shelf has been on the market since 2003, but initially it was used only for fast-moving goods and stock replenishment. There are three elements in smart shelf systems: an RFID tag, an antenna, and an RFID reader.

RFID tags with microchips are attached to the products. An RFID reader is capable of reading these data from the microchips (this pull-based reading requires no battery or power in the RFID tag, makes it very low cost, and weighs much less). Finally, the information collected from RFID tags is transmitted to the IoT server for further processing and analysis. The shelves keep track of products and keep in-store inventory counts accurate and up to date in real time. Smart shelves mainly help in handling inventory, which has long been an expensive and repetitive operation. Smart shelves automatically track inventory and send warnings to managers if a certain item runs low or if its date expires early. Linked devices are therefore essential to prevent oversupply and lack of products.

That's not all, though. To really make a store smart, we need to make shelves smarter. We need to incorporate AI, machine learning, and computer vision by adding more digital displays to it, like LCD panels to show ads, digital coupons that consumers can easily add to their mobile devices, and changing prices on the fly. Smart shelves equipped with image recognition cameras make it easier for customers to navigate the retail environment, and apply AI technologies to provide customers with personalized recommendations. With the data collected, retailers can modify their pricing strategies, offer promotions customers are truly interested in, and thus optimize revenue per square foot.

Smart shelves also play a significant part in delivering insightful insights into consumer behavior. The devices will provide retailers with information they never had before. Do you remember the last time you picked up a bottle of tomato sauce but put it back because you didn't like percentage of sodium in it or the overall content didn't meet your cooking requirements? We now have access to data about how many customers pick up merchandise versus how many sales occur.

Use Case 2: Digital Signage

Digital signage systems offer personalized media playlists to one or more digital displays, allowing a network manager to display content at a specific time and place to a target audience. Digital signage is often used to deliver a personalized content mix that includes product ads, news, and upcoming events. It is used in a wide range of applications, from targeted retail advertising to internal communication with employees and remote training.

The best use of digital signage is when it is combined with closed-circuit cameras and connected to cognitive services from a cloud provider to get information about customers' gender and approximate ages, as shown in Figure 12-1. It recognizes customers' movement in the store; additionally, it can be connected with beacons to collect customer data, calculate when customers generally group particular items, and display not only commercials and catalogs, but also personalized promotions based on the collected data.

Figure 12-1. *Information about a customer's gender and approximate age using Microsoft's Cognitive Services*

In the photo shown in Figure 12-2, object detection is used to determine whether objects are present in an image. With more customized solutions you can find the brand of consumer wear; based on these data you can predict the buyers' choices.

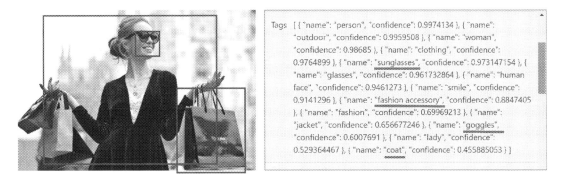

Figure 12-2. *Object detection and brand detection*

Digital signage can overdeliver retailers if used with Cognitive Services. Marketers save costs related to conventional print media with digital signage technologies, and drive customer interaction to the next level. Digital signage solutions can be used as a single mechanism for displaying the advertisements and enhancing the in-store experience. For instance, they can move ads and price adjustments into real-time markets.

Use Case 3: Virtual Dressing Rooms and Augmented Reality

Something like mobile notification seemed revolutionary only a decade ago, and now it is routine. Retail is one of the world's largest industries and therefore the perfect testing ground for the introduction of new technologies. The retail industry needs to be competitive, so keeping the cost aside, they need to use every new technology that has even a slight chance of success.

For example, in-store navigation is one of the most complex aspects of customer service. Sometimes, this really cannot be physically overcome. Augmented reality (AR) will make things much simpler. AR routing will show a customer where to find and item. AR routing can also be used to create an optimized shopping route that is a blessing for busy shoppers. In the "gamification" of the client experience, the path leads not only to the desired commodity, but perhaps to some fun rewards or discounts.

Product search and customization assistance is another important thing AR can do. AR can streamline the discovery factor in the process of finding the correct product. AR retail extensions could have a huge effect on product customization. A dress might only be available with a specific color in-store, but AR could allow a customer to try the same dress in different colors.

There is limited space for product information on the packaging. Any effort to include detailed product knowledge is the most effective way to incorporate AR into the consumer in-store experience. Not all products can fit the product information in more than two languages, so having AR to read product information in customers' choice of language is a big advantage to gain their confidence in a product.

I love the concept of virtual dressing rooms or virtual fittings. Some products are hard to purchase online because customers don't know how they will look on them. In addition, not all colors and styles are physically available. There are thousands of small to midsize retailers that don't have the budget and space to keep a wide range of products, styles, and colors in stock. Returns (reverse logistics) are costly and a bad shopping experience for the customer. The virtual dressing room is an in-store concept and an online feature that can solve all of these problems. Yes, you can take the dressing room home, but retailers still like consumers to come to the store to try things on. For example, if you need new glasses, you can just upload a headshot and match frames to your face online instead of visiting a store. What if you would like to purchase a party gown or tailored suit? You will want expert guidance as well as a bigger screen to view the products. You might not be able to confirm size precisely, but you can try various colors and styles within minutes. Beyond clothing, cosmetics, jewelry, and fashion accessories can benefit from this technology.

Lab: Visual Analytics Using Cognitive Services

In this lab we will do multiple things. To start with, we create a Computer Vision project that can detect human faces within an image and generate the age, gender, and rectangle for each detected face.

Then we will perform brand detection, a specialized mode of object detection that uses a database of thousands of global logos to identify commercial brands in images. The built-in logo database covers popular brands in consumer electronics, clothing, and more.

By combining both of these features, we will be able to determine the gender and age of your customer, in addition to learning what brands he or she are currently wearing.

Note   No machine learning expertise is required.

Getting an API Key

The first thing you need is Cognitive Services. Azure Cognitive Services enables developers to build intelligent applications powered by AI and machine learning. It offers capabilities across the areas of vision, speech, language, Web searching, and decisions available in the form of SDKs and APIs, thereby making AI and maching learning more accessible for developers at large. Because of its vast capabilities, Cognitive Services is a multiservice resource. There are 19 single-service resources like Face or Speaker Recognition. If you are only interested in a specific resource like Face, then Azure Portal allows you to create only that resource. In this lab, I am using a multiservice resource, Cognitive Services.

1. On Azure Portal, log in to your Azure Subscription and click Create A Resource on the dashboard page. On the Create page, shown in Figure 12-3, provide the required information.

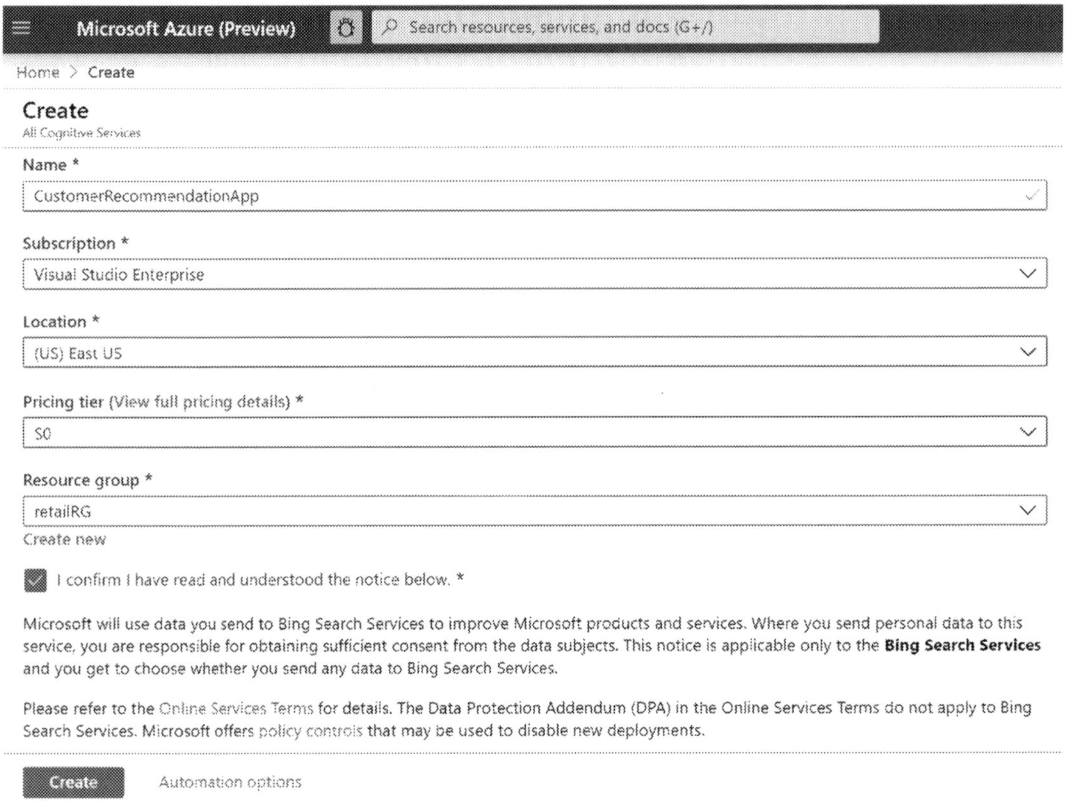

Figure 12-3. *Creating Cognitive Services*

2. Click Create.

3. It will take less than a minute to complete the deployment. After your resource is successfully deployed, under Next Steps, click Go To Resource. In the Quick Start dialog box that opens, you can access your key and endpoint as shown in Figure 12-4.

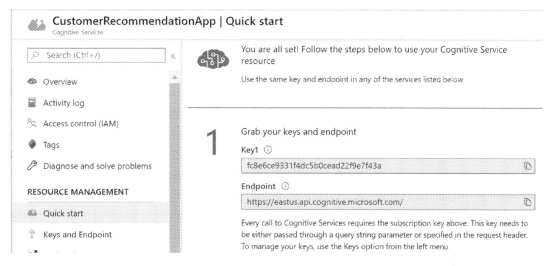

Figure 12-4. *Endpoint and key of Cognitive Services in Quick Start dialog box*

Facial Recognition

The next step is to write code using Visual Studio for facial recognition. Face detection algorithms perceive faces and attributes in a given image. Additional features are emotion recognition, face landmark recognition, and more. Of all of these face landmark recognition is different and very technical. It is an array of 27-point landmarks on the face at the important positions. The face landmarks include positions of each face component like pupils, eyebrows, mouth, nose, and so on.

Microsoft provides a rich SDK in .NET, Python, Java, Node.js, and Go. We are using the .NET SDK using C# for the Face API to perform all the operations. Let's go step by step to see how this can be done.

1. Open Visual Studio (I am using Visual Studio 2017 Professional). Create a console application and name it CustomerRecommendationApp or the name of your choice.

2. Right-click the project in Visual Studio and add the nuget package `Microsoft.Azure.CognitiveServices.Vision.Face` as shown in Figure 12-5. At the time of writing, the nuget is in preview and prerelease.

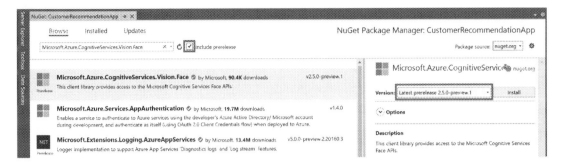

Figure 12-5. *Microsoft.Azure.CognitiveServices.Vision.Face nuget package*

3. Once done, open `Program.cs` and add namespaces.

```
using Microsoft.Azure.CognitiveServices.Vision.Face;
using Microsoft.Azure.CognitiveServices.Vision.Face.Models;
using System;
using System.Collections.Generic;
using System.IO;
using System.Threading.Tasks;
```

4. Then add the following code.

```
static readonly string SUBSCRIPTION_KEY = "YOUR KEY";
static readonly string ENDPOINT = "YOUR ENDPOINT";
static List<FaceAttributeType> returnFaceAttributes;
static IFaceClient client;

static async Task Main()
{
    client = new FaceClient(new ApiKeyServiceClientCredentials(SUB
    SCRIPTION_KEY)) { Endpoint = ENDPOINT };

    returnFaceAttributes = new List<FaceAttributeType>
    { FaceAttributeType.Age, FaceAttributeType.Emotion,
    FaceAttributeType.Gender };
    var faceList = await DetectFacesAsync(client);

    foreach (var face in faceList)
    {
```

```
        Console.WriteLine($"A {face.FaceAttributes.Gender} id
        {face.FaceId} of age {face.FaceAttributes.Age} " +
            $"at location {face.FaceRectangle.Left}, {face.
            FaceRectangle.Left}, " +
            $"{face.FaceRectangle.Top + face.FaceRectangle.Width},
            {face.FaceRectangle.Top + face.FaceRectangle.Height}"
            +
            $" having Happiness {face.FaceAttributes.Emotion.
            Happiness * 100}%");
    }

    Console.ReadKey();
}

/// <summary>Detect faces with all attributes from local image
</summary>
/// <param name="client">Authenticated Face Client object</param>
/// <returns></returns>
private static async Task<IList<DetectedFace>>
DetectFacesAsync(IFaceClient client)
{
    var imageFilePath = @"<LocalImage>";
    using (Stream imageFileStream = File.OpenRead(imageFilePath))
    {
        return await client.Face.DetectWithStreamAsync(imageFileSt
        ream, true, false, returnFaceAttributes);
    }
}
```

I defined returnFaceAttributes with three attributes (i.e., Gender, Age and Emotion). Other facial attributes you can use are Accessories, Blur, Exposure, FacialHair, Glasses, Hair, HeadPose, Makeup, Noise, Occlusion, and Smile. Or you can target fewer attributes, like only Glasses.

This code will take an image from your local path and detect faces. If you have files uploaded at some online shared location, then use the following code.

```
/// <summary>Detect faces with all attributes from online image
</summary>
/// <param name="client">Authenticated Face Client object</param>
/// <returns></returns>
public static async Task<IList<DetectedFace>> DetectFacesAsync
(IFaceClient client)
{
    var remoteImageUrl = @"https://images.pexels.com/photos/972995/
    pexels-photo-972995.jpeg";

        return await client.Face.DetectWithUrlAsync(remoteImageU
        rl, true, false, returnFaceAttributes, RecognitionModel.
        Recognition01);
}
```

Another thing to notice in this new function is RecognitionModel.
There are two RecognitionModels: Recognition01 and
Recognition02. Recognition02 is more optimized, but at the time
of writing, it does not contain all the features.

5. Compile and press F5 to execute. You will see the result shown in
    Figure 12-6.

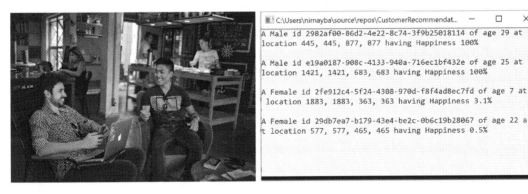

Figure 12-6. *Result of face detection*

Brand Recognition

The next step is to write code using Visual Studio for brand recognition. This is a specialized mode of object detection that uses a database of thousands of global logos to identify commercial brands in images or video.

1. Right-click the project in Visual Studio and add the nuget package `Microsoft.Azure.CognitiveServices.Vision.ComputerVision`, as shown in Figure 12-7.

Figure 12-7. `Microsoft.Azure.CognitiveServices.Vision.ComputerVision` *nuget package*

2. Once done, open `Program.cs` and add namespaces.

```
using Microsoft.Azure.CognitiveServices.Vision.ComputerVision;
using Microsoft.Azure.CognitiveServices.Vision.ComputerVision.
Models;
using System;
using System.Collections.Generic;
using System.IO;
using System.Threading.Tasks;
```

3. Then add the following code. Use the same key and endpoint you generated in the previous section.

```
static readonly string SUBSCRIPTION_KEY = "YOUR KEY";
static readonly string ENDPOINT = "YOUR ENDPOINT";
static List<VisualFeatureTypes> returnAttributes;
```

```
static async Task Main()
{
    ComputerVisionClient client = new ComputerVisionClient(new
    ApiKeyServiceClientCredentials(SUBSCRIPTION_KEY)) { Endpoint =
    ENDPOINT };
    returnAttributes = new List<VisualFeatureTypes>() {
    VisualFeatureTypes.Brands };

    var analysis = await AnalyzeImageAsync(client);
    Console.WriteLine($"Brands identified are: {String.Join(", ",
    analysis.Brands.Select(x => x.ToString()).ToArray())}");
    DisplayResults(analysis);

    Console.ReadKey();
}

/// <summary>Analyze a local image</summary>
/// <param name="client">Authenticated Computer Vision Client
</param>
/// <returns></returns>
private static async Task<ImageAnalysis> AnalyzeImageAsync
(ComputerVisionClient client)
{
    string localImagePath = @"<LocalImage>";
    using (Stream imageStream = File.OpenRead(localImagePath))
    {
        return await client.AnalyzeImageInStreamAsync(imageStream,
        returnAttributes);
    }
}
```

This code will take an image from your local path and detect brands. If you have files uploaded at some online shared location, then use the following code.

```
/// <summary>Analyze a remote image</summary>
/// <param name="client">Authenticated Computer Vision Client
</param>
```

```
/// <returns></returns>
private static async Task<ImageAnalysis> AnalyzeImageAsync(Compute
rVisionClient client)
{
    var remoteImageUrl = @"https://images.pexels.com/
    photos/972995/pexels-photo-972995.jpeg";
    return await client.AnalyzeImageAsync(remoteImageUrl,
    returnAttributes);
}
```

The Computer Vision service detects commercial brand logos in a given image and returns the brand name, a confidence score, and the coordinates of a bounding box around the logo. The built-in logo database covers popular brands in consumer electronics, clothing, and more. As shown in Figure 12-8, you can display this information using the following function.

```
// Display the most relevant caption for the image
private static void DisplayResults(ImageAnalysis analysis)
{
    foreach (var brand in analysis.Brands)
    {
        Console.WriteLine($"Logo of {brand.Name} at location " +
            $"{brand.Rectangle.X}, {brand.Rectangle.Y}, " +
            $"{brand.Rectangle.X + brand.Rectangle.W}, " +
            $"{brand.Rectangle.Y + brand.Rectangle.H}");
    }
}
```

That's it. Press F5 to see the result, as shown in Figure 12-8.

Figure 12-8. *Result of brand detection*

Notice that the algorithm only detected the brands Apple and Corona. It was unable to detect famous footwear brand Nike and known coffee chain Illy. Unlike `RecognitionModel` in Face API, Computer Vision Api unfortunately does not provide any other model to select. Although the Computer Vision API is production ready, it is unreliable at the time of writing.

Virtual Dressing Rooms

Earlier I enumerated the benefits of virtual dressing rooms for retail businesses. The benefits of using virtual dressing rooms go beyond clothing, and some cosmetic brands and accessories have also included this technology in their strategies. For example, Sephora allows you to try on your own range of makeup and different colors using their mobile application. Ray-Ban, a well-known brand of sunglasses, allows you to try on sunglasses through their website's Virtual Model page if you have a webcam.

In this last part of the lab, let's try to overlay sunglasses on a photo, just like Ray-Ban is doing. You will see how simple and easy it is. The same sample could be extended to other accessories like jewelry, hats, and so on.

Extending the same example we earlier wrote for facial recognition, change project to Windows Form Project and replace the `DetectWithStreamAsync` call with

```
return await client.Face.DetectWithStreamAsync(imageFileStream, true, true);
```

Here we changed the third parameter returnFaceLandmarks from false to true, to get landmarks of eye and eyebrow in the image. Second, we removed the returnFaceAttributes parameter, because we no longer need gender, age, and other information from the face.

Finally, add the following function.

```
private void DisplayFeatures(string imageFilePath, IList<DetectedFace>
detectedFaces)
{
    Bitmap glassImage;
    var glassFilePath = @"<LocalImage>\glass.png";
    using (FileStream glassStream = new FileStream(glassFilePath,
    FileMode.Open, FileAccess.Read))
    {
        glassImage = new Bitmap(Image.FromStream(glassStream));
    }

    Bitmap finalImage;
    using (FileStream pngStream = new FileStream(imageFilePath,
    FileMode.Open, FileAccess.Read))
    {
        finalImage = new Bitmap(Image.FromStream(pngStream));
        using (Graphics g = Graphics.FromImage(finalImage))
        {
            var face = detectedFaces[0];
            int x1 = (int)face.FaceLandmarks.EyebrowLeftOuter.X;
            int y1 = (int)face.FaceLandmarks.EyebrowLeftOuter.Y;
            int x2 = (int)face.FaceLandmarks.EyebrowRightOuter.X;
            int y2 = (int)face.FaceLandmarks.EyeRightBottom.Y;

            g.DrawImage(glassImage, new Rectangle(x1-5, y1, x2 - x1,
            y2 - y1));
        }
    }

    //Draw the final image in the pictureBox
    //pictureBox.Image = finalImage;
}
```

To get the correct overlay, we used the coordinates of `EyebrowLeftOuter` as our starting point and coordinates of `EyebrowRightOuter` as our endpoint. The height of the sunglasses is defined using the coordinates of `EyeRightBottom`. If you save the final image or have `PictureBox` on the form, you will see the image as shown in Figure 12-9.

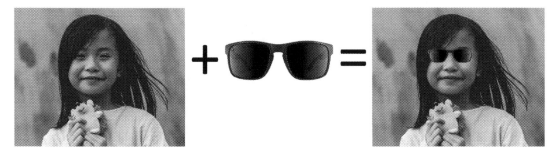

Figure 12-9. *Overlay glasses over the eyes based on eye `FaceLandmark`*

AR is a very powerful tool for both retailers and e-commerce. This example will need more polishing if you have picture other than a straight headshot, but finishing this code is outside the scope of this chapter.

Exercises

Feeding data from closed-circuit cameras to Azure Cognitive Services, you were able to obtain information about customers' gender and approximate age. Next, record time customers spent in each department.

Finally, retailers need to analyze the presence of consumers in their physical stores. This information on customer demography and moving patterns helps retailers provide brand-specific deals and plan dynamic pricing. It can also help retailers understand their market and which type of customer visits more, which could eventually help in making appropriate arrangements of stock and manpower.

Benefits of IoT in Retail

IoT will dramatically transform and innovate the retail industry in the coming years. There are numerous benefits of integrating the technology as part of the retail sector.

- *Reduced fraud:* Shrinkage and fraud are ever-present challenges in retail stores, whether by customers or employees. IoT brings an additional layer related to traceability and visibility. NFC tags have already saved more than $1 trillion annually through improved tags.

- *Efficient use of the staff in store:* IoT uses various devices such as cameras, sensors, and other algorithms to recognize a shopper. Staff should be able to make strategic decisions and engineer the environment inside the store effectively.

- *Personalization:* Using the data retailers generate with sensors and IoT-enabled devices, they will acquire loads of information about their consumers and their behavior. These data can be used to help create personalized marketing and advertising campaigns to more accurately target consumers.

- *Connecting experiences online and in store:* In the retail sector, IoT allows consumers to take advantage of brand-related digital technologies with the help of physical stores. In this way, companies can create harmonious interactions online as well as in stores.

- *Customer experience:* One of the advantages of online shopping is being able to drive items and deliver them to consumers rather than waiting for them to discover them on their own. It helps grab consumer interest at the right moment and significantly boost sales. Sensors placed on shelving units can help monitor current stock of items and refill them before they are gone.

Challenges of IoT in Retail

Listed here are some of the key challenges associated with IoT in retail.

- *Infrastructure:* Many brick-and-mortar retailers lack infrastructure and require significant amounts to implement any IoT project. For example, to digitize retail stores, merchants will need a stable network, cloud platforms, and mobile point of sale (mPOS). All these things will necessitate substantial expenditure.

- *Security:* Most retailers are wary of IoT-related protection and privacy concerns. The implementation of the General Data Protection Regulation (GPDR) has intensified those fears. Access to consumer data offers retailers new incentives but at the same time opens the door to risks of cyberattacks and legal problems.

- *Data management:* Due to a lack of appropriate skills and expertise, carrying out timely and effective IoT data analysis poses a major challenge for retail enterprises. There is not enough technological and analytical ability at hand to obtain useful information from the vast volume of data that IoT collects.

Summary

Implementing IoT technologies will provide retailers with useful insights. These approaches will make customer service better while improving profits. In this chapter I covered how brick-and-mortar stores are digitizing traditional business with various IoT applications, which can have an enormous ROI, like increased marketing conversions and more. As a result, it is clear that IoT-enabled technologies have the ability to improve consumer engagement and increase brand loyalty.

Next, I provided three use cases that are innovating in the retail market. Integrating IoT solutions would allow the companies dealing in the retail sector to create successful customer-behavior-based marketing campaigns, improve inventory management, deliver enhanced services, and also reduce overall operating costs.

In the lab in this chapter I used the Face API and Computer Vision API to provide very simple but effective implementation. I hope you have learned how to analyze an image (local or remote) using the Face SDK and Computer Vision SDK. You don't need knowledge of machine learning or AI, nor do you need giant computers to make such analysis. Yet you can still deliver compelling personalized experiences to your customers.

CHAPTER 13

IoT Applications in Transportation

This is the last chapter to explore applications of IoT in various industries. So far, we have seen that IoT has transformed almost every industry, and the transportation industry is no exception. The transportation industry is the second-largest segment investing in IIoT.

In this chapter I present the application of IoT in various types of transportation; that is, industrial transportation and public transportation, including air and water transportation. Huge monetary investments are taking place in this industry and I will give information on the positive changes IoT is making to make transportation safe, secure, and eco-friendly.

In this evolving world, with the adoption of the latest emerging technologies, every process is being automated so that the physical tasks that were previously required of people can be minimized. It is mainly due to the fact that humans are busy with so many other essential activities that they don't have much time to focus on repetitive, physical regular or basic tasks. The main topic of discussion in this chapter is the role of IoT in the transportation industry.

This chapter focuses on various use cases to dive deep into the significance of IoT in the transportation sector and highlight multiple applications where IoT architecture can be deployed; for example, the impact of IoT on vehicles that change the way one interacts with a vehicle and utilization in traffic management, such as traffic lights and cameras embedded with IoT.

Due to its various benefits, we have adopted and widely applied the idea of smart transportation. At the same time, smart transportation problems are emerging, and IoT is providing a new direction for its development. Later in this chapter I discuss some benefits and challenges of IoT in this industry.

© Nirnay Bansal 2020
N. Bansal, *Designing Internet of Things Solutions with Microsoft Azure*,
https://doi.org/10.1007/978-1-4842-6041-8_13

Transportation

When the car was invented, I am sure that our elders thought that it would never take hold in our society. The car was revolutionary, though, as were the truck, train, ship, and airplane. Transportation allows us to access public transit, helps us in shipping, allows us to share rides, and provides an immeasurable amount of convenience.

I have covered lot of industries thus far and have given examples of small Things like starting a coffee machine or heater while you are driving to your home on a cold evening, having your refrigerator place an order when you are low on eggs, and monitoring your heart rate, blood pressure, and the calories you are burning. Don't be surprised, though, that I have not dedicated a separate chapter to the smart city. I believe the smart city is a combination of making every other service smarter; that is, smart agriculture, smart retail, smart medical, smart homes, and definitely smart transportation in the city. Looking beyond the minor home improvements from the previous chapters, transportation is arguably the sector where we would like to see the greatest transformation. The reduction in prices of sensors and improved coverage of faster Internet makes the adoption of IoT in the transport sector predictable.

In the world, the transportation industry is considered to be one of the nonnegotiable requirements, as it is essential in transporting various type of goods as well as people around the world. It was critical during the lockdowns during the COVID-19 pandemic that this industry kept working to move food and medicine and evacuate citizens from red zones. Consider another example of a company that is manufacturing something essential like seafood, but the company is located in a country where air transport is closed. Thus, the role of water transportation comes into play, by which these essential products can easily be transported to any location around the globe. In this mode of transportation, though, many variables changed. One of the most important factors is time, as it increased multifold as compared with air transport. How to keep this seafood fresh for such a long journey, though? There are various other aspects that have to be considered for accomplishing a proper transportation process, such as having controlled refrigeration, the position at which it must be kept, quality considerations of the items during and after the shipment, and so on. All these aspects are essential in the accomplishment of successful transportation of seafood to the desired destination. To manage all these new variables, we need a new, improved technology, planning, and methods, that can efficiently manage all of these factors. As consumers we expect even more convenience, safety, and commitment from business.

Wearing a business hat, we should understand the importance of these technologies early and capitalize on them as early adopters.

IoT was not alone; it had lot of friends, including sensors and an improved Internet network, pushing it to its boundaries. Finally, IoT found a dream partner, 5G. 5G has improved speed of by a factor of ten as compared with current 4G (LTE) and its latency improved by a factor of 100. This marriage gave birth to other opportunitys like connectivity between vehicles and roads, an essential element for autonomous driving. GPS was developed and launched in 2004 using a code-division multiple access (CDMA) system. The friendship of GPS with IoT enhanced tracking services can be used for a variety of applications including fleet management to answer when, locating a personal car to answer where, elderly patient monitoring to answer how, and pet recovery. Autonomous driving is another big leap in this industry.

5G will change maritime transportation as well. Currently, oceans are not covered by mobile networks, so geostationary satellites provide the vast majority of bandwidth to ships sailing in deep oceans, with limited Internet speed of a few hundred kb/s. With a growing number sensors, though, it could be anywhere between 10,000 and 20,000 sensors per ship. Low Earth orbit (LEO) satellites are being deployed that can provide speeds of up to 1 Gb/s, but this will take time. Another technology to cover maritime transport is 5G at sea, which could be provided by balloons or drones that need not leave Earth's stratosphere, but stay just 20 km above ground. Therefore, 5G would be comparatively cheap and easy to expand. Another advantage of 5G is that it will be able to provide the on-board coverage needed to serve the dense needs of completely connected cargo with up to 20,000 containers.

Applications

IoT in transportation basically allows data to be collected from each entity. The availability of a wider collection of real-time data and the ability to analyze it will enhance strategic decision-making capabilities for logistics and supply chain companies. Thus, in the following sections, my discussion will be based on some associated use cases. First, let's look at the vast and ever-growing network of connected entities in transportation.

Industrial Transportation

Issues with poor fleet management could be eliminated with scheduling, routing, monitoring, and maintenance of vehicles through technology. Fleet management technology is slowly and progressively being adopted with the associated improvements in operational efficiency, maintenance costs, fuel consumption, regulatory compliance, and faster accident response time. GPS tracking, geofencing, customized dashboards, and real-time business decisions are some of the key features any fleet management solution offers. Companies with fleets of vehicles spend millions of dollars in unnecessary costs when their vehicles suddenly break down while in route. Companies can also optimize other factors beyond vehicle health, such as idle time. This not only helps cut costs for the business, but also relieves drivers of monotonous and often error-prone tasks like manual reporting. Multiple IoT technologies can be employed to track shipments, optimize delivery and shipping routes, reduce costs associated with inefficiencies in logistics, and improve bottom lines. Incorporating data from weather advisories and road closure memos can help operations run smoother. It could also inform stakeholders of the status of operations in real time.

Transporters can attach internal and external sensors to gather and store real-time data on everything from temperature and humidity to carbon dioxide levels. It also facilitates real-time GPS tracking of containers, provides automatic notifications that keep cargo owners aware of any deviations in temperature, enables them to take immediate action, and thus improves product quality and security.

Earlier I used the word *geofencing*. When GPS captures the location coordinates of an asset or device, geofencing helps in generating alerts when an asset deviates from the prescribed path, as in the case of cargo destined for Europe offloading at a port in Japan. As it can prevent delays in delivery time and reduce accidental loss, geofencing is very important.

Rail Transport

IoT applications in the field of rail transport include monitoring train speed and automatically shifting routes. Integrating sensors to predict the failure of rail machinery and railway tracks helps maintenance departments to take preventive action. This also results in fewer maintenance breakdown delays, better safety, and higher reliability. Sensors and the connection between the server and the rail improve passenger and rail safety. The subway in Times Square, New York City, has a frequency of two to ten minutes during rush hours. Currently almost all mass transit systems lack integration of passenger data with transit data. The opportunity here is to use passenger data to predict the number of passengers in each train, thus avoiding over- or undercrowding in stations. This is much needed mass transit systems everywhere.

Road Transport

Available parking spots in the cities across the world are hard to find, especially in the central city during peak hours, as well as during special events. Sensors make parking management easier with their ability to determine if a spot is available. This can be done using cameras and ground sensors to determine whether or not a car is parked in a spot, along with the spot's exact location. Going a step further, IoT can help drivers get smartphone alerts about the availability of parking spots, including information about the fees required. Real-time spot availability displays not only save time, but save fuel, reduce traffic, and cut down on roadway congestion.

IoT devices can not only be installed on public transport vehicles like buses and trains, but also can be incorporated into the city infrastructure. Sensors on roads, streetlights, railway platforms, bus stops, and other parts of travel routes can enable transport regulators to conduct traffic flow analysis of the public transportation system. This traffic flow analysis can be used in automatic control of traffic signals. Smart cities are equipped with a complex network of road sensors that can communicate congestion and hazard data to other vehicles and to traffic lights, rerouting and load-balancing traffic throughout the city in real time. These are called connected cars.

Toll systems employing technology can adjust pricing based on congestion and facilitate real-time payment. I-405 in Seattle is a good example of this. The toll price ranges from 75 cents up to $12 during peak hours.

Public Transport

Public transit systems offer many benefits to passengers and to the environment. Tracking the real-time location of a bus and knowing when it will arrive at a stop was always a challenge. As real-time tracking of vehicles is possible with the help of IoT in transportation, location data are sent to a central system and it is then shared to Internet-enabled mobile devices and digital signboards at stops. IoT is eradicating challenges of public transit systems and has enabled rerouting features to help people make alternate arrangements as real-time tracking of vehicles common. To encourage ride sharing, some governments are providing incentives, including free use of toll lanes and ride-sharing cars (including gas expenses).

Water Transport

A ship is no longer a ship; it is now a network of thousands of connected devices. Ship owners use sensors to submit verified emissions data to the European Maritime Safety Agency for each voyage they undertake within the European Union. Ship owners use technology for vessel tracking, emissions control, predictive maintenance, supply chain visibility, and safety. Sensors measuring vibration, sound, and temperature in the engine room provide real-time alerts and actionable insights for predictive maintenance.

Note   When 80 percent of the world's cargo is shipped by sea, then it should be efficient and safe.

Ride-Sharing

Dedicating a section to ride-sharing is appropriate for this mode of transport. We are now transforming the meaning of vehicle ownership. One of the more interesting and recent applications of IoT in transportation is vehicle ownership. Due to the growing cost of a title, insurance, maintenance, gas, and parking, urban dwellers are selling or resisting purchasing their own cars. They're choosing to ride with vehicle-sharing platforms like Uber and Lyft, in addition to relying on steadily improving public transportation services in the city. Ride-sharing is becoming cost-competitive with the total cost of car ownership. With a higher number of companies turning to IoT, these platforms will continue to expand, multiply, and get cheaper, driving down the demand for car ownership. This platform is using a business model that includes flexible pricing based on the time of day and vehicle tracking. Did you notice the notification "Your ride is five minutes away"? This is called vehicle-to-person communication.

I am an MBA graduate, so I must look for opportunities for vehicle insurers here. In Chapters 10 and 11 I covered advantages of IoT for insurance companies in the financial and medical sectors, respectively. Similarly, if vehicle insurers could get data about vehicle health and drivers' operating habits, they could manage risk by analyzing those data. Through OBD devices, insurers have real-time insights into driver behavior, including factors like driving miles, speed, braking, tailgating, and frequency of night driving. OBD devices also help in improving fuel efficiency, predicting maintenance, and suggesting repairs. They can even help determine the meaning of a code from a check engine alert.

Applications

At a national level, governments around the world are starting to pilot IoT transportation initiatives. There are other applications of IoT in transport that are worth mentioning here, though. The following are the selected unique use cases associated with IoT applications in transportation.

Use Case: Transportation-as-a-Service

We used to know this using the simple word taxi or yellow cab. The definition of a taxi is enhanced under Transportation-as-a-Service (TaaS), though. This is another name for Mobility-as-a-Service (MaaS). It refers to the buying of miles, trips, or experiences, and none of these comes with the responsibility of car ownership. I agree that due to the TaaS model, car ownership is shrinking and creating an existential crisis within the transportation sector worldwide. Thinking about it differently, though, it is just a natural extension like in any other business. When a business process changes, we don't call it disruption, we call it improvising. The automobile industry was working with the same model for decades and it was just waiting to be changed. From where I am looking, it is providing new business opportunities in this industry.

Thinking by numbers, an average U.S. family will save more than $5,600 per year in car ownership costs, equivalent to a wage increase of 10 percent. This cost of ownership includes parking and repairs. This money will go into other business and boost the economy overall.

Examples of TaaS are delivery services, ride-sharing services, rental transportation, car subscription services, bike shares, and private car rental (peer-to-peer rentals).

What is IoT doing in this use case? It starts with travelers; they can access schedules by smartphone to plan their trip based on real-time information from the transportation systems. Providers are next. With the use of IoT, vehicle pooling providers such as Uber will be able to keep track of rider and driver involvement during the course of travel. Rental companies can schedule vehicle maintenance based on actual utilization, which reduces disruptions from unexpected breakdowns. When accidents do occur, insurance telematics make for faster recovery, often at a reduced cost.

Use Case: V2X Communication

Vehicle-to-everything (V2X) occurs when a vehicle transmits messages to any potential entity that might affect that vehicle, like traffic lights, streetlights, and other vehicles. As shown in Figure 13-1, it consists of various type of communication. Vehicle-to-vehicle (V2V) technology is new.

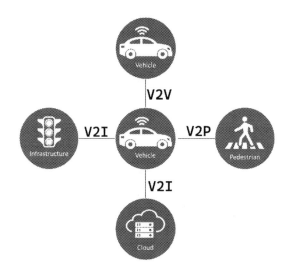

Figure 13-1. *Types of V2X communication*

It means that a vehicle will transmit speed and position data to other surrounding vehicles on the road, thus preventing accidents using dedicated short-range radios. This is the core of automated cars (self-driving cars) and driverless public buses providing 360° situational awareness on the road. In vehicle-to-pedestrian (V2P) communications, a signal from the beacon will be released from the person and the car will detect it to avoid accidents.

Use Case: Location Tracking

As already discussed, transportation is a department that is functional around the clock, even during the time of a pandemic. Every day there is delivery of a vast number of items and movement of cargo as well as vehicles from any source to any destination around the world. In a condition in which there are a large number of items kept in a single place, then it is very difficult to find anything out. The packages can be integrated with a QR or barcode that can be scanned by cameras; further, accurate information can be delivered to the responsible authority. However, you cannot track its present location.

Now, in accordance with this provided case, IoT can help in maintaining a location record by using the sensors that are integrated in the warehouse, products, cargo, and vehicles. Thus, this integration of IoT in locating items is definitely considered a favorable use case.

In the lab that follows, we explore low-cost options to develop a location-aware application.

Lab: Logistics Monitoring

In 2016 at Seattle Code Camp, I presented a session on IoT. Most of my demo in that session was done using a smartphone, the cheapest IoT device anyone can have. This inexpensive IoT device comes with a touch screen display, full Android or iOS operating system, better memory, CPU power, battery, and all types of network connectivity, like Wi-Fi, Bluetooth, and NFC. In this lab I am once again using a smartphone to show how to track the location of a Thing. There are many different ways that you can track location data. Location data are important in every industry—we also learned of its importance in Chapters 9 and 10. In transportation, location data are now nonnegotiable data.

In this lab I am using Xamarin, the ultimate cross-platform mobile development platform for .NET developers. It creates a native application that is developed using the tools specified by the creator of the platform, such as an application developed for iOS with Objective-C, or an Android app developed with Java. Xamarin does produce a native app using a Windows app developed with .NET. It is a developer platform that is used for developing native applications for iOS (Xamarin.iOS), Android (Xamarin. Android), and macOS (Xamarin.Mac). One excellent feature of Xamarin is that it allows us to access both platform-specific APIs and platform-independent parts of .NET, including, for example, namespace systems. We can share a lot of code like business logic and network calls between our target platforms by keeping code in a common project. Code sharing leads to shorter development times and higher quality.

As a manager you would like to cover the maximum number of users for your product, like a full range of Android and iOS devices. At the same time, you need to keep the cost of development and cost of maintenance down. You also want to reuse the current talent pool in the organization. That's where Xamarin enters the picture. Because there are more .NET developers than Objective-C developers, it would be easier to find new developers. The in-house .NET developers can start building native mobile applications by just learning few APIs for the mobile platforms.

During installation of Visual Studio 2019, as shown in Figure 13-2, make sure to select the Mobile Development With .NET workload. If you already have Visual Studio 2019 installed, open Visual Studio Installer and click Modify to select Mobile Development With .NET.

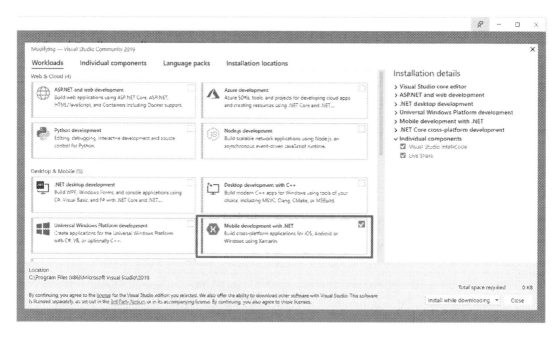

Figure 13-2. *Mobile development with .NET*

Let's see how to access location coordinates in your device in the Xamarin UWP application using Visual Studio 2019. For example, this project can be installed on the smartphone of a public bus or school bus driver, to track the location and time-of-arrival at a stop to avoid a long wait on cold winter or hot summer days.

Follow these steps to create a new Xamarin app.

1. Open Visual Studio 2019.

2. Select Create A New Project.

3. From the Project Type drop-down list, select Mobile.

4. Select the Mobile App (Xamarin.Forms) template and click Next.

5. Enter RouteMonitoringApp as the project name and click Create.

6. As shown in Figure 13-3 select the Shell template. Ensure that the Android and iOS check boxes are both selected. Ensure that the Include ASP.NET Core Web API Project check box is selected and click OK.

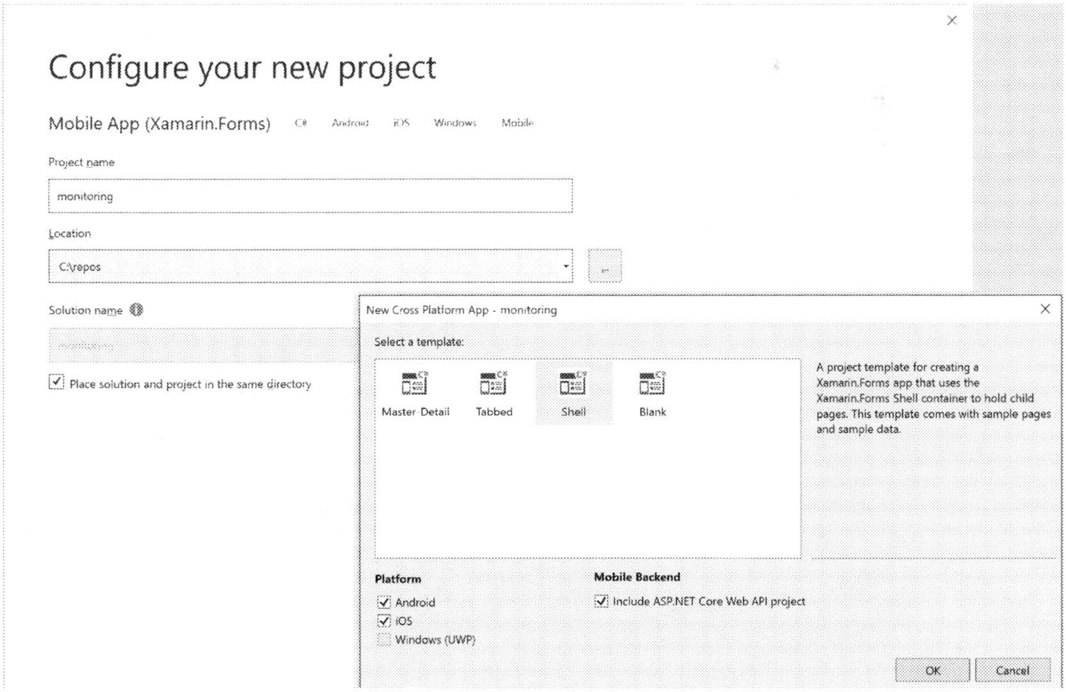

Figure 13-3. *Creating a new Xamarin.Forms app*

7.   Wait until the nuget packages are restored (a "Restore completed" message will appear in the status bar). When asked, specific versions of the Android SDK are required to build projects. If your machine is missing the required SDK, you'll see a prompt while the new project is loading. Click Accept to begin the automatic installation.

Your project is ready, as shown in Figure 13-4. You will see an Android project along with iOS and Web projects. The common code is shared between Android and iOS.

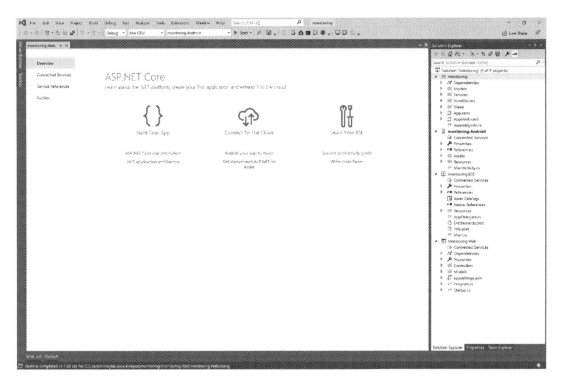

Figure 13-4. *Xamarin Forms project with Android and iOS forms*

8.   New Visual Studio 2019 installations won't have an Android emulator configured. On the Debug button, click the drop-down arrow and choose Create Android Emulator, as shown in Figure 13-5, to launch the emulator creation screen shown in Figure 13-6.

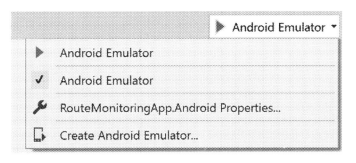

Figure 13-5. *Android Emulator to install and debug application*

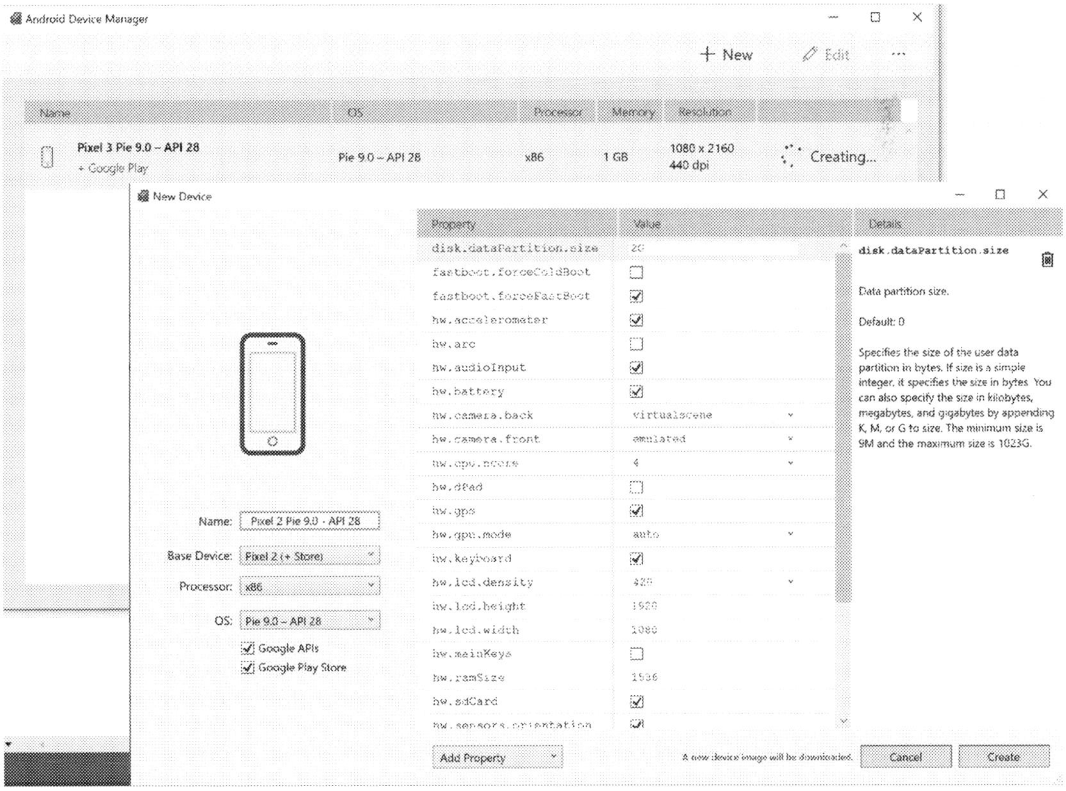

Figure 13-6. *Android Device Manager to create a new emulator*

Permissions can be set either from the Android Manifest tab in the properties
of the RouteMonitoringApp.Android project or via the AndroidManifest.xml
file in the Properties folder. When changes are made on the Android Manifest
tab, the changes will be written to the Manifest file as well, so it doesn't matter
which method you prefer.

9. Open `AndroidManifest.xml` under `RouteMonitoringApp.Android` and give permission for Location and Coarse Location services.

```
<uses-permission android:name="android.permission.
ACCESS_FINE_LOCATION" />
<uses-permission android:name="android.permission.
ACCESS_COARSE_LOCATION" />
```

10. Depending on the use of Wi-Fi and a network to send these data to a server, you also need to give permission for Wi-Fi and network services.

```
<uses-permission android:name="android.permission.ACCESS_NETWORK_
STATE" />
<uses-permission android:name="android.permission.ACCESS_WIFI_
STATE " />
```

11. Right-click the project in Visual Studio and add the nuget package `Xamarin.Essentials`.

12. Open `MainPage.xaml.cs`. Under Common Project Name, add the following namespaces.

```
using System.Net.Http;
using Xamarin.Essentials;
```

13. Paste the following code.

```
HttpClient client = new HttpClient();
public static string AzureBackendUrl = DeviceInfo.Platform ==
DevicePlatform.Android ? "http://10.0.2.2:5000" : "http://
localhost:5000";

Device.StartTimer(TimeSpan.FromSeconds(30), () =>
{
    Task.Run(async () =>
    {
        await SendLocationToServer();
    });
```

```
        return true; // True = Repeat again, False = Stop the timer
    });

    public async Task SendLocationToServer()
    {
        client.BaseAddress = new Uri($"{AzureBackendUrl}/");

        try
        {
            var request = new GeolocationRequest(GeolocationAccuracy.
            Medium);
            var location = await Geolocation.GetLocationAsync(request);

            if (location != null)
            {
                var locationTuple = $"{location.Latitude}, {location.
                Longitude}, {location.Altitude}";
                var response = await client.PostAsync($"api/location",
                new StringContent(locationTuple, Encoding.UTF8,
                "application/json"));
            }
        }
        catch (Exception)
        {
            // Unable to get location
        }
    }
```

14. To set the emulator device location, click ... next to the emulator
    and select a location. I am setting a location of Pike Market,
    Seattle, WA, as shown in Figure 13-7, which will send location
    Latitude, Longitude and Altitude "47.609655, -122.342151666667,
    0" to the API.

Note   For brevity in this chapter I am not showing you how to create a .NET Core
Web POST API, which takes this location and save it in some storage for further
processing.

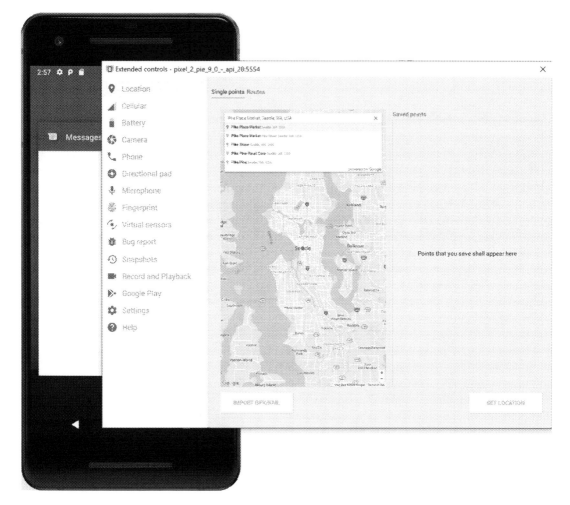

Figure 13-7. *Setting an Android emulator device location*

That's it. From the menu, select Debug ➤ Start Debugging or simply press F5 to see the result of your web API. Congratulations! You've built and run your first Xamarin app to track your location using an inexpensive IoT device, a smartphone.

To implement geofencing, Android supports multiple active geofences, with a limit of 100 per app, per device user. Geofencing is the combination of current location latitude and longitude with proximity to the location as a radius. The latitude, longitude, and radius define a geofence, creating a circular area, or fence, around the location of interest. Android provides entering and exiting events out of the box. Many open source and nuget packages available make it even simpler. I leave the implementation of a geofence in the preceding project for you to try.

Usually this kind of application should be able to run in the background. We can also enable background mode in our app with some more coding efforts. With Android, you need to create a JobService and schedule it. I am leaving the background scheduler for you to practice.

Lab: Working with Sensors (Smart Parking)

In this lab, I am using an ultrasonic ranging module (HC SR04) to measure the distance of a car from the sensor and print the result. Ultrasonic ranging modules use the principle that an ultrasonic signal will reflect when it encounters an obstacle.

We start counting the time when the signal is transmitted, and we finish counting after the signal is received back. The time difference is the total time of the ultrasonic signal from transmission to reception. Because the speed of sound in air is constant, and is about v = 340 m/s, we can calculate the distance between the model and the obstacle with the formula s = (v*t)/2.

We are using the same setup as in the lab in Chapter 6.

As shown in Figure 13-8, the ultrasonic sensor has four legs. HC-SR04 takes a 5V input and echo a 5V signal. From left to right, connect VCC to 5V. Connect the legs Trig and Echo to GPIO pins 23 and 24, respectively. Finally, connect GND to GND of GPIO.

Figure 13-8. *Circuit diagram of ultrasonic sensor connected with GPIO*

1. Create a new project with File | New Project.

2. Select the template Blank App (Windows Universal).

3. Add a new class.

```
using System.Threading;
using Windows.Devices.Gpio;

class UcHCSR04Sensor
{
    GpioController gpio = GpioController.GetDefault();
    readonly GpioPin TriggerPin;
    readonly GpioPin EchoPin;

    public UcHCSR04Sensor(int triggerPin, int echoPin)
    {
        TriggerPin = gpio.OpenPin(triggerPin);
        EchoPin = gpio.OpenPin(echoPin);

        //Sets the drive mode of the general-purpose I/O (GPIO) pin
        //The drive mode specifies whether the pin is configured
          as an input or an output
        TriggerPin.SetDriveMode(GpioPinDriveMode.Output);
        EchoPin.SetDriveMode(GpioPinDriveMode.Input);

        TriggerPin.Write(GpioPinValue.Low);
    }

    public double GetDistance()
    {
        ManualResetEvent mre = new ManualResetEvent(false);
        mre.WaitOne(500);

        Stopwatch pulseLength = new Stopwatch();

        //Send pulse
        TriggerPin.Write(GpioPinValue.High);
        mre.WaitOne(TimeSpan.FromMilliseconds(0.01));
        TriggerPin.Write(GpioPinValue.Low);
```

```
//Receive pulse
while (this.EchoPin.Read() == GpioPinValue.Low) { }
pulseLength.Start();

//Read the signal from the sensor
while (this.EchoPin.Read() == GpioPinValue.High) { }
pulseLength.Stop();

//Speed 17,000 miles/hour or 27,350 kilometers/hour
//Calculating distance with sound speed 340m/s
double distance = pulseLength.Elapsed.TotalSeconds * 17000;

return distance;
    }
}
```

Here the write and read drives the specified value onto the GPIO
pin according to the current drive mode for the pin.

If the GPIO pin is configured as an output, the method drives the
specified value onto the pin according to the current drive mode
for the pin.

If the GPIO pin is configured as an input, the method updates the
latched output value for the pin. The latched output value is driven
onto the pin when the configuration for the pin changes to output.

4. Add the following code in `MainPage.xaml`.

```
<Grid Background="{ThemeResource
ApplicationPageBackgroundThemeBrush}">
<TextBox x:Name="LocationBox" HorizontalAlignment="Left"
Margin="431,405,0,0" Text="TextBox" VerticalAlignment="Top"
Height="95" Width="406" FontSize="36"/>
 Grid>
```

5. Add the following code in `MainPage.xaml.cs`.

    ```
    var uc = new UcHCSR04Sensor(23, 24);

    var dist = uc.GetDistance();
    LocationBox.Text = dist;
    ```

    To compile and deploy the project you need to follow the steps given in Chapter 6. The final hardware setup is shown in Figure 13-9.

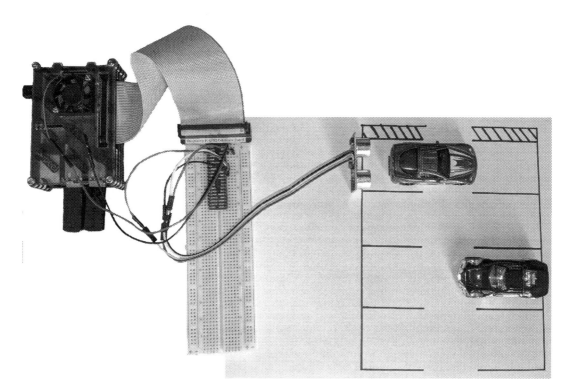

Figure 13-9. *Smart parking using an ultrasonic sensor connected with Raspberry Pi*

Congratulations! You just deployed your smart parking UWP application to a device running IoT Core and finished reading ultrasonic sensor data.

Note   You can connect multiple ultrasonic sensors with the Raspberry Pi.

Benefits of IoT Application in Transportation

After discussing the various use cases associated with this assignment, I present here a few ways in which IoT in transportation can benefit all the stakeholders involved. Based on the application, the benefit is classified into a different category, like traffic congestion, automotive telematics, reservations, tolls, ticketing, security, and surveillance.

Benefits to Commuters

Quite often public transportation commuters leave their homes or workplaces well ahead of time and are forced to wait at the train station or bus stop, wasting their valuable time. The primary reason for this is the highly unpredictable status of buses and trains. In the case of buses, although riders know the standard schedules, they don't know if the buses are sticking to those schedules at any given time. Many cities are investing in IoT technology to solve this problem by relaying this information to passengers via mobile applications, digital signage at stops, or both. A few cities are also providing information on the number of passengers currently waiting and also recommending the best time to travel.

Mechanical breakdowns cause delays and frustrate passengers. Implementing modern maintenance techniques such as preventive and predictive maintenance help monitor the different health parameters of vehicles and infrastructure can help identify potential problems in advance. This leads to longevity of the vehicles, high uptime of services, minimal disruptions, and greater safety for passengers.

Benefits to the Environment

In reference to the preceding benefits, once we know the number of passengers on bus stops, a routing system could allocate the appropriate number of vehicles to different routes. When buses are filled, drivers can be alerted to skip stops and take shorter routes or take the fastest route based on traffic and signal information.

Similarly, railways take advantage of passenger data and decide how many seconds to wait at each spot. Trains can also increase or decrease their speed to efficiently utilize capacity.

City administrators use the same data to plan new routes and increase the number of buses and trains and the frequency of existing ones.

Citizens are also using public transportation to contribute to reducing pollution and helping to preserve the earth. On the other hand, cities have a similar responsibility and therefore provide reliable and predictable commuting options and attempt to reduce the number of private vehicles on roads. Cities use the same data to reduce their carbon footprint.

Benefits to Businesses

Through a rapidly increasing number of connected devices, embedded sensors, and analytics technologies, companies in the transportation sector can enjoy unprecedented visibility in almost every aspect of their business. The ability to control goods across the logistics can improve protection as well as product quality. Advanced telematics systems and GPS tracking sensors can be used to capture real-time data for monitoring and evaluating vehicle performance.

Different countries have different compliance requirements for businesses. Using sensors to record speed, distance, and driver activity ensure regulatory compliance and accurate recordkeeping for the entire fleet. These data are also shared with insurance companies to create customized insurance plans like user-based insurance (UBI) or models like pay as you drive (PAYD) and pay how you drive (PHYD).

Businesses reduce risk by identifying hazardous areas and damaged machinery so that it can be replaced in a way that causes little or no threat to employees like engineers and crew members. For example, drones can be used to identify leaks in an oil tanker and could also be used to patch the leak remotely.

Challenges of IoT Application in Transportation

Although IoT technology is exciting and futuristic, it comes with its own share of challenges. Referencing various advantages of IoT in transportation, there are various challenges as well. Let's discuss challenges faced by companies while implementing IoT technology in their business activities.

- *Liability:* Semiautomatic or self-driving vehicles are designed to reduce accidents and eliminate loss of life, but accidents are inevitable. The responsibility of liability is a hotly debated topic. In the absence of a real driver behind the wheel, the other stakeholders are the car manufacturer, the passenger as a standby driver, or the communication system. The lines are blurred, but for now we hold the passenger as standby driver responsible, and the reputation of the manufacturer could be damaged.

- *Network infrastructure cost:* Replacing existing towers with the new, sophisticated technology required for enabling 5G and laying fiberoptic cables throughout a city requires significant infrastructure upgrades and investment. Cameras and sensors are required for each parking spot to facilitate smart parking, an expensive proposition.

- *Employee training:* Although the use of IoT could be a lot of help, it will still require experience and knowledge of predictive maintenance charts and alerts, as the wrong interpretation of any condition could further damage the machinery and lead to costly repairs, which might be unacceptable to the company. Companies not hiring the right talent to deal with IoT work could see a delay in ROI. With more Edge computing coming into the picture, we need talent with knowledge of programming and cloud computing, or existing employees should be continuously adapting and learning. Companies might have to accept that they need a part-time consultant (or full-time employee in a larger organization) to work on AI, machine learning, and data analytics technologies to harness the true value of data.

- *Security:* Due to the involved sensors and devices connected to vehicles, the data are vulnerable to interruption and coordinated malware attacks. A malicious hacker could sell or exploit your location data. In case the of semi- or fully autonomous cars, hackers could even take over the operations of the car. Organizations need to implement processes to protect sensitive data and networks. Proper data governance and firewalls are essential to overcome this challenge.

Summary

Transportation is beginning to rely more heavily on IoT. The applications run far beyond those listed here. Any company working within the industry will soon learn, if they haven't already incorporated IoT into their business, that this is the best way to beat the competition and future-proof their company.

When cities integrate wireless technology into traffic management and emergency response, the effect of IoT on transportation efficiency is projected to be immense. In this chapter, we have learned about the use of IoT in TaaS and how it is the backbone of V2X communication.

After practicing content from the lab section of this chapter, you should now have a good grasp of all the steps involved in creating a Xamarin.Forms application from scratch for Android and iOS devices. Using the knowledge gained from this chapter, you should be able to create any location-aware app you like.

To visualize what location data our app tracked, you will use the .NET Core API and a low-latency database.

This is the last chapter that discusses IoT in various industries. In the next chapter, you will take these concepts further and see the risks and challenges involved in implementing an end-to-end IoT project in an organization.

CHAPTER 14

Risk

The previous chapters revealed the size, use cases, and potential of IoT in various industries, having billions of devices connected. In the discussion of challenges in every chapter, I touched on the provisions of securing the system. This chapter is dedicated to types of risk that can do minor to major damage, agnostic to the type of industry. For an IoT environment, security is an ongoing process in which a proactive attitude and forward-looking actions are nonnegotiable, and there is no true definition of done.

Later in this chapter, we discuss the security provisions in an industrial control system (ICS) at three levels: network and communication, computer systems, and sensors. Architects or managers are responsible for understanding the end-to-end IoT technology stack and securing them from any type of possible exploitation. In an IoT project, security must consider a wider range of issues as compared with traditional IT cybersecurity, because it involves all three of these layers.

IoT technology is no longer in its infancy stage; now that is just an excuse. All of the challenges with this technology are solvable. Here I present how to use the Threat Modeling tool and empower you with all types of STRIDE threats, including step(s) to mitigate them. You can use this tool for any project.

I will finish this chapter and conclude the book with details on the available IoT standards and regulations.

Note   From this book, if there is one key concept to grasp in implementing any IoT project in your organization, it is the importance of security.

This book has attempted to provide practical advice for designing and deploying many types of secured IoT systems.

© Nirnay Bansal 2020
N. Bansal, *Designing Internet of Things Solutions with Microsoft Azure*,
https://doi.org/10.1007/978-1-4842-6041-8_14

Risk

When a burglar invading your home, you don't find who the burglar was; first you find the place he or she entered the house. Similarly, you don't wait for it to happen; you secure your house to minimize the risk in the first place. This is the same way we need to secure our IT infrastructure in the first place. In this example, the burglar is not the threat; instead, the actions he or she can perform is the threat. In the context of IoT, the threats are that someone can get to the sensors, hold the data hostage, and reduce reliability of service.

The possibility of a problem and expectation of loss due to that problem is called *risk*. In Figure 14-1, which displays a risk flowchart in software, we identify risk and use qualitative (i.e., probability and impact matrix) or quantitative methods (i.e., Expected Monetary Value (EMV), Monte Carlo, and decision tree) for evaluating risk. If it goes above a threshold value, then there are five main methods to manage that risk: accept, avoid, transfer, mitigate, or exploit.

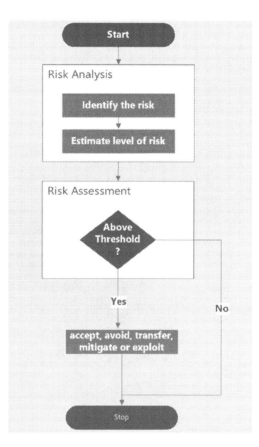

Figure 14-1. *Risk flowchart*

Accepting the risk sounds bad because you log it and take no action. The transfer method is unacceptable, as you transfer the impact and management of the risk to someone else, and I am not covering any risk that can be exploitable here. This leaves you with only two choices: Avoid risk by changing your plans completely or mitigate risk by limiting the impact of a risk, so that if it does occur, the problem it creates is smaller and easier to fix.

We need to systematically evaluate the security and potential attacks. As part of the security development life cycle, Microsoft developed a Threat Modeling tool that can be downloaded from `https://aka.ms/threatmodelingtool`. It allows software architects to identify and mitigate potential security issues early when they are relatively easy and cost-effective to resolve. Threat modeling helps identify the vulnerable entry points in all the assets within a system.

Referring back to the Azure IoT architecture I described in Chapter 3, the threat model of that architecture will look like Figure 14-2.

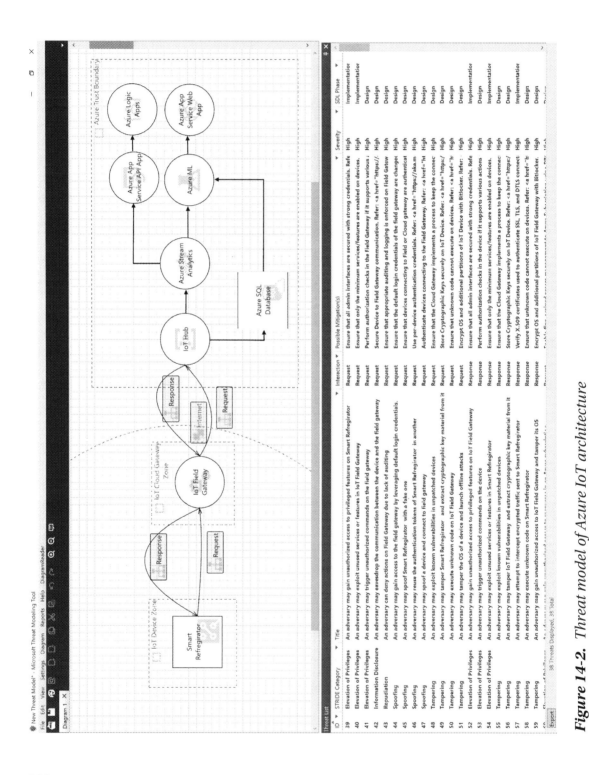

Figure 14-2. *Threat model of Azure IoT architecture*

Threat modeling provides us with a methodical approach to performing a security evaluation of a system or system design. To illustrate the threat modeling process, we will evaluate threats to a smart refrigerator, which orders milk from your favorite grocery store based on a real-time analysis of the re**frigerator's** contents and your purchasing and consumption history.

For example, I am taking only one use case of smart refrigerator to place an order of milk when it goes below the threshold limit, as shown in Table 14-1.

Table 14-1. *Use Case of Smart Refrigerator*

Use Case	Placing Order
Preconditions	Customer has grocery store and payment information registered with refrigerator.
Action	Smart refrigerator communicates with and collects data from sensors, and places order if low quantity is found.
Postconditions	Credit card is charged, and order is placed.

After creating a threat model and generating a threats list, the tool will display the threats at the bottom of your threat model, as shown in Figure 14-2. All elements in the architectural diagram are subject to various threats, but I am only listing few of them that support our use case in Table 14-2. The category is based on the STRIDE Model. You can apply the the STRIDE threat model to each entry point in your architecture.

Table 14-2. *Example of STRIDE Threats*

Category	Title	Interaction	Security Development Life Cycle Phase
Spoofing	An adversary might spoof the sSmart refrigerator with a fake one.	Request	Design
Spoofing	An adversary might spoof a device and connect to a field gateway.	Request	Design
Tampering	An adversary might exploit known vulnerabilities in unpatched devices.	Request	Design
Repudiation	An adversary can deny actions on the field gateway due to lack of auditing.	Response	Design
Information disclosure	An adversary might eavesdrop on the communication between the device and the field gateway.	Request	Design
Elevation of privileges	An adversary might trigger unauthorized commands on the device.	Response	Design
Elevation of privileges	An adversary might gain unauthorized access to privileged features on the smart refrigerator	Request	Implementation

The possible mitigation is also listed in the Threat Modeling tool. For example,

- To mitigate a ***spoofing*** attack, we need ensure that devices connecting to the field or cloud gateway are authenticated and authenticate devices connecting to the field gateway.

- To mitigate a ***tampering*** attack, ensure that the cloud gateway implements a process to keep the connected devices' firmware up to date.

- To mitigate a ***repudiation*** attack, ensure that the appropriate auditing and logging is enforced on the field gateway.

- To mitigate ***information disclosure***, an adversary might eavesdrop and interfere with the communication between the device and the field gateway and possibly tamper with the data that are transmitted.

- To mitigate an ***elevation of privileges*** attack, perform authorization checks on the device if it supports various actions that require different permission levels and ensure that all admin interfaces are secured with strong credentials.

You now have the choice to avoid risk by changing your plans or mitigate risk as recommended by the Threat Modeling tool.

Privacy

The confidentiality of data has always been and remains a primary concern. For any organization, small or large, there are legal, regulatory, and commercial obligations to protect intellectual property and customer data, especially intellectual property, financial, and health care data. This emphasis is applicable to data collected manually or by IT systems. Among all the issues, intellectual property confidentiality and human privacy are critical.

Privacy is the most important subject we discuss today. Organizations are even more responsible to protect the privacy of users. Unfortunately, the definition of privacy is vague, changes from person to person, and has different ranking levels. is the definition is so vague that something we share on social media, we assume cannot be shared by an organization. In fact, many countries have privacy legislation, and therefore it is a fundamental human right. I am not debating the true definition of privacy here, but would like to mention the GDPR legislation passed in 2016.

Individual certification as a Certified Information Privacy Professional (CIPP) from the International Association of Privacy Professionals (IAPP) focuses on data privacy.

Safety

Safety and security are closely related linguistically, so here I use them interchangeably. The safety focus is frequently driven by the security impacts that an organization has historically experienced, known as reactive actions. Most of the time, managers understand security only after critical data are exposed to the public, corrupted, or deleted. At that point they start making security a priority and start approving budgets for security-related projects. By that time, though, damage has already been done.

Networks, computer systems, and sensors are typical IoT or industrial system assets, and security begins with these assets. In most cases there exists a tight coupling between network design and operational processes; therefore, to avoid any business process impacts, securing the network and all communication channels is even more important.

Securing a network sounds simple when talking about a small, confined environment like a few buildings situated within a known boundary (e.g., a manufacturing unit). Disconnecting an internal network from a public network is as simple as said it seems. In geographically distributed environments, it is not possible to disconnect from the public network entirely. For those networks, we need sophisticated network devices and explicit partnering with Internet service providers. Modern networking equipment offers a rich set of access control and secured communications capabilities.

There are various types of attacks that can be carried out against a network and assets. In the real world, most attacks are highly customized and are not yet publicly known; this is called *vulnerability*. Some common types of cyberattacks on IoT projects are listed here.

- *Botnets:* Talking about Botnets brings Mirai to mind. It continues to be a problem today with millions of IoT devices affected. Mirai has the capability to use smart, connected devices to transfer private and sensitive data, which could be sold on the dark web, or to disable a device. Botnets are networks of systems, such as those used for denial-of-service (DoS) attacks explained later in this list.

- *Man-in-the-middle:* Man-in-the-middle attacks are the most common in IoT systems. In this type of attack, a hacker breaches communication between a sensor and a system and tricks the recipient into thinking they are receiving a legitimate message. An example might be sending the wrong D2S message to IoT Hub about a critical physical condition like heat or vibration, or sending the wrong S2D message to a sensor to switch off. These can be dangerous attacks because a hacker can trick the recipient into thinking they are still getting a legitimate message. As in the previous example, these attacks can be extremely dangerous in the IoT, affecting things like garage door openers and industrial machinery.

- *Firmware hijacking:* Firmware is the piece of code that runs on startup and later subverts the operating system. BIOS is not the only firmware in our system; it is the very core of every hardware device.

For example, your noise-canceling headphones, printer, and security camera all have their own firmware. Therefore, firmware is the most vulnerable attach point to access your system before it has even booted up. Once in, a hacker could change the firmware for good, target sections of the OS, or stop antimalware software to execute and steal CPU processing power (e.g., cryptomining). Because firmware is installed on a special chip attached to the system on a chip (SOC), replacing a hard drive or reinstalling the OS won't help. Many manufacturers release updates regularly based on newly discovered vulnerabilities, but in some cases if a company goes out of business or discontinues supporting a product, you are widely exposed. With proper IT processes in place to look for updates and update your firmware to the latest versions quickly and often, you can close off lax security avenues and keep the system running smoothly.

- *Ransomware:* Ransomware is a type of malicious software that cybercriminals use to block users from accessing their own files, usually by encrypting them with a key. Then they share instructions with the user on how to pay a ransom to get the decryption key. This type of attack is a hostage-like situation and comes with a price, depending on how badly the user needs those files back. For example, hackers might be able to access a power grid and blackmail the utility company by causing a complete blackout if they refuse to pay the ransom using cryptocurrency.

- *Denial of service:* A DoS attack happens when a service becomes unavailable, usually due to capacity overload. A large number of requests are made to a service (target) at the same time. In comparison to other hacking attacks like phishing or brute-force attacks, DoS is not interested in stealing any information; it just tries to bring a system down, causing damage to a company's reputation and seriously affecting the business.

Whether you're just getting started with an IoT project or you've already implemented it, it's important to regularly perform a cybersecurity audit to determine whether you need to take additional steps to protect your devices.

IoT Standards and Regulations

The National Institute of Standards and Technology (NIST) defines national standards on security, encryption, and networking. The organization also provides guides for the security of connected devices. They also maintain national and internationally recognized standards regarding security. Supporting materials can be found at `http://csrc.nist.gov`.

The U.S. Department of Homeland Security mandates guidance for Congress, other agencies, and the private sector regarding cybersecurity standards under the National Security Telecommunications Advisory Committee. Supporting materials can be found at `https://www.dhs.gov/topic/cybersecurity`.

A part of the U.S. Department of Commerce called the National Telecommunications and Information Administration controls U.S. radio spectrum allocation, domain naming, and security. More information can be found at `https://www.ntia.doc.gov`.

In Europe, the European Union Agency for Cybersecurity issues standards and publications on various information security practices. In Australia, the IoT Alliance Australia maintains a set of guidelines and practices.

IEEE IoT is a multidisciplinary organization comprised of academic institutions, government bodies, and industry and engineering professionals to drive IoT development. More information is available at `iot.ieee.org`.

The Computer Emergency Response Team identifies and responds to national high-impact computer security emergencies (`https://www.us-cert.gov/ncas/current-activity`).

The Children's Online Privacy Protection Act (COPPA) requires that operators provide notice to parents and obtain verifiable parental consent prior to collecting, using, or disclosing personal information from children under 13 years of age.

HIPAA covers regulations and guidance on anything related to health care. It is applicable to wearables to. The HIPAA Security Rule identifies 18 criteria that define Protected Health Information (PHI).

GDPR, mentioned earlier, outlines a set of data subject rights. These include breach notifications, right to access, right to be forgotten, data portability, and privacy by design.

Bonus Read: Azure Sphere

I know you need help protecting your data, privacy, physical safety, and infrastructure, and you are looking for an end-to-end solution. Azure IoT Edge allows you to offload most of the cloud processing near the device. Therefore, we need even more security on an Edge device and Azure Sphere aims to provide security solutions for such IoT devices. This bonus read is about Azure Sphere, a comprehensive IoT security solution including hardware, OS, and cloud components developed by Microsoft.

The Azure Sphere platform, shown in Figure 14-3, consists of the integration of three key technical components working as one: a brand new secured silicon chip, the Azure Sphere OS, and the Azure Sphere Security Service.

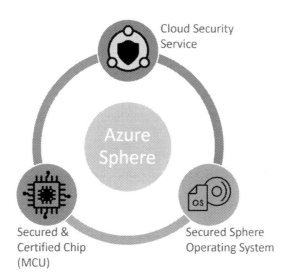

Figure 14-3. *Azure Sphere*

The Azure Secured Sphere OS is based on Microsoft's custom Linux-based microcontroller OS that is built for security and agility to create a trustworthy platform for new IoT experiences. It runs a custom Linux kernel developed by Microsoft fit in just 4 MB of RAM and based on mainline Linux 4.9. Every device has a certificate on it and is known by Microsoft before that Azure Sphere is sold. Therefore, Microsoft maintains the OS and updates it using over-the-air (OTA) updates. It connects to the other components and the Azure Sphere Security Service (AS3).

AS3, the Cloud Security service layer on Azure Sphere communication between Azure and the device, uses HTTPS and the same trusted certificates for authentication. It is integrated with Azure IoT Hub for device provisioning and machine-to-machine (M2M) communication. Although Azure is the preferred cloud for Sphere, it can be connected to any cloud-based device management layer.

Secured and Certified Azure Sphere's chip (MCU) is built by Microsoft's silicon partners, so they possess the hardware root of trust needed. Currently the certified chip is MT3620AN, where Microsoft will support OS and security service updates through July 2031. The custom Linux-based OS mentioned earlier runs on this certified chip.

I believe security should start with hardware and extends to your solution end to end to deliver a holistic, secure system that protects you from almost all threats. Most of the time we put effort into building a perfect architecture and developing a solution, but we ignore the hardware piece. With many IoT devices suffering from security vulnerabilities and trojans, this MCU is a solution. These three components create and provide a complete, secure software environment for IoT application development.

So far in this book we have used Raspberry Pi. Is Raspberry Pi different from Azure Sphere? Yes, these are two different platforms. However, they both offer a few similar features for building IoT solutions. For example, they both have processing units, RAM, connectivity like Wi-Fi, GPIO ports to extend the capability, and so on. The biggest difference is the security features of the Azure Sphere platform that do not exist for Raspberry Pi. There are many cases where either a Raspberry Pi or Azure Sphere device could be used to build an IoT solution. If security is important to your IoT project, however, Azure Sphere might be the best platform.

Even if the price is your primary decision factor, Azure Sphere is not too costly. At the time of writing, there were two approved Azure Sphere development kits recommended by Microsoft (see `https://azure.microsoft.com/en-us/services/azure-sphere/get-started/`) and available for less than $100, and a mini board is available for less than $35, which is sufficient for any regular project. There are no ongoing subscription fees or consumption fees associated with your Azure Sphere purchase or the Azure Sphere Security Service from Microsoft. Pricing and support for Azure Sphere certified MCU MT3620AN is less than $8.65. This is already included in the purchase price of the development kit.

Getting Your Device Ready

As I mentioned, there are broadly two development kits available. You've probably got one from Avnet and Seeed from their available device options. This lab can be run on any of these. As shown in Figure 14-4, I am using Avnet because the Avnet Azure Sphere starter kit contains a MediaTek MT3620 MCU and includes a three-axis accelerometer, three-axis gyro, temperature sensor, and ambient light sensor.

Figure 14-4. *Avnet Azure Sphere starter kit*

You can use Visual Studio or the Visual Studio Core CLI command to develop Sphere security-enabled applications on a certified board. Developing solutions for Azure Sphere requires Visual Studio Enterprise, Professional, or Community 2019 version 16.4 or higher.

Download the Azure Sphere SDK from `https://aka.ms/AzureSphereSDKDownload`. You will see the Azure Sphere Developer command prompt shortcut on your Start menu.

Download the Azure Sphere SDK extension for Visual Studio from `https://marketplace.visualstudio.com/items?itemName=AzureSphereTeam.AzureSphereSDKforVisualStudio2019`.

Claiming a Device

An Azure Sphere can be claimed only once; that is, once activated, the device cannot be sold or transferred to another person or organization. If you are purchasing a preowned device, make sure it is not yet claimed. The process of claiming is not straightforward and not well documented online.

If you try to register and claim the device using a `.hotmail.com`, `.live.com`, or `.outlook.com` account using the command `azsphere login --newuser <your account>@hotmail.com`, you will see this error:

```
AADSTS50020: User account '<your account>@hotmail.com' from identity
provider 'live.com' does not exist in tenant 'Azure Sphere' and cannot
access the application '0b1cxxxx-xxxx-xxxx-xxxx-7d7dxxxxc87f'(Azure Sphere
Utility) in that tenant. The account needs to be added as an external user
in the tenant first. Sign out and sign in again with a different Azure
Active Directory user account.
```

First, log in to your Azure Portal (`https://portal.azure.com`) using your `live.com` account. If you are using a work account, you need administrative privileges on Azure Active Directory. Most of the organization would not provide this level or role on Azure Active Directory; therefore, for this lab I am using a personal Azure account.

1. Search for and select Azure Active Directory.

2. In the left pane, under Manage, select Users.

3. Click +New User

4. Select the Create User option. Notice in Figure 14-5 that the domain is already present with the name <your account>hotmail.onmicrosoft.com.

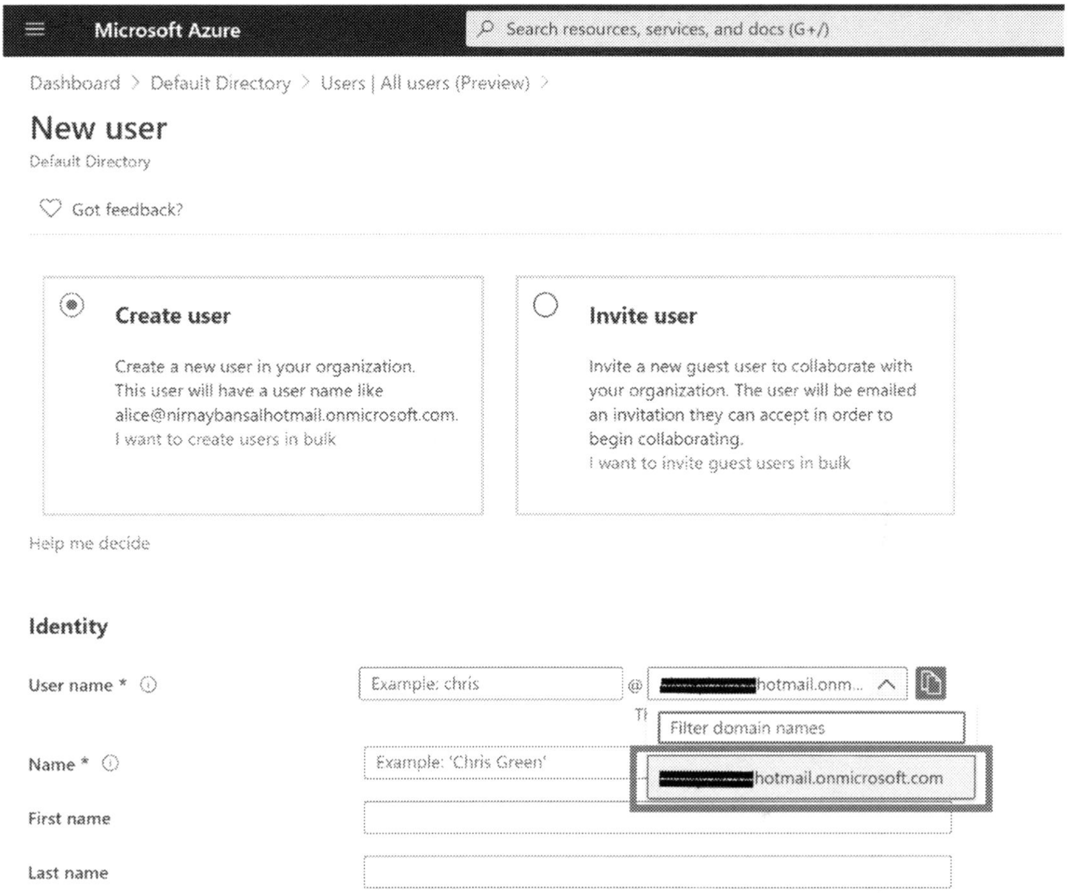

Figure 14-5. *Creating a new user in Azure Active Directory*

> 5. On the User page, enter the user information as shown in Figure 14-6.

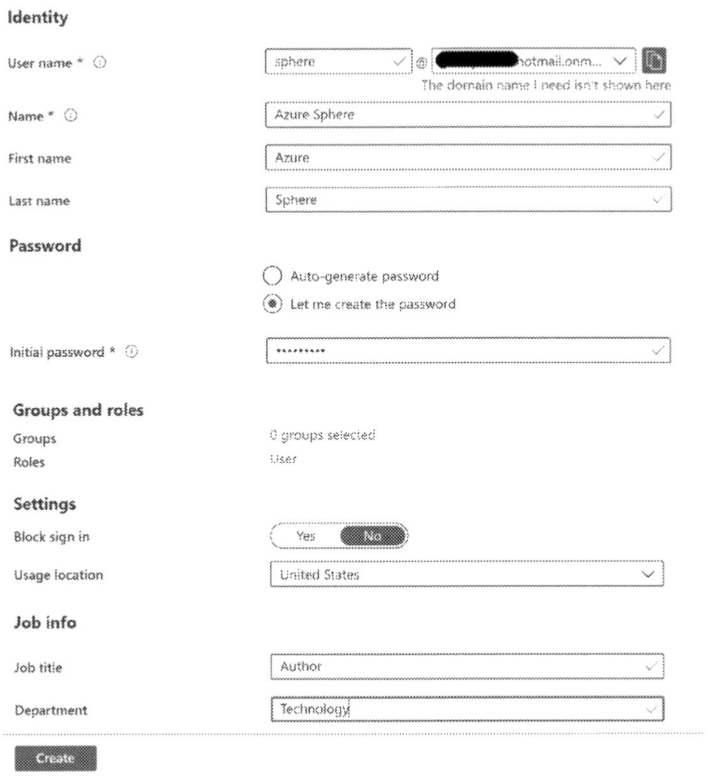

Figure 14-6. *Adding user information*

6. Click Create to add the new user to your Azure Active Directory
    organization, as shown in Figure 14-7.

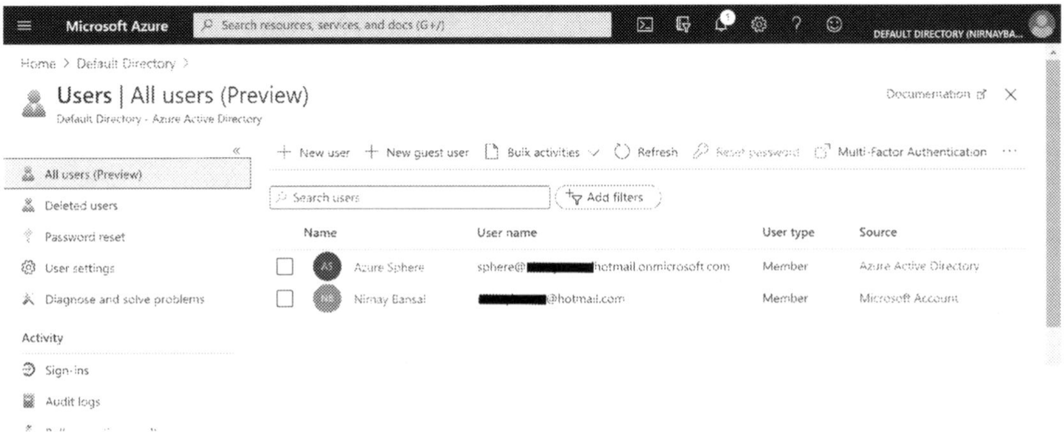

Figure 14-7. *Azure Active Directory users list*

7. Open the Azure Sphere Developer command prompt.

8. Execute the following command to log in to Azure Sphere using a new user account.

```
D:\>azsphere login --newuser sphere@<your account>hotmail.
onmicrosoft.com
Registration successful. Press any key to log in with your new
account.
>
Login successful as 'sphere@<your account>hotmail.onmicrosoft.com'.
warn: You don't have access to any Azure Sphere tenants.
warn: Type 'azsphere tenant create --name <name>' or, if you have
used Azure Sphere before, type 'azsphere tenant migrate'.
```

9. Use your browser to complete the sign-in process and change the user password when prompted, as shown in Figure 14-8.

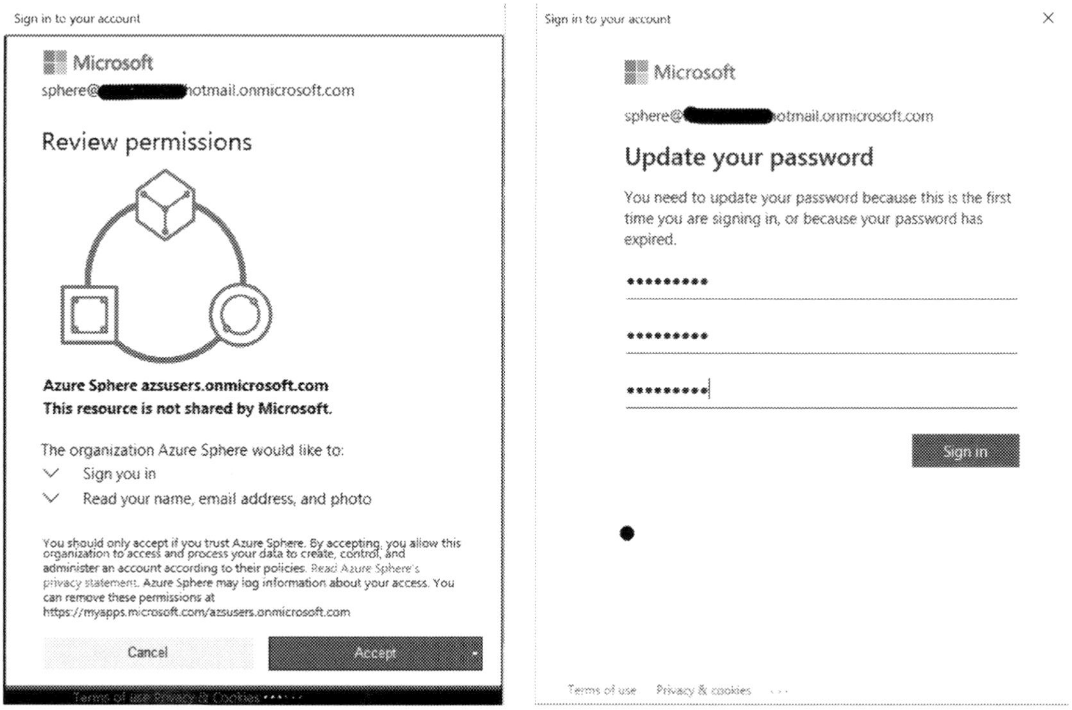

Figure 14-8. *Azure Sphere login prompt and first-time password change screen*

10. Next, create a new tenant:

```
D:\>azsphere tenant create --name iotazurespheretenant
warn: You have logged in with the following account:
warn: sphere@xxxxxxxxhotmail.onmicrosoft.com (21b1xxxx-xxxx-xxxx-
xxxx-5225xxxx4c1e)
warn: Do you want to use this account to create a new Azure Sphere
tenant using the attached device?
warn: You cannot change the tenant name 'iotazurespheretenant'
once it has been created.
Enter 'yes' to continue. Enter anything else to exit.
> yes
Created a new Azure Sphere tenant:
 --> Tenant Name: iotazurespheretenant
 --> Tenant ID:   '65axxxxx-xxxx-xxxx-xxxx-f49xxxxfb851
Selected Azure Sphere tenant 'iotazurespheretenant' as the
default.
You may now wish to claim the attached device into this tenant
using 'azsphere device claim'.
```

When you create a new tenant, your user identity is automatically
made an administrator of the tenant. Make sure your tenant is
created.

```
D:\>azsphere tenant list
ID                                         Name              Roles
--                                         ----              -----
'65axxxxx-xxxx-xxxx-xxxx-f49xxxxfb851 iotazurespheretenant
Administrator
```

11. Claim your device

```
D:\>azsphere device claim
Claiming device.
Successfully claimed device ID '5E1Exxxxxxxxxxxxxxxxx8B' into
tenant 'iotazurespheretenant' with ID '65axxxxx-xxxx-xxxx-xxxx-
f49xxxxfb851'.
```

Between the time when the device is manufactured and it is sold to you, Microsoft might have issued multiple updates that were missed for your device. We need to check and update the OS to avoid any errors like this:

```
error: The device did not accept the device capability configuration.
Please check the Azure Sphere OS on your device is up-to-date using
'azsphere device show-deployment-status'.
```

Execute the following command to find out which version of the Azure Sphere OS your device is currently running.

```
D:\ >azsphere device show-deployment-status
Your device is running Azure Sphere OS version 19.05.
The Azure Sphere Security Service is targeting this device with Azure
Sphere OS version 20.05.
warn: Your device is running an older Azure Sphere OS version (19.05). It
has not yet started receiving the available update to version 20.05.
warn: Your device is not connected to Wi-Fi. Your device may be connected
via Ethernet. If not, please check the Wi-Fi configuration on your device
and try again.
Go to https://aka.ms/AzureSphereUpgradeGuidance for further advice and
support.
```

Add your Wi-Fi network to the device. Replace <yourSSID> with the name of your network. Note the network SSIDs are case-sensitive. Replace <WifiPassword> with your WPA/WPA2 key. Azure Sphere devices do not support wired equivalent privacy (WEP).

```
D:\ >azsphere device wifi add --ssid "<yourSSID>" --psk "<WifiPassword>"
```

```
Add network succeeded:
SSID                    <yourSSID>
Configuration state     enabled
Connection state        unknown
Security state          psk
Targeted scan           False
```

Confirm if Wi-Fi is working on your Azure Sphere device.

```
D:\ >azsphere device wifi show-status
```

SSID	<yourSSID>
Configuration state	enabled
Connection state	connected
Security state	psk
Frequency	5765
Mode	Station
Key management	WPA2-PSK
WPA State	COMPLETED
IP Address	192.168.0.31
MAC Address	xx:xx:xx:xx:xx:xx

It is time to relax. The Azure Sphere device is now checking for any available updates for Azure Sphere OS. Download and installation could take as much as 15 to 20 minutes and might cause the device to restart. Actually, the device checks in three different ways:

1. Each time the device boots.

2. When it connects to the Internet for the first time.

3. Once every 24-hour interval thereafter.

Execute show-deployment-status again to make sure the latest OS deployment update has completed.

```
D:\ >azsphere device show-deployment-status
Your device is running Azure Sphere OS version 20.05.
The Azure Sphere Security Service is targeting this device with Azure
Sphere OS version 20.05.
Your device has the expected version of the Azure Sphere OS: 20.05.
```

Finally, enable app development on the device. This will assign the device to the default Development device group and adds the device capability to accept applications for debugging.

```
D:\ >azsphere device enable-development
Device ID: '5E1Exxxxxxxxxxxxxxxxx8B '
Downloading device capability configuration.
Application updates have already been disabled for this device.
Enabling application development capability on attached device.
Applying device capability configuration to device.
The device is rebooting.
Installing debugging server to device.
Deploying 'C:\Program Files (x86)\Microsoft Azure Sphere SDK\DebugTools\
gdbserver.imagepackage' to the attached device.
Image package 'C:\Program Files (x86)\Microsoft Azure Sphere SDK\
DebugTools\gdbserver.imagepackage' has been deployed to the attached device.
Application development capability enabled.
Successfully set up device for application development, and disabled
application updates.
(Device ID: '5E1Exxxxxxxxxxxxxxxxx8B ')
```

If you see any error in executing this command, that means the OS is still updating and requires a manual reset.

Congratulations! Your Azure Sphere device is now enabled and ready for debugging and closed to cloud application updates until you explicitly change that setting using the `azsphere device enable-cloud-test` command.

Currently custom applications can only be developed in C. You can now proceed to explore device capability by creating sample applications using the new Project type Azure Sphere MT3620 Blank template in Visual Studio 2019, as shown in Figure 14-9.

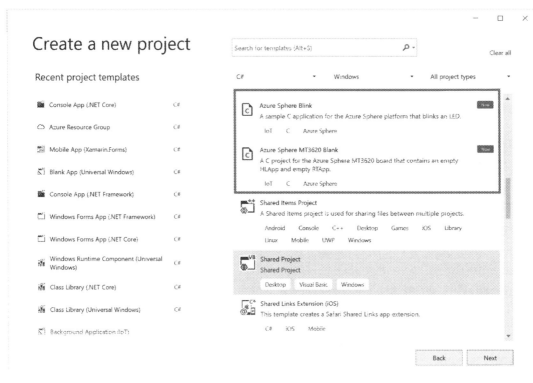

Figure 14-9. *Azure Sphere MT3620 Blank solution*

C-based solutions are usually lengthy and require significant knowledge of the language. Building applications using C is outside the scope of this book. There are quite a few samples provided by Avnet (`https://github.com/Avnet`) and third-party developers to clone, and they can be executed on your device as is.

Summary

This chapter detailed the risks of IoT security. IoT projects are more vulnerable because of their surface area, from hardware to software and everything in between. Therefore, an architect must be cognizant of security at each level.

Protecting privacy is challenging for the IoT, and you need to budget time and money for this important task. In this chapter, we've covered identifying risk, threats, and how to mitigate them. You can use the Threat Modeling tool to flag all the threats and learn how to mitigate them. I provided a list of government and private organizations that provide standardization and technical roadmaps of this technology.

As a bonus, I added a brief introduction to Azure Sphere, the security offering from Microsoft.

This book has attempted to provide practical advice for designing and deploying many types of complex IoT systems. I have thoroughly enjoyed presenting unique use cases and solving them practically with different technology in each chapter. I hope you enjoyed learning them, too.

Index

A

Acceleration sensors, 24

Acoustic sensors, 23

Advanced Message Queuing Protocol (AMQP), 26

Advanced telematics systems, 260

Agriculture
  action, 96, 97
  applications, 97, 98
    hydroponics, 99
    livestock monitoring, 98, 99
  drones, 96
  farmers awareness, 95
  Green Revolution seeds, 94
  implementation, 96
  IoT challenges, 113
  natural resources, 93
  precision farming, 94
  robots, 97
  smart farming, 94

Air-as-a-Service (AaaS), 77

AIVisionDevKitGetStartedModule module, 190, 191

Amazon AWS IoT, 27, 28

Amazon Echo, 135, 139

Amazon FreeRTOS, 27

AMQP over WebSocket, 27

Apple watch health data, 206, 207

Application programming interface (API), 18

Applications
  agriculture (*see* Agriculture)
  energy
    catalyst in reducing energy losses, 120, 121
    consumption-based production, 118–120
    drone-mounted cameras, 121–123
  financial (*see* Financial services industry)
  manufacturing
    predictive maintenance, 78, 79
    subscription economy, 77, 78
    unlocking innovation, 76, 77

Augmented reality, 223, 224

Awareness, livestock management, 95

AWS IoT Greengrass, 28

Azure Active Directory
  adding user information, 278
  user creation, 277
  users list, 278

Azure function app, 168–170

Azure IoT edge
  creation
    AIVisionDevKitGetStarted Module, 190, 191
    device, adding, 188
    edgeAgent and edgeHub modules, 189
  prerequisites, 187

© Nirnay Bansal 2020
N. Bansal, *Designing Internet of Things Solutions with Microsoft Azure*,
https://doi.org/10.1007/978-1-4842-6041-8

Printed in the United States
By Bookmasters